Women and Workplace Discrimination

Women and Workplace Discrimination

Overcoming Barriers to Gender Equality

Raymond F. Gregory

Rutgers University Press

New Brunswick, New Jersey, and London

Library of Congress Cataloging-in-Publication Data

Gregory, Raymond F., 1927–
    Women and workplace discrimination : overcoming barriers to gender
equality / by Raymond F. Gregory.
        p. cm.
    Includes bibliographical references and index.
    ISBN 0-8135-3136-5 (cloth : alk. paper) — ISBN 0-8135-3137-3
(pbk. : alk. paper)
        1. Women employees—United States. 2. Sex discrimination against
women—United States. 3. Sex discrimination in employment—
United States. 4. Sex discrimination in employment—Law and legislation—
United States. I. Title.

HD6095 .G733 2003
331.4'133'0973—dc21

                                                                    2002024834

British Cataloging-in-Publication data for this book is available from the British
Library.

Manufactured in the United States of America

For Mary, wife, as well as best friend, for nearly fifty years

Contents

Women and Workplace Discrimination

Introduction

Why bother writing a book that condemns employer acts of discrimination against working women? Women's problems in the workplace have been largely resolved, have they not? Haven't women already achieved workplace equality? These are typical of the reactions I have encountered while writing this book, and they appear to reflect the current opinion of women and men alike.

Title VII of the Civil Rights Act of 1964 and various state anti-discrimination laws prohibit discrimination in employment based on sex, as well as on race, national origin, and religion.[1] Coincident with the advent of Title VII, sweeping economic and social trends induced, if not compelled, women's entry into the national workforce in vast numbers, and the female proportion of the workforce has continued to increase to this day. Women have gained access to positions formerly barred to them, and the past four decades have witnessed the elevation of women to corporate and professional levels formerly unheard of. During this time, discrimination against women in the workplace has abated.

Federal and state anti-discrimination laws have performed a critical role in expanding workplace opportunities for women. As an old cigarette commercial exulted, "You've come a long way, baby." Yet women are still denied full equality in the workplace. Even though they can now secure powerful professional, academic, and corporate positions once reserved for men, the ever-present "glass ceiling" still deters the advancement of large segments of the female workforce. Sex discrimination may have subsided, but it surely has not been eliminated. As one law professor, commenting on current workplace conditions, aptly put it, "The present day finds us not at the end of the path, but navigating a crucial bend in the road."[2] But many women, especially young women entering the workplace for the first time, are unaware that the end of the road is still distant and that substantial obstacles to attaining complete equality remain firmly in place.

If you have any doubt about the continuing presence of sex discrimination in the workplace, consider the following. Although recent years have seen some narrowing of the long-standing gap between compensation paid to men and that paid to women, female workers still receive substantially less than men. In 1985 the average income of women was 68 percent of that of men. By 1999 it had risen to 77 percent.[3] At this rate, another fifty years will elapse before women achieve pay equality. The youngest women now working cannot reasonably expect to achieve income parity in their lifetimes.

Or consider this. Although women made up 46.5 percent of the U.S. workforce in 2000, women held only 11.7 percent of board of director positions of Fortune 500 companies, and only 12.5 percent of the corporate officers of those companies were female. Ninety of those companies did not have a single female officer. Given the average rate of increase in appointments of women to corporate offices, it has been projected that in 2020, when more women than men will be employed in the workforce, men will still hold nearly 75 percent of such positions in Fortune 500 companies.[4]

Are these appalling statistics attributable to sex discrimination? Critics of federal and state anti-discrimination laws struggle mightily to convince the public that social and cultural factors substantially contribute to the existence of a second-class status for working women. But even if social and cultural mores are contributing elements, discrimination against women remains the major barrier to their full equality in the workplace.

The major premises of this book are these. First, sex discrimination against working women persists. Second, it exists at all levels of employment and in nearly all job categories. And third, if the workplace is ever to be free of gender inequality, working women must commit themselves to opposing employer discriminatory conduct, policies, and practices.

My primary purposes in writing the book have been to show that sex discrimination continues as a major disruptive force in the lives of working women; to demonstrate that the most effective method of eliminating it from the workplace lies in vigorous opposition to all employer discriminatory conduct, policies, and practices, wherever and whenever they appear; and to persuade women victimized by acts of sex discrimination that they can best oppose such conduct, polices, and practices through legal challenges based in the federal anti-discrimination laws.

The chapters are divided into seven groups:

- The types of sex discrimination currently prevalent in the workplace (chapters 1 and 2)
- The enactment and subsequent development of the federal anti-discrimination laws (chapters 3 through 5)
- Discrimination against certain groups—older women, women of color, women in the professions, pregnant women, and women with children (chapters 6 through 10)
- Sex discrimination at various stages of the employment relationship (chapter 11)
- Sexual harassment in the workplace (chapters 12 through 15)
- Employer retaliation against workers who claim sex discrimination (chapter 16)
- Proving sex discrimination and the remedies available to successful litigants (chapters 17 through 19)

Law school students studying for admission to the bar learn by the case-book method; they read the official reports of court cases. In this book, I use a modified form of this method by summarizing court cases to illustrate aspects of sex discrimination as they emerge in the workplace. As you review these case summaries, you will come to understand the basic concepts that underlie the anti-discrimination laws and learn to identify sex-discriminatory conduct. Women readers will then be equipped to undertake measures appropriate to circumstances encountered in the workplace and, if necessary, to help their lawyer develop a solid legal case for presentation in court.

The use of court cases in this fashion has a negative aspect—we do not always learn the final outcome of the cases under review. If a jury verdict is upheld by an appellate court, the final outcome of the case is public knowledge. But during the course of many, if not most, employment discrimination cases, the defendant employer strives to have the plaintiff's case dismissed on legal grounds, so that no jury trial is necessary. These employer attempts more often than not fail, and at this point in the litigation employers often agree to settle the worker's claim. As a condition of settlement, employers frequently demand that the settlement terms remain confidential. The general public, therefore, never learns the outcome of the case. Some of the cases reviewed in the chapters that follow conclude with the court's denial of the employer's motion to dismiss. Although these cases illustrate the point under discussion,

I am not always able to tell you how the worker fared in the end. This is frustrating, of course, but a consequence that cannot be avoided.

This book is aimed primarily at the lay person, not the lawyer. I have tried to eliminate technical language and legal jargon and to avoid drowning you in legal intricacies and technical data. In areas of the law where you need some technical knowledge of the law of sex discrimination, such as those related to the methods used by lawyers to prove sex-discriminatory conduct, I have emphasized the general applicability of the law, without regard to its exceptions. The broad picture takes precedence over special circumstances that may be relevant only to a limited number of instances.

Since Title VII of the Civil Rights Act of 1964 has largely preempted state anti-discrimination statutes, this book focuses on federal rather than state law, and thus most of the court cases reviewed in the book were decided pursuant to Title VII and litigated in the federal courts.

The anti-discrimination laws were intended to eradicate sex discrimination in the workplace. They have accomplished much, but we will see an end to sex discrimination only if working women regularly challenge employer acts of sex discrimination. I have written this book to encourage working women to commit to that course.

One

Trends in Workplace Discrimination against Women

Many Americans believe that sex discrimination no longer presents a significant problem for working women. Increasingly common are newspaper and other media accounts of women who receive high-level appointments in academia and in the other professions, and who advance to upper-level corporate positions. The appointment in July 1999 of a woman as president and chief executive officer of Hewlett-Packard, the world's second-largest computer company, was greeted with the pronouncement that "the glass ceiling finally had been shattered," and that the appointment reflected the absence of barriers that blocked women from promotion to middle and senior management positions.[1] But, the elevation of a woman to a CEO position clearly is not an everyday occurrence. In fact, Hewlett-Packard was only the third of the Fortune 500 companies to turn to a woman for leadership at the highest level.[2] The glass ceiling may have been cracked in this instance, but to characterize it as "shattered" is to engage in gross exaggeration.

Certainly, we should celebrate the appointment of a woman to a leadership position in a company as large as Hewlett-Packard and in an industry historically dominated by men as a significant step toward workplace gender equality. But this appointment hardly means that women no longer confront barriers in achieving equal workplace status with men. Although the past thirty-five years have witnessed much progress, sex discrimination—blatant, subtle, and covert—continues to plague working women. Nearly all still encounter obstacles to job advancement, whether the obstacles be glass or cement ceilings or ordinary brick walls.

Little support exists for those who would argue this point. If by the end of 2001, five Fortune 500 companies had elevated women to top leadership positions, 495 were still led by male CEOs.[3] Of the hundred largest New York City law firms, one was led by a woman and ninety-nine by men.[4] Across the country, five of the hundred largest law firms have selected women as chairpersons; ninety-five still rely on men in the top spot.[5] In 1998, it was widely reported that women filled 11 percent of senior executive positions at Fortune 500 companies, but not that men filled the other 89 percent.[6]

Discriminatory workplace policies and practices adversely affect older women, women of color, pregnant women, and women with children, as does discriminatory conduct at all points of the employment relationship. Sexual harassment of women continues, despite the wake-up calls engendered by the congressional hearings for the appointment of Clarence Thomas to the Supreme Court, as well as the recent major sexual harassment cases argued before that Court.

Many women remain mired in lower-level positions—even at Hewlett-Packard. At about the same time the company was being lauded for elevating women to senior executive positions, a case pending against it in federal court in New York presented a different picture. A former sales representative in Hewlett-Packard's Long Island office alleged that company policies and practices barred female sales representatives from promotion to sales managerial positions. Although female sales representatives often received the highest performance ratings, not one of them had ever been promoted to a management post. Evidence supported the worker's claim that female sales representatives had been adversely impacted by these policies and practices.[7]

Disparities between the compensation paid to women and men substantiate the continued discrimination against women in the workplace.

- In 1993, a survey conducted by the Colorado Women's Bar Association disclosed a large economic gap between the state's male and female lawyers of comparable years of experience and types of legal practice. The average income of female lawyers was only 59 percent of that of male lawyers. A 1998 study attributed at least part of this pay disparity to law firm decisions calculated to provide advantages and protections for those in power, typically men. Moreover, a law firm's economic decisions were most often made by male-dominated executive committees, while women were generally excluded from participation in those decisions. The value of a female lawyer's performance and the monetary award attached to it were based on the expectations and perceptions of those in power—the male lawyers in the firm.[8]

- Although nearly 4 percent of the highest-ranking corporate officers of Fortune 500 companies in 1999 were female, women comprised only 2.7 percent of the highest-paid corporate officers.[9] Thus, even at the highest levels of the corporate hierarchy, women are paid less than men.

- The average lifetime cumulative earnings of a fifty-year-old woman is $496,000, while that of a fifty-year-old man is $1.1 million. Because of a lifetime history of lower pay, women retirees earn less than one-half the pension income of men.[10]

- The compensation gap between African American women and white men stood at 62 percent in 1985, at 66 percent in 1999.[11] At this rate of progress, African American women will not achieve parity with white males until well into the twenty-second century.

- Hispanic women are even more disadvantaged; moreover, the gap between their compensation and that of Hispanic men actually increased between 1990 and 1997.[12] On average, Hispanic women with college degrees earn less than white male high school dropouts.[13]

- A survey conducted by the Hudson Institute in 1993 disclosed that men with college degrees earned 34 percent more than women with comparable degrees.[14]

- The Department of Labor's 2000 statistical data on men and women in the workforce disclosed that 1,214,000 men, representing 3.4 percent of all workers, were employed at or below minimum wage levels; the number of women employed at those levels exceeded 2,126,000, or 5.9 percent of the workforce.[15]

- A *Business Week* study found that female business school graduates with MBA degrees earn 12 percent less than male graduates.[16] Because these graduates were all new hires directly out of school, this salary disparity reflected neither experience nor performance, only corporate management's decision to favor men over women.

- A survey made by the American Association for the Advancement of Science in 2001 reported that women employed in the life sciences—biology and medicine—earn 23 percent less than their male counterparts. Among life-science professors who rated themselves as at the peak of their careers, women earned 14 percent less than men, regardless of the size and prestige of the university.[17]

- Even federal government employment policies favor men over women. In 1994, women filled 56 percent of the government's lower-paying positions (grades 1 through 12), while men held nearly 77 percent of the mid-level positions (grades 13 through 15) and 83 percent of its senior-level posts.[18]

Can we attribute these compensation disparities to workplace discrimination? Some legal commentators argue that the personal choices made by women outside work have important implications for earnings and promotions in the work environment, and that these personal choices, not workplace discrimination, account for the persistent income gaps. This argument relies primarily upon the contention that opportunities for promotion may not be as great for women who choose to leave work for extended periods to take care of their children. These commentators also observe that women who plan to interrupt their careers to bear children may select occupations where job flexibility is high but compensation is low. In either event, it is argued, free choice rather than sex discrimination accounts for workplace disadvantages suffered by women.[19]

Undoubtedly, young mothers confront a disproportionate share of job disadvantages. Whether or not, in individual cases, these disadvantages exist as a consequence of discriminatory intent, no existing data support the proposition that long-standing compensation gaps between male and female workers occur as a direct consequence of career choices freely made by working women with children. Rather, as court cases in subsequent chapters demonstrate, employers often discriminate against working mothers.

These commentators also contend that linking male-female pay gaps to workplace discrimination ignores the "pipeline theory." They observe that senior management positions typically require twenty-five or more years of service, and most women have been in the pipeline—that is, on a career path to upper-management positions—for shorter periods. Under the pipeline theory, women will achieve pay parity in due course.[20] But these commentators ignore an aspect of the pipeline theory that works against women. The critical career paths for senior management positions begin with line positions, such as those in marketing, sales, and production, or with critical control functions such as accounting or finance. Women are more likely to be placed in support-staff positions, such as personnel, human resources, public relations, communications, and customer relations.[21] Since movement between staff and line positions seldom occurs in most major companies, women are less likely during the course of their careers to be assigned pipeline positions that lead to senior management. The pipeline, therefore, actually perpetuates the barriers that have traditionally kept women from moving up the corporate ladder.

The continuing disadvantages encountered by women in the workplace are typified by Mary Ann Luciano's experience with the Olsten Corporation in New York, an employment agency for temporary employees. Olsten hired Luciano as director of field marketing, and her excellent performance appraisals suggest that she had worked well in that position. Two years after Olsten hired her, another company offered her a vice presidency. Olsten's CEO decided to match the offer to induce Luciano to remain. However, several of Olsten's male senior executives were not pleased with the prospect of Luciano's promotion to vice president, and they persuaded the CEO to convince her to accept a lower position temporarily, with a written commitment for promotion to a vice presidency in a year's time, provided her performance continued to be acceptable.

During that year, three of Olsten's senior vice presidents formulated a new job description for Luciano, incorporating duties upon which she would be evaluated prior to promotion to vice president. It was designed to ensure unsatisfactory performance. Still not satisfied, they later increased Luciano's job responsibilities but withheld the support staff she required to perform the additional duties. Even then, they refused to proceed with Luciano's performance appraisal, but instead terminated her, allegedly because her position had been eliminated in a corporate reorganization.

Olsten then assigned Luciano's job responsibilities to two male senior vice presidents, one of whom Olsten had recruited from outside the company. Although Luciano was qualified for both positions, Olsten rejected her, and even though she also was qualified for other open positions in the company, she was not considered for any of them. After experiencing all these adverse actions, Luciano sued the company, claiming she had been the victim of sex discrimination.

At the trial, Luciano's lawyers presented the jury with a vast amount of evidence supporting her sex-discrimination claim. In addition to the machinations of the three senior vice presidents, the jury learned, Olsten had promoted men with poor performance records to senior management positions, and in the reorganization that cost Luciano her job, new positions were created for male employees whose jobs had been similarly eliminated. The jury also considered statistical data that reflected a glass ceiling firmly in place for female employees.

- More than 80 percent of Olsten's 200 Office Services Division field offices were headed by women, who were considered "junior management." No woman had ever been elevated from a junior management position to a vice president or senior vice president postion in the Office Services Division.
- At its corporate headquarters, Olsten had assigned seventeen vice president and senior vice president positions to men, but only one to a woman. In contrast, although 70 percent of Olsten's middle-management workforce was female, women were rarely promoted to positions above the middle-management level.

- In some job categories, a $10,000 wage disparity existed between the average salary paid to men and to women.

With all this evidence at hand, the jury had little difficulty in arriving at a verdict in favor of Luciano, awarding her substantial damages, including punitive damages.[22]

This case is typical in that Luciano encountered obstacles that barred her advancement to a higher position and were designed to disadvantage her, while protecting the positions of fellow male workers. Women encounter similar circumstances every day. But the case is atypical in that the measures undertaken to bar Luciano's promotion were overt, with little regard to concealing conduct clearly discriminatory. More frequently, decisions contrived to impair the advancement of a woman are subtle, secretly formulated and covertly implemented. Because employers generally hide discriminatory conduct, those against whom it is directed and other workers not directly involved rarely see it. Many workers, therefore, erroneously assume that discriminatory conduct is absent from their workplaces. This assumption in turn leads to the mistaken belief that sex discrimination no longer presents a material bar to women's promotions.

Since its initial formulation, the concept of the glass ceiling has grown to include disadvantaged racial minorities as well as women, and its focus has expanded to include all promotional opportunities, not merely those pertaining to senior management positions.[23] The concept caught the attention of congressional leaders in 1991 when it was considering amendments to the 1964 Civil Rights Act. Ultimately, Congress created a Glass Ceiling Commission to study and recommend measures to eliminate "artificial barriers to the advancement of women and minorities" and to increase and foster their advancement in the workplace. In 1995, the commission issued its fact-finding report, which affirmed the continuing presence of such barriers.[24]

One of the areas upon which the commission focused was typical employer-held perceptions of working women. Convinced that these perceptions tended to perpetuate the existence of the glass ceiling, the commission undertook to determine whether they had any basis in fact.[25] To the contrary, the commission concluded, such perceptions arose out of commonly held false stereotypes, including notions that women

- do not want to work;
- are less committed to their careers than men;
- are not tough enough to succeed in the business world;
- generally are unable or unwilling to work long or unusual hours;

- are unable or unwilling to relocate geographically;
- are unable or unwilling to make decisions;
- are not sufficiently aggressive; rather, they are too passive;
- are too emotional.

Why do these stereotypes persist? "In the minds of many white male managers," the commission concluded, "business is not where women . . . were meant to be—certainly not functioning as the peers of white men."[26]

Not only do employers hold false assumptions regarding the role of the female worker, but they also perceive conflicts between the child-rearing responsibilities of working mothers and their job responsibilities. Until these stereotypes are eliminated from the workplace, discrimination against women will continue.

Because acts of sex discrimination are frequently subtly conceived and not readily detectable, women often remain unaware that sex discrimination constitutes a moving force in their work lives, and, as a result, they seldom seek legal redress for it.[27] Some women who do recognize the effect of discrimination on their careers are reluctant to become involved in complex legal proceedings. Others may lack the financial resources to retain an attorney. Others believe family responsibilities would make it impossible for them to become involved in extended litigation. Some women fear losing their jobs, while others believe that all workplaces are infested with sex discrimination, so why bother to contest it. As a result, unlawful employer policies and conduct often remain unaddressed. Employers are well aware of these circumstances, and since they have little to fear by allowing their unlawful employment policies to continue, they frequently remain unmotivated to rid their workplaces of discriminatory conduct.

The number of women who suffer acts of sex discrimination greatly exceeds the number who file discrimination claims against their employers. Women's failure to act—whatever the reason—unwittingly serves to perpetuate discriminatory conduct, policies, and practices.

Sex discrimination will become a more disruptive feature of the workplace as the number of female workers increases in the years to come. In 1999, women represented 46 percent of the entire workforce.[28] U.S. Department of Labor projections show that this trend will continue, and by 2005, the workforce will be 48 percent female.[29] The rise inevitably will be followed by increased incidents of sex discrimination, further disrupting the workforce.

Women are rapidly becoming better educated than men. Women already earn more than one-half of all bachelor's and master's degrees; they lag behind only in the number of doctorates conferred.[30] Women, therefore, will be better qualified than men to assume positions of authority. Will an increasingly better-educated corps of women be more inclined to seek legal redress against employer discriminatory policies and practices? I believe so. Better-educated women are less likely to accept career barriers created by such discrimination, more likely to recognize discrimination for what it is, and more likely to act on the conviction that sex discrimination has no place in their lives.

The female worker of the future is likely to be a mother of young children. Already, 64 percent of all married women with young children are working mothers;[31] 77 percent of divorced, separated, and widowed mothers with young children are working or looking for work.[32] These women are not likely to readily accept employment policies formulated on the assumption that a working mother's child-rearing responsibilities necessarily conflict with her work responsibilities. Since these women are better educated than past generations of working women, they are more likely to appeal to the courts to obtain legal relief from all employer-initiated discriminatory conduct, policies, and practices.

For nearly four decades, this country has been engaged in creating workplace equality for persons of different races and ethnicities, and it has achieved some success in that regard. At the same time, we have been engaged in creating a workplace that will take full advantage of and fairly compensate women. Whether we will succeed in achieving either of these goals remains an open question.

Two

Sex Discrimination in Today's Workplace

In 1994, male members of the faculty of the School of Sciences of the Massachusetts Institute of Technology outnumbered women twelve to one. Of the 252 men on the MIT faculty, 194 were tenured; of the 22 faculty women, 15 were tenured. Nancy Hopkins, a prominent DNA expert and one of the tenured women, over a period of years had designed and taught a course very popular with MIT students. When the number of students enrolled in it exceeded one thousand, the School of Sciences administrators designated a male professor to assist her. Despite Hopkins's role in developing and teaching the course, MIT later informed her that they had designated her male assistant, not her, to turn the course into a book and a CD-ROM.

Hopkins was bitter. While discussing the quality of her professional life with another female professor, she discovered that her colleague, like herself, felt that over the years she had been targeted for adverse treatment, and that MIT had not treated her nearly as well as men faculty. Discussion with a third female faculty member, who also acknowledged unhappiness with her life as an MIT professor, led the three to poll the tenured School of Sciences female professors and analyze their positions at MIT. To their amazement, their efforts disclosed the following:

- The School of Sciences paid male faculty members more than female faculty members.
- On average, research monies allotted to men exceeded those allotted to women.

- The School of Sciences had never appointed a woman to head a department.
- MIT assigned female faculty members less office space than their male colleagues. Although MIT insisted that office space was assigned equally, it later conceded that School of Sciences administrators had included lab space in their measurements of the office space assigned to women, but not in the measurements of that assigned to men.
- Male professors who received job offers from other institutions were given raises as inducements to remain with MIT; women were not.
- Women were rarely appointed to important committee seats. As a result, they felt marginalized and excluded from significant roles in their departments.
- Marginalization was often accompanied by fewer awards granted to women, despite professional accomplishments equal to or surpassing those of their male colleagues.
- Compared with fifty-five men, only seven women were then on a tenure track.
- For the past ten years, and perhaps longer, only 8 percent of the faculty of the School of Sciences had been female.

Following discussions with women faculty members of other MIT Schools, it became apparent to Hopkins and the other female professors that sex-based measures had long adversely affected women throughout the university. A long-term pattern of discrimination based on gender was indisputable.[1] Based on their findings, the women were convinced that their gender, rather than their talents or abilities, had been the guiding force in the development of their professional lives—lives substantially inferior to those of their male colleagues. They then resolved to effect changes. They charged the School of Sciences with discriminatory conduct and set forth a proposal to eliminate such conduct from the daily lives of the female faculty:

> This proposal has been developed by the tenured women faculty in the School of Sciences. It speaks to our serious concerns about the small number of women professors at MIT, and about the status and treatment of the women who are here. We believe that unequal treatment of women faculty impairs their ability to perform as educators, leaders in research and models for women students. . . .
>
> We believe that discriminatory attitudes operate at the time of hiring junior faculty and influence the experiences of the women who are hired. . . .
>
> Thus, we need to develop safeguards to prevent, detect, and promptly correct the experiences that together constitute gender discrimination. . . .
>
> We believe that unequal treatment of women who come to MIT makes it

more difficult for them to succeed, causes them to be accorded less recognition when they do, and contributes so substantially to a poor quality of life that these women can actually become negative role models for younger women.

Lest there be any doubt that these women were charging MIT with unlawful discrimination, they made the charge explicit: "The heart of the problem is that equal talent and accomplishment are viewed as unequal when seen through the eyes of prejudice. . . . Currently, a glass ceiling exists."[2]

School of Sciences officials, without admitting that they had deliberately discriminated against female faculty, responded positively to the proposal. Their written response emphasized "our collective ignorance" as the basic cause underlying the long-standing discrimination against female faculty members. MIT's president, Charles M. Vest, remarked: "I have always believed that contemporary gender discrimination within universities is part reality and part perception . . . but I now understand that reality is by far the greater part of the balance." The dean of the School of Sciences, Robert J. Birgeneau, commented: "I believe that in no case was this discrimination conscious or deliberate. Indeed, it was usually totally unconscious and unknowing. Nevertheless, the effects were real."[3]

The faculty chair, Lotte Bailyn, was of a similar mind:

> The key conclusion that one gets from the [proposal] is that gender discrimination in the 1990s is subtle but pervasive, and stems largely from unconscious ways of thinking. . . .
>
> This makes the situation better than in previous decades where blatant inequities . . . were endured but not spoken of. We can all be thankful for that. But the consequences of these more subtle forms of discrimination are equally real and equally demoralizing.[4]

In subsequent remarks and statements issued by administration officials, the discrimination experienced by the MIT women was described as "unconscious and unknowing," neither "deliberate" nor "blatant," and although it was "subtle," it nevertheless was "pervasive." One wonders how several generations of MIT male administrators could have been unaware that the School of Sciences practices and policies adversely affected the professional lives of its women professors. Is "collective ignorance" an adequate explanation? How could these administrators not have known that they had assigned female faculty members less office space than their male colleagues, that the School of Sciences paid male faculty more than female faculty, that research monies allotted to men exceeded those allotted to women, that administrators had never appointed a woman to head a department, that women rarely were appointed to important committee seats, and that for ten or more years the proportion of women on the faculty had remained at approximately 8 percent? Even if MIT administrators had failed to realize the full effect and consequence of these practices and policies, is it conceivable that they could have been totally unconscious of their existence? MIT's written response to the women's claims is mostly silent in this regard, but one comment is revealing: "Some argued that it was the *masculine culture* at MIT that was to blame and little could be done to change that."[5]

False assumptions regarding women's work ethic prevail in a masculine work culture, and thus men working in such a culture are likely to remain oblivious to the needs and concerns of female workers. Although males may remain insensitive to the adversities suffered by women employed in such a culture, and although they may at times remain largely unaware that practices and policies benefiting men at the same time negatively affect female workers, their conduct is no less pernicious. Acts of sex discrimination committed by men working in a masculine culture generally are subtly conceived and not readily discernable, and thus their existence may be difficult to establish. Consequently, discrimination committed in a masculine work culture, as at MIT, frequently remains unaddressed for extended periods of time.

Men working in a masculine culture tend to emphasize the differences between the gender-role expectations of men and those of women as they relate to child-rearing responsibilities, and they conclude that a woman's family obligations conflict with her work responsibilities, thus requiring the assignment of women to less-demanding positions. Still other false perceptions of working women lead to unrealistic conclusions regarding women's "proper" role in the workplace.[6]

Such faulty perceptions and stereotypes distinguish sex discrimination from acts of discrimination based on race, national origin, or religion, which are grounded in emotional and subjective prejudice. Sex discrimination emanates from an acceptance of false stereotypes pertaining to characteristics thought to be common to working women. These false stereotypes arose in an era when brawn was apt to be more highly valued in the workplace than brains. Physically demanding jobs could often be better performed by men. The economy's shift in emphasis from manufacturing to service industries was accompanied by the expansion of white-collar positions at the expense of blue-collar jobs, and this led inevitably to an expanded role for women in the workplace. Service jobs, however, are filled on the basis of subjective judgments. Almost all upper-tier jobs, for example, require a subjective judgment of a worker's ability to make decisions in unanticipated conditions. As the court cases later reviewed show, subjective judgments in personnel decisions are often influenced, consciously or unconsciously, by false stereotypes relating to such attributes as aggressiveness, leadership ability, the capacity to adapt to unforeseen circumstances, and the ability to handle interpersonal relationships. Women are decidedly disadvantaged when hiring and other employment decisions are influenced by such stereotypes.[7]

Furthermore, male managers—still primarily responsible for most hiring and other workplace decisions—are more likely to attribute to other men than to women the qualities and characteristics they deem necessary for a position. This attribution is based on what Rutgers University professor Alfred W. Blumrosen describes as

> a deep-rooted assumption that those whose backgrounds are similar to their own or familiar to them are likely to do a better job than those whose background and experience are different. This tendency to identify with persons "like ourselves" and to project upon them characteristics and attributes which we believe we have, is an important element in the necessarily subjective judgments which predict future performance. The higher the job level, the more visible will be the performance of the person selected, and the greater the pressures on the selecting personnel will be to demonstrate their acumen. This pressure increases the likelihood that a "bias toward the familiar" will occur in the selection process.[8]

These same male managers, consciously or unconsciously, may accept as true any number of false assumptions pertaining to the traits, characteristics, and work habits of female workers. One of the most pernicious of these false assumptions undermines and devalues the work roles of mothers with young children.

Because women traditionally have assumed primary familial responsibility for the rearing of their children, men, relieved of such responsibilities, have performed well in jobs requiring a near total commitment to the workplace. An employer may structure a job description that demands an uncompromising work commitment, while ignoring the impact of such a commitment upon the (presumed male) worker's family, as the employer may safely assume that the worker's wife will accept all child-rearing responsibilities. This is no longer the case in our society. The male worker's wife is now more likely to be employed herself and thus is no longer available for full-time child care. But unenlightened employers persist in requiring the acceptance of a work ethic that establishes the job as the central, if not the sole, priority in a worker's life. Those who agree to function in such a capacity are sometimes referred to as "ideal workers."

A workplace structured on the ideal-worker concept is based on the assumptions first, that the ideal worker is a man, and second, that, if the ideal worker is married, he can depend on his wife to fulfill all, or nearly all, child-care responsibilities, thus freeing him to work extended days, maintain inflexible work schedules, travel frequently, and work unimpeded by any concerns for the daily welfare of his children. Because employers perceive working mothers as confronting a conflict of loyalty between home and work, they assume that these women, regardless of their circumstances, lack the commitment required of the "ideal worker," and thus they exclude women as candidates for positions structured for such workers.[9]

A work environment grounded in the ideal-worker concept materially limits the employment role of the working mother. Mothers with young children, compelled to work in an environment designed for men without child-rearing responsibilities, are relegated to positions perceived as consistent with the fulfillment of family responsibilities, and these positions generally are inferior and lower paying. Because such a work environment adversely impacts women, an employer who fails to structure its workplace to accommodate the responsibilities of working mothers will likely, sooner or later, be charged with sex discrimination.

Because the devaluation of the workplace role of women is often subtle and thus difficult to establish, the courts have been slow to recognize this type of employer conduct as discriminatory. Except for issues pertaining to discrimination against pregnant women, the courts have rarely considered the concept of motherhood as it relates to sex discrimination. Yet this unequal treatment, built into the practices and procedures of male-dominated organizations, routinely disadvantage female workers, since the central features of these practices and procedures have been constructed by men according to norms that exclude or degrade the experiences and perceptions of women. In such an environment, women are generally subordinated and devalued. This is the essence of sex discrimination.

Although women have forced some employers to reevaluate the need for such male norms, other employers have rejected all efforts to restructure their workplaces to eliminate conditions and practices that adversely affect women. An attitude that denies the need for change—an attitude based on an assumption of male superiority—leads to even higher expectations of men's abilities, while women are categorized as fit for employment only in specified lower-paying, lower-status positions.

_____ *Table 1* _____
Percentage of Women in Nonprofessional Positions

Occupation	1983	1999
Bookkeepers	91.0	91.4
Payroll and Time Keeping Clerks	82.2	88.2
Billing Clerks	88.4	92.0
Telephone Operators	90.4	83.7
General Office Clerks	80.6	81.4
Bank Tellers	91.0	87.7
Child Care Workers	96.9	97.4
Cleaners and Servants	95.8	94.4
Kitchen Workers (food preparation)	77.0	70.4
Dental Assistants	98.1	96.1
Nursing Aides and Orderlies	88.7	89.9
Dietitians	90.8	84.0

Source: U.S. Bureau of the Census, *Statistical Abstract of the United States, 2000* (Washington, D.C.: Bureau of the Census, 2000), table 669, pp. 416–418.

Historically, employers have tended to categorize women as capable only of "women's work," positions that exist in relatively few occupations and rank among those with the lowest status and compensation. The assignment of women to such positions results in the segregation and stratification of women in the workplace. The consignment of women to occupations disproportionately female tends to extend their segregated and stratified roles.

Until recently, 95 percent of all secretaries, stenographers, and typists were women. Although a significant reduction in job segregation has occurred in professional positions, it continues in many other job categories.[10] The Census Bureau's 2000 *Statistical Abstract of the United States* reveals the breakdown shown in table 1. Although Census Bureau statistics disclose some improvement in the hiring of women in some other job categories, women are still generally excluded from the male-dominated positions (table 2).

Undoubtedly, some women who anticipate that they will be called upon to fulfill family responsibilities freely choose to work in lower-paying and lower-status positions; they may be reluctant to make a significant investment in job training or to make the commitments necessary to attain higher-paying and higher-status posts. But women's careers are equally likely to be shaped by the job opportunities that employers historically have made available to women. Employers who falsely perceive women as exhibiting less commitment to their jobs feel justified in assigning them to high-turnover positions with low-turnover costs, and these jobs generally carry low pay and little status. Women who accept these positions are merely responding to employer expectations, rather

——————— *Table 2* ———————
Percentage of Women in Male-Dominated Occupations

Occupation	1983	1999
Airplane Pilots and Navigators	2.1	3.1
Firefighters	1.0	2.8
Mechanics	3.0	4.8
Motor Vehicle Operators	9.2	11.5
Engineers	5.8	10.6
Police and Detectives	9.4	16.9

Source: U.S. Bureau of the Census, *Statistical Abstract of the United States, 2000* (Washington, D.C.: Bureau of the Census, 2000), table 669, pp. 416–418.

than expressing a lack of interest in attaining better-paying positions. Relying on false stereotypical assumptions about working women's traits and characteristics, these employers shape women's work aspirations by creating a work environment that undermines the female work role.[11]

In addition to encountering glass ceilings, male-dominated work environments, and job segregation and stratification, working women also confront other areas of discrimination in today's workplace—discrimination against older women, against women of color, against professional women, and against women who are pregnant. To exacerbate matters, sexual harassment of women—of all ages, of all skin colors, in all job categories, and in all occupations and professions—pervades the workplace.

In the workplace, women get "old" at a younger age than men. Age is as likely as gender to disadvantage older working women, and in many instances, an older woman faces discriminatory conduct on account of both age and sex. Some employers who prefer attractive female employees hold older women, but not men, to a standard of attractiveness equated with youth; such an employer may be guilty of age as well as sex discrimination against its older female workers.[12]

Only 3 percent of female executives are African American.[13] They are paid less, rated lower in performance evaluations, and subjected to biased promotion practices. More impenetrable than glass ceilings, African American women view barriers to promotion as "concrete ceilings" that bar them from advancement. As a consequence of these barriers, a large number of African American women remain in lower-paying clerical and sales positions.

Discrimination against women in all professions persists, but it remains particularly egregious in the legal profession. A recent survey of the Association of the Bar of the City of New York disclosed that glass ceilings had been consciously imposed by senior male attorneys to deter the elevation of women in their firms. Sex stereotyping and perceptions about motherhood and its incompatibility with the professional life of a lawyer were found to present serious obstacles to the upward mobility of female lawyers.[14]

Pregnancy is often perceived by management as a disruptive event in the workplace and, as a consequence, women who announce their pregnancies often find they are less than welcome to continue in their positions. It is not uncommon for a woman returning to work after childbirth to find her job materially altered or even eliminated. The law requires employers to apply its policies relating to leave, seniority, compensation, and benefits to pregnant workers on the same terms as to workers with temporary disabilities. An employer who treats a pregnant worker less favorably than a similarly situated nonpregnant worker is guilty of sex discrimination. The law is clear, but employer compliance with the law remains less than complete.

Sexual harassment is particularly widespread and more likely than not will present a problem for nearly every working woman at some point in her life. Such harassment generally reflects an unequal relationship between a male manager and a subordinate female employee, with terms of employment that tend to create a hostile or offensive work environment for the woman. As Mona Harrington noted in her book *Women Lawyers*: "Sexual harassment of women by male co-workers expresses the ancient rule that women *should* be sexually available to men. And at the same time, it reminds the professional woman especially that while she appears in the workplace as the supposed equal of her male colleagues, she is not really an equal. It tells her that although she is gaining some economic independence, . . . she is still subject to an old order in which she is ultimately subordinate to men, ultimately and naturally defined by her body as a male possession."[15]

Sexual harassment denies equality. It conveys the message that a woman is not regarded as a respected colleague but rather as a sexual object. Even though sexual harassment cases often evolve into events of notoriety for the harasser, this conduct nevertheless widely persists in the workplace.

The case of the MIT professors raises another issue typical in sex-discrimination cases—women who are subjected to acts of discrimination often remain unaware that they have been victimized because of their gender. Although the MIT female professors eventually concluded that sex discrimination was the source of their plight, they endured several years of unhappiness with their professional lives before registering a complaint. How was it possible, especially in light of the adversities placed in the paths of these women, that they failed to realize that the mistreatment they experienced occurred on account of their gender? How could these women, obviously among the intellectual elite, have continued to endure this treatment for years without complaining or trying to eliminate its source?

Some female workers assume a "Don't rock the boat" attitude, consciously deciding to endure the adverse conditions of their employment. Others fail to act because they mistakenly believe that the adversities associated with sex discrimination in employment no longer exist, and thus their unhappiness with the circumstances of their employment must arise from another source. Other women realize they have been subjected to sex bias, but their personal circumstances or family responsibilities prevent them from devoting the time and effort necessary to effect a plan of action to eliminate the discrimination. Others simply lack the courage or energy to challenge their employer's conduct. All too often, women accept discriminatory conduct without complaint, and this usually leads to additional discriminatory conduct. Unless charged with discrimination and confronted with a lawsuit or the threat of a lawsuit, an employer is not apt to direct any of its resources to removing discrimination from its work site, since the costs of eliminating it may exceed the costs of permitting it to continue.

Women have the power to eliminate sex discrimination in the workplace, and they must avail themselves of the resources at hand—the laws outlawing employment discrimination. Almost all employers contest any claim of discrimination. They put such a claim in the same category as charges of theft, fraud, or grand larceny. They resolutely contest all claims of discrimination. Thus, a woman who elects to enforce her right to work in an unbiased environment must be prepared for battle; she must be prepared to participate in an extended period of intense and bitter litigation.

On rare occasions, as in the case of MIT, an employer may agree to mend its ways, rendering litigation unnecessary. But even the actions MIT has agreed to undertake to eliminate sex discrimination from its campus will take years to fully implement. If MIT's School of Sciences continues to hire women professors at its current rate, which represents a significant increase since the charges were made, it will be 2040 before even as much as 40 percent of its faculty is female. A masculine culture does not die easily.[16]

We have examined, in broad outline, sex discrimination in today's workplace. Before we look at the ways women have used and are now using the antidiscrimination laws to contest workplace discrimination, we need to become familiar with those laws and follow their development in the courts over the last four decades.

Three

Enactment of the Federal Anti-Discrimination Laws

The exclusion of women from the workforce dates to the beginning of the industrial era in the early nineteenth century. For the next 150 years, women were openly discriminated against by employers, who either refused to hire them under any circumstances or who rejected them if they were married or had children. The exclusion of women from the labor market was reinforced by state statutes later held constitutional by the Supreme Court.

Illinois was one of many states that barred felons and women from becoming lawyers. In 1872, the Supreme Court affirmed Illinois's rejection of Myra Bradwell's application for a license to practice law in the state and took the opportunity to fix women's proper place in society:

> The natural and proper timidity and delicacy which belongs to the female sex evidently unfits it for many of the occupations of civil life. The constitution of the family organization, which is founded in the divine ordinance, as well as in the nature of things, indicates the domestic sphere as that which properly belongs to the domain and functions of womanhood. The harmony, not to say identity, of interests and views which belong, or should belong, to the family institution is repugnant to the idea of a woman adopting a distinct and independent career from that of her husband.

To make certain that all citizens understood women's proper place, the Court added: "The paramount destiny and mission of woman are to fulfill the noble and benign offices of wife and mother. This is the law of the Creator."[1]

Other state laws restricted women to certain occupations and specified the number of hours they were allowed to spend in the workplace. Again, the Supreme Court led the way in limiting the work roles of women when it upheld the constitutionality of an Oregon statute that barred women from working more than ten hours during any one day in "any mechanical establishment, or factory, or laundry":

> That woman's physical structure and the performance of maternal functions place her at a disadvantage in the struggle for subsistence is obvious. . . . [H]istory discloses the fact that woman has always been dependent upon man. He established his control at the outset . . . and it is still true that in the struggle for subsistence she is not an equal competitor with her brother. . . . Differentiated . . . from the other sex, she is properly placed in a class by herself, and legislation designed for her protection may be sustained, even when like legislation is not necessary for men, and could not be sustained. It is impossible to close one's eyes to the fact that she still looks to her brother and depends upon him. . . . This difference justifies a difference in legislation, and upholds that which is designed to compensate for some of the burdens which rest upon her.[2]

The Supreme Court persisted well beyond the nineteenth century in expressing its conviction that women are dependent upon men. As late as 1948, the Court upheld a Michigan statute that barred a woman from employment as a bartender unless the male owner of the bar was either her father or her husband.[3]

Typical of barriers to female employment were those that applied to women attorneys. Law firm interviewers did not hesitate to tell female applicants that their firms did not hire women, or that "they already had one." Some firms simply posted "No Women" notices in their entrances and in their help-wanted ads.[4] When Supreme Court justice Sandra Day O'Connor graduated from Stanford Law School at the top of her class and applied to major West Coast law firms, the only offers she received were for the position of legal secretary. Nanette Dembitz—who later became a New York judge—was unable to obtain a position with a Wall Street law firm, even though she had been an editor of the *Columbia University Law Review* and, as the niece of Supreme Court justice Louis Brandeis, had excellent family connections.[5]

Women seeking industrial positions met with other employment prohibitions. By 1964, more than forty states had adopted laws or regulations limiting the daily or weekly hours women were permitted to work. Some states also barred women from engaging in hazardous occupations. Others required mandatory rest periods, barred night work, and limited the amount of weight a woman could be required to lift. Although intended to protect women, these laws and regulations reduced the value of the female worker, thus severely limiting her employment opportunities.[6]

African Americans confronted even greater obstacles to finding suitable employment. Although every president from Franklin Roosevelt to Lyndon Johnson issued executive orders relating to equal employment opportunity, jobs in the federal government nevertheless remained largely segregated. In private industry, as well as in local and state governmental agencies, segregation and discrimination in employment remained intact until the early 1960s.[7] Generally, blacks were excluded from traditionally "white" positions and were relegated to less desirable, lower-paying jobs. In 1962, nonwhite male workers earned less than 60 percent the income of white males. Nonwhite females fared even worse, earning less than 25 percent of that earned by white males.[8]

Until 1964, Congress failed to act to eliminate race or sex discrimination from the workplace. State legislatures, however, were more active. In 1945, New York enacted the first fair-employment law that covered private employment, creating a state agency to eliminate and prevent further discrimination in employment "because of race, creed, color, or national origin."[9] Noticeably absent was any reference to discrimination by reason of sex. The New York law became the prototype for statutes enacted in other states.[10] These statutes, however, generally lacked adequate enforcement procedures and thus were largely ineffective in eliminating ongoing patterns of workplace discrimination.

Still, the social impulse toward equality for African Americans gained strength between the end of World War II and the early 1960s. Rutgers University law professor Alfred W. Blumrosen attributes this trend to four factors:

1. The disclosure of Nazi atrocities committed in the name of "racial superiority" created a more sympathetic environment for those challenging racial discrimination in the United States.
2. A generation of African Americans committed to ending racial discrimination was given support by the Supreme Court decision in *Brown v. Board of Education,* which held that racially segregated schools violated the Fourteenth Amendment.
3. The refusal of Rosa Parks to move to the back of the bus in Montgomery, Alabama, and her subsequent arrest and conviction, became a symbol of oppression that intensified Americans' perception that the failure to grant African Americans racial equality was no longer an option.
4. The Montgomery bus boycott catapulted Martin Luther King Jr. into a leadership role in the civil rights movement, which later fueled demands by African Americans for the elimination of segregation and discrimination. Later, television displays of attacks on civil rights demonstrators with

clubs, dogs, and water hoses culminated in proposals for congressional action to end racial discrimination.

But, while the social impulse toward racial equality grew and extended across the nation, the public did not take seriously the notion that women also should receive equal treatment.[11]

In 1963, President John Kennedy proposed congressional passage of a Civil Rights Act, and President Johnson later pressed Congress to include in the act legislation that barred discrimination in places of public accommodation, voting rights, schools, and employment. Recognizing that African Americans had been too long deprived of opportunities readily available to other citizens, Congress, reflecting the public's mood, was ready to act.

The Department of Labor submitted to the House Judiciary Committee, then considering the proposed legislation, data that demonstrated widespread employment discrimination against African Americans. Nonwhite unemployment stood at 11.4 percent, while only 4.9 percent of whites were jobless.[12] Because employed nonwhites held mainly semi-skilled and unskilled positions, the median annual income of nonwhite males was less than 60 percent of that of white males, and the median annual income of nonwhite women was approximately 50 percent that of white women. Republican members of the committee pointed out that these discriminatory practices not only kept U.S. industry from obtaining the skilled workers it needed, but also limited the purchasing power of African Americans, thus acting as a brake on increases in the gross national product. The Republicans concluded: "Aside from the political and economic considerations, however, we believe in the creation of job equality because it is the right thing to do. We believe in the inherent dignity of man. He is born with certain inalienable rights. His uniqueness is such that we refuse to treat him as if his rights and well-being are bargainable. All vestiges of inequality based upon race must be removed in order to preserve our democratic society, to maintain our country's leadership, and to enhance mankind."[13]

Despite this lofty language, the proposed legislation did not prohibit discrimination in employment *based on sex*. Apparently, preserving our democratic society and our country's leadership and enhancing mankind were possible without granting women equality with men. The House Judiciary Committee simply ignored Department of Labor data that showed the median income of white females in 1960 was approximately 50 percent of that of white males, and that the medium income of nonwhite females was 41 percent of that of nonwhite males and only 24.8 percent of that of white males.[14]

Even with growing support for a Civil Rights Act, the proposed legislation was not without its opponents and detractors. Representative Howard Smith of Virginia, a leading opponent of the law, proposed an amendment that added sex to the prohibitions against employment discrimination. His intent was not to advance the interests of women, but to defeat the entire bill by complicating the debate and confusing some representatives who, although fully supportive of the provisions insuring equality for African Americans, were less certain of the need to expand the act to include protections for women.

Smith showed contempt for his own amendment when he said he had received a letter from one of his female constituents complaining about the "grave injustice" of having more females than males in the country, which prevented every woman from having a husband. This story was greeted with laughter on the floor of the House, but also with anger from the few women serving in Congress. Smith's ploy backfired. Once the question of discrimination against women was placed on the House floor, it was difficult for many representatives to ignore it, and ultimately Smith's amendment was adopted. Thus, what was first intended as a joke culminated in legislation that provided the broadest set of legal protections ever granted to U.S. women.[15]

The Civil Rights Act of 1964 was signed into law by President Lyndon Johnson on April 2, 1964, to take effect one year later. Title VII of the act barred discrimination in employment, and its principal goal was to achieve true equality in workplace opportunities for women and racial, religious, and national minorities. Blumrosen believes that the "effort to ameliorate long standing patterns of race and sex subordination [through enactment of Title VII] is perhaps *the most ambitious social reform effort ever undertaken in America.*"[16]

Title VII has had an enormous impact in securing employment opportunities for women. Ingrained employer practices accepted thirty-five years ago are now inconceivable. Sex stereotyping that once went unquestioned is no longer tolerated. But Title VII, even after more than thirty-five years, has not succeeded in eliminating all discrimination against women in the workplace. We now turn to a review of the law's many successes and failures.

Four

Sex Discrimination after the Enactment of Title VII

When Congress enacted Title VII of the Civil Rights Act of 1964, it declined to enumerate or restrictively to define discriminatory employment practices. Concerning sex discrimination against women, Title VII makes it unlawful for an employer "to discriminate against any [woman] with respect to [her] compensation, terms, conditions, or privileges of employment, because of [her] . . . sex, . . . or to . . . limit, segregate, or classify [its] employees . . . in any way which would deprive any [woman] of employment opportunities or otherwise adversely affect [her] status as an employee, because of [her] sex."[1] These few words proscribe all sex discriminatory workplace policies, practices, and behavior.

Congress was convinced that a broad, rather than a restrictive, definition of discriminatory practices and conduct was necessary, reasoning that workplace discrimination would surely change with time.[2] This has proved to be the case. Sex discrimination claims in the years immediately following passage of Title VII bear little resemblance to those of today.

Congress created the Equal Employment Opportunity Commission (EEOC) to administer Title VII and to process race, national origin, religious, and sex discrimination claims filed pursuant to the statute. More than nine thousand discrimination complaints were filed with the EEOC in its first year of existence, when only two thousand had been anticipated.[3] Not surprisingly, most of these claims charged employers with race discrimination.

In 1964, the unemployment rate of nonwhite workers was twice that of white workers.[4] Earlier Census Bureau statistics had disclosed that only 12 percent of nonwhite workers held professional, managerial, and other white-collar positions, whereas 42 percent of white workers were so employed. Almost one-half of all nonwhite employees worked at unskilled jobs.[5] Because African Americans had for years experienced workplace discrimination, they were among the first workers to take advantage of the new anti-discrimination law. At first, the EEOC had no alternative but to focus its efforts on race discrimination complaints.

At first, the EEOC did not take seriously female worker claims that sex discrimination constituted a substantial issue for women in the workplace. The first director of the EEOC, reflecting upon the manner in which sex discrimination had been added to the Civil Rights Act through the antics of Virginia representative Howard Smith (see chapter 3), characterized the prohibition against sex discrimination as a statutory "fluke . . . conceived out of wedlock."[6] This attitude motivated the EEOC in the early days to devote far less effort to eliminating sex discrimination than to eradicating race discrimination from the workplace.

The EEOC's irresolution in addressing discrimination against women was reflected in the original EEOC guidelines, which did not favor women. The EEOC assumed that when Congress enacted Title VII, it had not intended to disturb state protective laws, such as those that restricted women's work hours and places of employment. Employers had responded to these laws by assigning female workers to "women's jobs," and positions thus classified generally paid less than those designated as "men's jobs." Early on, the EEOC announced that it would not consider it inconsistent with Title VII for a state law to prohibit women from working in jobs that required them to lift more than a specified weight.[7] Thus, in the early stages of the EEOC administration of Title VII, state protective laws remained significant barriers for working women.

The failure of the EEOC to treat sex discrimination with the urgency with which it addressed race discrimination was one of the factors in the formation of the National Organization for Women (NOW) in 1966 by a group of women's rights proponents. NOW first focused its attention on the EEOC's hesitancy to address sex discrimination issues effectively. The EEOC came under still greater pressure when in 1972 Congress passed the Equal Rights Amendment. Although ultimately not adopted by a sufficient number of state legislatures to become an amendment to the Constitution, the ERA garnered enough mass support to greatly increase society's concern for women in general. The social impulse toward equality for African Americans that existed before the enactment of Title VII now broadened to include equality for women. At this point, the EEOC's attitude toward sex discrimination began to shift in favor of issues supported by women.[8] Women responded to the change by filing an increasing number of sex discrimination complaints, and by 2000 nearly 32 percent of all Title VII complaints were sex related, a filing rate slightly less than the 36.2 percent for race complaints.[9]

With the EEOC's attention redirected to Title VII's prohibitions against sex as well as race discrimination, it remained for the courts to determine whether to limit the application of the statute to the most blatant, and therefore the most obvious, forms of discriminatory conduct, or to extend its reach to less obvious violations. In 1971, this issue came before the Supreme Court.

After reading a local Florida newspaper help-wanted advertisement placed by the Martin Marietta Corporation, Ida Phillips applied for the position of assembly trainee. Shortly thereafter, she was notified that female applicants with preschool children were not being considered for the job. When she learned that men with preschool children were being interviewed and hired as assembly trainees, Phillips sued Martin Marietta for sex discrimination.

In response to Phillips's lawsuit, Martin Marietta pointed to the many women it had hired for the assembly trainee position, arguing that it had refused to hire Phillips, not because she was a woman, but solely because she had preschool children at home. An employer may be found guilty of sex discrimination, the company urged, only when it used gender, and only gender, as the basis for its action; because Phillips's gender had not been the basis for its refusal to hire her, it had not violated the statute. The Supreme Court rejected this argument, ruling that an employer that promulgates one hiring policy for women and another for men violates Title VII, even though the difference in the hiring policies relates to a factor other than sex—in this case, the presence in the home of preschool children.

If the Court had acceded to Martin Marietta's argument, the scope of the statute would have been materially limited. As stated by Justice Thurgood Marshall in his concurring opinion: "By adding the prohibition against job discrimination based on sex to the 1964 Civil Rights Act, Congress intended to prevent employers from refusing 'to hire an individual based on stereotyped characterizations of the sexes.' . . . Even characterizations of the proper roles of the sexes were not to serve as predicates for restricting employment opportunity. . . . When performance characteristics of an individual are involved, even when parental roles are concerned, employment opportunity may be limited only by employment criteria that are neutral as to the sex of the applicant." Thus, the Supreme Court firmly stamped its approval on the side of an expansive, rather than a restrictive, interpretation of the statute. It also established the rule that the differential treatment of women on the basis of their child-caring responsibilities constitutes a violation of Title VII.[10]

Another issue soon threatened to undermine the scope of Title VII. Congress had added an exception to the statute's proscriptions of sex discriminatory practices by permitting employers to deny employment to women when the nature of the job required the physical attributes of a man to perform the job's functions: "Notwithstanding any other provision of this [statute], it shall not be an unlawful employment practice for an employer to hire or employ employees on the basis . . . of sex . . . in those certain instances where . . . sex . . . is a *bona fide occupational qualification* reasonably necessary to the normal operation of that particular business or enterprise" (emphasis added).[11] If broadly interpreted, the bona fide occupational qualification (BFOQ) exception would justify the exclusion of large numbers of women from many jobs, particularly some jobs that required the performance of physically demanding tasks.

When Dianne Rawlinson applied for the position of prison guard in the Alabama prison system, her application was rejected because she failed to meet the state's minimum 120-pound weight requirement as well as its minimum height requirement of five feet, two inches. Rawlinson sued, claiming that the weight and height requirements disproportionately excluded women from eligibility for employment as prison guards.

Data submitted to the trial court showed that the five-foot-two minimum height requirement excluded more than 33 percent of working women from prison guard positions, but only slightly more than 1 percent of male workers. Similarly, the 120-pound minimum weight requirement eliminated 22.29 percent of female workers, but only 2.35 percent of male workers. When the height and weight requirements were combined, more than 41 percent of the working female population would fail to qualify for the position, while less than 1 percent of working males would be barred. The Alabama Board of Corrections argued that the weight and height requirements were bona fide occupational qualifications directly related to the prison guard position, thus justifying the rejection of Rawlinson's application. However, the board failed to offer the court any data that correlated the height and weight requirements with the strength necessary to perform the functions of the prison guard job.

When the case reached the Supreme Court, the justices pointed out that if the strength of a prison guard were truly job related and constituted a BFOQ, the board could have adopted tests to measure each applicant's strength directly: "Such a test, fairly administered, would fully satisfy the standards of Title VII because it would be one that measures the person for the job, and not the person in the abstract." The Supreme Court ruled that if the board wished to rely on the BFOQ defense in denying these positions to women, it must conduct individual evaluations of each female applicant to determine that applicant's qualifications for the position.[12]

This was the first of many court rulings holding that an employer must evaluate a female worker as an individual, rather than rely upon stereotypical characterizations of female worker capabilities. An employer may not validly assert the BFOQ defense on the assumption that all women, as a class, possess identical or even similar attributes. As the Supreme Court emphasized, the BFOQ defense is based on an extremely narrow exception to the general prohibition of discrimination on the basis of sex, and for an employer to rely upon that exception, it must prove a female job applicant is specifically unqualified for the position in question. It is impermissible under Title VII to refuse to hire a woman on the basis of a stereotypical characterization of the female sex.

When may the BFOQ exception be validly asserted? Under Alabama law, Dianne Rawlinson had a second hurdle to negotiate before she could qualify for the prison guard position. The Supreme Court noted that Alabama's prison system was "a peculiarly inhospitable one for human beings of whatever sex." Because of insufficient staffing and inadequate penal facilities, the Board of Corrections had not undertaken to segregate inmates according to their offenses and, as a result, male sex offenders—20 percent of the prison population—were scattered throughout the prison's dormitory facilities. Were these circumstances such as to render the prison guard job too dangerous for women? Ordinarily, as the Court observed, whether a particular job is too dangerous for women is a decision that an individual woman should make for herself. But in this case, more was at stake. The Court felt that sex offenders who had criminally assaulted women in the past would be moved to do so again if they had access to women within the prison. There also was the risk that other inmates, deprived of a normal heterosexual environment, would assault women guards. "In a prison system where violence is the order of the day, where inmate access to guards is facilitated by dormitory living conditions, . . . and where a substantial portion of the inmate population is composed of sex offenders mixed at random with other prisoners, there are few visible deterrents to inmate assault on women custodians." Therefore, the Court concluded, Rawlinson's "very womanhood" undermined her capacity to provide the security that is a primary responsibility of a prison guard. Since the use of women guards under the conditions in the Alabama prison system would pose a substantial security problem—a problem directly linked to the sex of the prison guards—being male was a bona fide occupational qualification for the prison guard position.[13]

There are not many positions in the business world where "womanhood" constitutes a disqualifying factor. The Court's decision in the Rawlinson case, along with other early court decisions emphasizing the narrow application of the BFOQ defense, have opened up many positions for women that formerly were reserved for men. Every policewoman, as well as all female school bus drivers, train engineers, conductors, construction and utility workers, and other female workers performing tasks that prior to the enactment of Title VII had been reserved for men, have the courts to thank for the limitations placed on the application of the BFOQ defense.[14]

Beginning with the Rawlinson case, the Supreme Court has repeatedly held that a woman must be evaluated as an individual and not as a member of a class or as a woman in the abstract. Stereotypical characterizations of female attributes may in certain instances be true of some women, but they are not true of all women.

The issue of sex stereotypes next came before the Court in connection with a challenge to a pension plan for employees of the Los Angeles Department of Water and Power. The pension plan was based on mortality tables, as well as on the department's own experience that women live longer than men. Because the department's female workers lived longer in retirement, the cost of a pension for the average female retiree was greater than that for the average male retiree. To compensate for the difference, the department required its women employees to make larger contributions to the plan. When greater amounts were withheld from their paychecks to finance their pension benefits, female workers received less take-home pay than their male co-workers. The women sued the Los Angeles Department of Water and Power.

The Supreme Court struck down the pension plan; it was a matter of sex stereotyping, the Court declared. The department's rationale for requiring larger pension contributions from women was based on the assumption that women live longer than men. But *all* women do not live longer than *all* men. As a group, women live longer than men, but this may not be true of many members of each group and it is certainly not true of all members of either group. It is impossible for an employer to forecast the life span of any particular woman employee. The Department of Water and Power was not justified, therefore, in using a group's average longevity in the computation of the cost of a particular woman's pension benefits. To do so was to consider her not as an individual, but as a member of a group. Employment decisions based on stereotypical assumptions pertaining to a group or class rather than upon an individual's particular circumstances are antithetical to gender equality.[15]

Other courts, following the Supreme Court's lead, have rejected employer initiatives based on sex stereotypes. United Air Lines adopted a no-marriage rule for its female flight attendants but declined to make the rule applicable to male flight personnel, including male flight attendants. United attempted to justify its no-marriage rule on the ground that it had received complaints from husbands of its flight attendants concerning their wives' work schedules and irregular hours. The federal court of appeals sitting in Chicago rejected United's position, noting that Title VII required employers to treat their employees as individuals: "United's blanket prophylactic rule prohibiting marriage unjustifiably punishes a large class of prospective, otherwise qualified and competent employees where an individualized response could adequately dispose of any real employment conflicts."[16]

Subsequent to these early cases, most courts have consistently rejected stereotype-based employment rules and regulations. But despite these rulings, stereotypes still frequently underlie current employment decisions that adversely affect women. The insidiousness of employer use of stereotypes must be fully grasped if we are to understand fully the nature of present-day workplace sex discrimination.

The use of stereotypes is common throughout the workplace, especially in connection with the employment of older workers. In fact, age stereotypes underlie nearly all acts of age discrimination. Stereotypical preconceptions consign to older workers of a particular age the physical and mental characteristics of the average worker of that age. Such thinking fails to distinguish between an older worker's physical and mental capabilities and those perceived to be common among members of that worker's age group. Negative employer perceptions of aging are expressed in these commonly held stereotypes:

- Older workers are stubborn, inflexible, resistant to change, and less likely to accept new technology.
- Older workers are less productive than younger workers.
- Older workers are less adaptable, and as they are slow learners they find it more difficult to learn new skills.
- If their skills become obsolete, older workers are more difficult to retrain.
- The cost of employee benefits for older workers are greater than those for younger workers.
- Older people are eager to retire at the earliest opportunity. They merely want to ride out what remains of their careers.
- Because their remaining tenure with the company will probably be short, it is economically unreasonable to invest in training older people in new technologies and processes.

Little evidence exists to support the validity of any of these age stereotypes. Except in jobs that demand strenuous physical labor, studies fail to show a correlation between age and ability to perform. Older workers consistently receive high ratings for job skills, loyalty, reliability, and lack of turnover. Other studies show that older workers who are continually challenged by their jobs demonstrate little or no decline in interest or motivation, are not resistant to change, and readily accept new technologies. Generally, the performance of older workers is at least as good as and sometimes better than that of younger workers.[17]

Although stereotypical thinking is especially pervasive in employment decisions that adversely affect the careers of older workers, it often underlies employment decisions that negatively impact female workers. As noted in chapter 2, employment decisions regarding women are frequently influenced by commonly held stereotypes that view women as lacking leadership ability, unable to adapt to changing circumstances, incapable of resolving problems that arise in difficult interpersonal relationships, and unable to balance work with the demands of motherhood, supposedly a detriment to long-term careers.

In spite of early Supreme Court rulings that firmly rejected sex stereotypes as a legitimate basis for employment decisions, a few courts have actually used these stereotypes to justify the rejection of sex discrimination claims. In 1986, the EEOC, acting on behalf of women employed as salespersons by Sears, Roebuck and Company, sued the company for sex discrimination, claiming that Sears had failed to promote women employed as noncommission salespersons to commission salesperson positions. Merchandise sold on a commission basis was usually more expensive, as commission selling generally involved big-ticket items, such as major appliances, air conditioners, and tires, while noncommission selling usually involved small-ticket items, such as clothing, linens, toys, and cosmetics. Commission sales positions were highly competitive, requiring salespersons with a high degree of motivation and enthusiasm as well as a willingness to depend for one's livelihood solely upon one's sales ability. Commission salespersons on average earned substantially more than noncommission salepersons.

Sears, in its attempt to justify its promotion of a far greater proportion of men than women from noncommission to commission sales positions, relied on certain stereotypical assumptions about women:

- Women tend to see themselves as less competitive, and thus are less likely than men to be interested in sales jobs involving a high degree of competition.
- Women often view noncommission sales as more attractive than commission sales.
- Women are less likely than men to be interested in working nights and weekends (required of sales commission positions) and are more likely to be interested in regular daytime work.
- Women are less likely than men to be motivated by the amount of the compensation provided by a job rather than by the nature of the job itself.

- Women tend to be more interested than men in the social and cooperative aspects of the workplace.

The court ruled that these "conclusions" supported Sears's contention that women were less likely than men to be interested in commission selling, thus explaining the company's employing a disproportionate number of men as commission salespersons.[18]

The court decided the case on a basis the Supreme Court had already ruled inappropriate—it evaluated Sears's female employees solely as members of a group, and not as individuals. Although it may be argued that a small element of truth lies in each of Sears's generalizations about women, these generalizations are nonetheless irrelevant to the issues relating to sex discrimination. A generalization true about some women may not be true about all women, and it certainly may not be true about a particular woman.

Even though an employer may refrain from discriminating against women in general, it may nonetheless be guilty of acts of discrimination that violate a particular woman's rights. Thus, even if an employer generally treats its female employees fairly and advantageously, it can never be justified in discriminating against a particular female worker. Each claim of discrimination must be examined in the circumstances confronted by the particular woman involved. As already noted, Title VII and the principles of nondiscrimination require that an employer consider a female worker on the basis of individual capabilities and not on the basis of any characteristics attributable to women in general. Stereotypical assumptions may play no role in this process.

In addition to adjudicating cases that involve sex stereotyping, the courts were required early on to consider the validity of state protective laws. As we have seen, these laws originally were intended for the general benefit of women, but restrictions on working conditions of female workers seriously undermined many women's career prospects. The initial EEOC guidelines were based on the assumption that Congress, in enacting Title VII, had not intended to invalidate these laws. The courts, however, believed otherwise, and most of the state protective laws soon met their demise. But, not long after, an analogous issue arose that also tended to limit the areas of female employment.

In the 1980s, an estimated twenty million jobs in the U.S. workforce involved exposure to toxic substances that presented reproductive hazards for workers.[19] Because of concerns for fetal health, many employers adopted fetal-protection polices that excluded women from jobs exposing them to these toxic substances.

Johnson Controls, Inc., manufactured batteries. Exposure to lead, a primary element in the battery-manufacturing process, entails health risks, including possible harm to the fetus of a pregnant worker. Concern for the unborn children of its employees led Johnson Controls to adopt a fetal-protection policy that excluded pregnant women, as well as women capable of bearing children, from jobs that would expose them to lead. Women working for the company objected to the policy, claiming that Johnson Controls was discriminating against its female employees by excluding them from higher-paying manufacturing jobs. They sued, claiming violation of Title VII.

Although Johnson Controls' fetal-protection policy was adopted for a good purpose, it nevertheless was discriminatory. Exposure to lead also has a deleterious effect upon the male reproductive system, but Johnson Controls did not exclude men capable of producing children from the exposure-to-lead positions. The company thus classified or segregated workers on the basis of gender. Because both men and women were at risk, individual workers should have been permitted to decide whether to accept or reject that risk. An employer may not assume that women are less capable than men of making that choice. It is for each woman, not her employer, to decide whether her reproductive role or her economic role is more important to her and her family.[20]

Thus, in the years immediately following the adoption of Title VII, the courts and the EEOC formulated broad legal principles applicable to issues relating to discrimination against women. To see how successful the courts have been in helping women eliminate sex discrimination from the workplace, we now turn to a review of court cases that have applied these principles in sex discrimination claims over the last three and one-half decades.

Five

Common Forms of
Sex Discrimination

Within fifteen years of the enactment of Title VII, the wage income of women increased by $22 billion, and more than four million women were working in higher job categories.[1] Although women have continued to experience improvement in working conditions, employment discrimination against women persists in various forms in at least three distinct categories: overt sex discrimination, sex stereotyping, and disparate treatment.

Overt and Blatant Forms of Sex Discrimination

For the most part, employers who discriminate against women endeavor to conceal their conduct. Others, however, have so little regard for the anti-discrimination laws that they openly flout them. Their conduct is overt and blatant, as Gendra Sennello found when she moved from Michigan to Florida and went to work as a sales agent with Reserve Life Insurance Company in Ft. Lauderdale. The following year, Reserve Life promoted her to a management position, and during the next seven years she gradually moved up the ranks to district manager of the company's Ft. Lauderdale office. Sennello's record at Reserve Life was exemplary. She effectively managed three offices, was often promoted, and was highly regarded by her colleagues. Then, suddenly, she was demoted and, shortly after, terminated.

The demise of Sennello's career at Reserve Life coincided with the arrival of a new regional manager. For many years, William Ebert worked for Reserve Life in regional manager positions throughout the country, and at this time he was appointed regional manager for Florida. Immediately after assuming his new duties, Ebert conferred with Sennello's direct supervisor, advising him that "we can't have women in management because women are like Jews and Niggers; they hire like themselves, and the trouble with that is that when they leave they take [the workers they hired] with them." Ebert criticized Sennello because in his eyes she had hired too many women. He was not happy with the "gender make-up" of her offices. He pressured Sennello to resign her management position, but to remain with the company as a sales agent. Sennello decided to accept the demotion, returning to the position she had filled when hired seven years previously. Six weeks later, Ebert fired her.

Ebert was not the only highly ranked employee at Reserve Life who expressed discriminatory animus toward women in management. At a company sales conference, Reserve Life's president, Douglas Pierce, while commenting on a critical letter Sennello had written, derisively remarked that he had not realized Sennello "was so high on the women thing." On another occasion, Pierce, responding to a comment of a woman employee, crushed out a cigarette with his shoe, stating, "That's why I don't like women in management—they keep grinding and grinding."[2]

Remarkably, neither Ebert nor Pierce attempted to conceal his bias against women in management; apparently, they felt they had little to fear from openly sexist behavior. They simply acted as if the laws barring discrimination in employment did not exist. Their conduct was unlawful, it was overt, and it was blatant. In the end, after Sennello sued the company for sex discrimination, Reserve Life suffered the consequences of their conduct.

A similarly blatant display of overt discrimination occurred in the case of Irene Spears, who taught in an elementary school in Pike County, Kentucky. Although she was consistently rated by her supervisors as a superior teacher, Spears's main interest was elevation to a principal's position. Two years after starting her teaching career in Pike County, Spears obtained a master's degree, and four years later a degree as an educational specialist. Subsequently, she attained the highest professional rating a teacher could achieve in Kentucky—a Rank I classification—and at that point the state certified her as qualified for an elementary-school principal position. Spears immediately sought promotion to an administrative role in the Pike County school system.

During the succeeding five years, nine administrative positions became available in the system, and in each instance the superintendent of schools appointed a man to the vacancy, while not considering Spears for any of them. Later, during the trial of Spears's sex discrimination suit against the county, the court ruled that in each instance Spears had been better qualified than the male employee who had received the appointment.

Statements made by the superintendent of schools in connection with the nine appointments were viewed by the court as discriminatory; they disclosed an illicit frame of mind. On one occasion, the superintendent commented that he wanted to appoint a man as principal of one of the county's high schools because he wanted someone who would instill "the discipline of a football coach." On another occasion, after Spears inquired about a vacant elementary-school principal's position, the superintendent told her he "needed a man up there."[3]

Although not as offensive as the discriminatory remarks made by the Reserve Life officials, the superintendent's statements nevertheless were blatant, clearly demonstrating a discriminatory animus toward women. It may appear surprising that a person in his position could be so insensitive to the demands of the anti-discrimination law, but such occurrences are common. In the case reports that follow, the prohibition against sex discrimination often is the farthest thing from the minds of employers, and in such circumstances, female workers inevitably are the targets of discriminatory behavior. Dana Throgmorton's story is a case in point.

United States Forgecraft Corporation, located in Arkansas, hired Throgmorton as a quality control clerk and, soon after, promoted her to coordinator of a computer system that Forgecraft used for production data. Throgmorton remained in the coordinator position until Forgecraft decided to discontinue use of its computer system, and at that point she was terminated. Forgecraft then eliminated some of Throgmorton's former job responsibilities and assigned others to a male employee.

Throgmorton sued Forgecraft, alleging that her termination occurred as a consequence of a general gender bias on the part of management, and that if she had been a man, she would have been transferred to another position rather than terminated. In support of her allegations of sex bias, Throgmorton testified that the company's chief operations officer had told her that women did not belong in management. This attitude appeared to reflect the views of the company's owner, whose testimony sounds as if it comes out of another century:

> Here she was a little old girl, a country girl, up there that didn't know anything from come sic' em and . . . here he wanted her to help him implement a very complex system. And so all she could do is follow one, two, three, four and, you know, what can you do with a girl who is nothing but a clerk and all she did was run copies. . . . I guess a man could have done that job, but it's more suited to a woman. . . .
>
> Shuffling paper and punching a keyboard is—most women have better dexterity than men and . . . you see more women clerks than you do men clerks. That's our history in business, isn't it?

If this attitude sounds as if women at Forgecraft were relegated to second-class status, that is precisely how it was described by a consultant for the company: "Women in that company were second class citizens, . . . treated like cattle, different than any company I've ever been in. [Women] appeared to understand that they were subservient to the men. No women could ever make a decision." Based on this testimony, the court ruled that Throgmorton's termination was gender related, as Forgecraft would have found another position for her had she been a man.[4]

A more egregious example of blatant sex discrimination may be difficult to find, and yet Forgecraft's owner freely testified to his sex-biased attitudes. He denigrated and ridiculed the company's female workers, disclosing a company bias against women. His decision to testify in this fashion exhibited either a contemptuous disregard for the law, an arrogant belief that he was free to act without regard to it, or gross ignorance of it. In any case, sex discrimination at his company was overt and blatant.

Another blatantly discriminatory case was that of Maureen Barbano, a social welfare examiner for Madison County in upstate New York. Responsible for determining the eligibility of individuals for public assistance, Medicaid, and food stamps, she was generally familiar with federal, state, and local laws pertaining to the operation of the public assistance programs in the county. After three years in this position, she learned of an opportunity for advancement at the Madison County Veterans Service Agency, which reported a vacancy for director of the agency, responsible for the supervision of veterans' welfare programs throughout the county. Barbano filed her application with the agency's six-man hiring committee and was scheduled for an interview.

Before entering the interview room, Barbano overheard one of the interviewers say, "Here are copies of the next resume," followed by the comment, "Oh, another woman." Early in the interview, one of the committee members, Donald Greene, told Barbano that he wanted to know what her plans were for having a family, since there were "some women" he was unwilling to consider for the position. As if this question were not sufficiently objectionable, he also asked Barbano whether her husband would object to her transporting male veterans around the county. Barbano responded that the questions were irrelevant and discriminatory. Greene demanded answers. When Barbano again declined to respond, Greene growled that the questions were relevant—he did not want to hire a woman who would get pregnant and then quit. Barbano advised the committee that if she decided to have a family, she would take no more time off than medically necessary. Greene once again asked whether Barbano's husband would object to her "running around the county with men" and declared he would not want his wife to do it. Barbano retorted that she was not his wife, and on that note, the interview was concluded.

The committee interviewed several other candidates, determining that all were qualified, and awarded the position to Allan Wagner, who for the previous six years had been a school bus driver and part-time bartender at the local American Legion. In contrast to Barbano's experience with county public assistance programs, Wagner had no knowledge of federal, state, or local laws pertaining to veterans' benefits and services and was generally unfamiliar with the county's welfare agencies.

After the committee rejected her, Barbano sued Madison County for sex discrimination. The court later ruled that Greene's questioning of Barbano, constituting nearly her entire interview, was discriminatory. His queries about a possible pregnancy and Barbano's husband's feelings about her "running around the county with men" were totally unrelated to any qualification for the director position. Thus, the committee's weighing of the relative merits of Barbano's and Wagner's qualifications were necessarily tainted with discrimination.

Perhaps Greene's attitude was an outgrowth of a lifetime of antipathy to women in the workplace. Although this would not justify his treatment of Barbano, it would tend to explain his conduct at the interview. But what about the other five committee members? Although they must have known that Greene's questions were discriminatory—in fact, Barbano told the committee they were—none voiced any objection to Greene's queries. They went along with this charade of an interview. Whether they acted in contemptuous disregard for the law, or as the result of a belief that they were free to act without regard to it, or simply in ignorance of the law, we do not know. Regardless, they violated the law, and Madison County paid the price for their conduct.[5]

Overt and blatant acts of sex discrimination also occurred in the Olsten case discussed in chapter 1. Three of Olsten's senior vice presidents were determined to prevent Mary Ann Luciano's promotion to vice president. They revised her job description to ensure an unsatisfactory job performance rating so as to preserve the all-male status of senior management in their division of the company. They undertook to achieve their goals by openly discriminating against Luciano.[6]

In another case, a woman applied for a vacant position on a small-town police force. In her interview with the police chief, he informed her that she was the most qualified of those applying for the position, but he also warned her that some of the town aldermen were opposed to women on the police force. Subsequently, the aldermen decided not to fill the vacancy. Even though the failure to fill the vacant position required other police officers to work substantial amounts of overtime, no new police officers were hired for the next eighteen months. The aldermen allowed these circumstances to prevail for a year and a half rather than place a woman on the police force.[7]

Incidents of blatant and overt discrimination against women have decreased as employers have discovered they are able to achieve their ends by acting covertly. As employers have become more proficient in concealing their discriminatory intent, their conduct has become less readily identified as discriminatory. As a result, victims of discriminatory behavior have found it more difficult to prove to a court or jury that they were actually victims of discrimination.

Sex Stereotyping

Sex discrimination in the form of sex stereotyping is often closely allied with acts of overt discrimination, as was true in three of the cases just reviewed. In the *Sennello* case, the newly appointed regional manager assumed that women tend to hire other women. In the *Spears* case, the school superintendent assumed that female teachers were incapable of coping with situations he felt could be handled adequately only by someone with a football coach mentality—in other words, solely by a man. In the *Throgmorton* case, the company owner assumed that women do not perform well as managers. As noted in the last chapter, the Supreme Court has repeatedly ruled that an employer may not lawfully make employment decisions based on stereotyped characterizations of the sexes.[8]

Yet gender stereotypes persist in the workplace. Personal attributes presumed necessary for higher-level positions in the business world are often seen as incompatible with personality characteristics generally associated with women. For example, women are viewed as nurturing and sensitive—traits often not looked upon favorably in the workplace. On the one hand, women are frequently perceived as lacking the aggressiveness and dedication necessary for success; on the other hand, women who are assertive and dedicated to their jobs are often viewed as overly aggressive, uncooperative, and unfeminine. Ann Hopkins confronted such a no-win situation.

Hopkins served as a senior manager in the accounting firm of Price Waterhouse. She had worked in the firm's Office of Government Services in Washington, D.C., for five years when the partners in that office proposed her as a candidate for partnership. They praised her character as well as her accomplishments, describing her as "an outstanding professional" who had a "deft touch," and a "strong character, independence and integrity." They also favored her for partnership because she had succeeded in obtaining major new clients for the firm, a record none of the other candidates for partnership could match.

When Hopkins was nominated, only 7 of the firm's 662 partners were female, and of the eighty-eight persons proposed for partnership, Hopkins was the only woman. When the partnership nominations were put to a vote, forty-seven of the candidates were admitted to partnership, twenty-one were rejected, and the remaining twenty—including Hopkins—were advised that their candidacies would be held for reconsideration the following year. One year later, all of the male candidates who had been placed on hold were renominated for partnership, but Hopkins was not. When she inquired about her rejection, she was told that difficulties she had experienced in interpersonal skills as well as her aggressive, tough behavior had contributed to the negative decision. Hopkins then sued the firm, alleging that stereotyped views of women and female behavior had played a substantial role in her rejection for partnership.

Evidence submitted to the court during the course of the litigation revealed that some of the firm's partners reacted negatively to Hopkins solely because she was a woman, and these partners had evaluated her on sex-based terms. Several partners criticized her use of profanity. One partner described her as "macho," another asserted that she "overcompensated for being a woman," and still another suggested that she take "a course at charm school." Hopkins was advised that if she wanted to improve her chances for partnership she should "walk more femininely, talk more femininely, dress more femininely, wear make-up, have her hair styled, and wear jewelry."

In previous years, Price Waterhouse had also evaluated female candidates for partnership on sex-based terms. These women were viewed favorably if they were perceived to have maintained their femininity while becoming effective professional managers. To be viewed as a "women's libber" was regarded negatively.

Ultimately, Hopkins's case reached the Supreme Court. In determining whether gender had played a motivating role in the decision to deny Hopkins partnership status, the Court first set out a rule of thumb to be followed in cases where it is necessary to decide whether a woman has been discriminatorily denied a job opportunity: "In saying that gender played a motivating part in an employment decision, we mean that if we asked the employer at the moment of the decision what its reasons were and if we received a truthful response, one of those reasons would be that [she] was a woman." As it would be somewhat naive to expect a totally truthful response to such a query, the Court examined the specific circumstances Hopkins confronted at the moment of Price Waterhouse's decision to reject her for partnership, and focused on the partners' stereotypical comments about her aggressiveness: "In the specific context of sex stereotyping, an employer who acts on the basis of a belief that a woman cannot be aggressive, or that she must not be, has acted on the basis of gender. . . . An employer who objects to aggressiveness in women but whose positions require this trait places women in an intolerable and impermissible Catch–22; out of a job if they behave aggressively and out of a job if they don't. Title VII lifts women out of this bind."[9]

The sex-based evaluations used by Price Waterhouse reflected negative stereotypes of female workers and, therefore, subverted the evaluation process of the female candidates for partnership. Price Waterhouse discriminated against Hopkins when it relied on these negative stereotypes to deny her partnership status.

Disparate Treatment

A third type of discrimination that women commonly encounter can be defined as second-class-citizen treatment. Some employers simply treat their male employees more advantageously than their female employees, paying them more and promoting them more frequently. These same employers relegate women to lower-paying, dead-end positions and generally refuse to promote them. An employer's different, or disparate, treatment of men and women constitutes the very essence of sex discrimination.

An example is the case of Mary Polacco, who after receiving a Ph.D. from Duke University and completing a postdoctoral fellowship at Yale, was hired by the University of Missouri as a research assistant professor in its Department of Biochemistry. The previous year, the university had hired her husband as a professor of biochemistry. Her husband's position was tenure track, Polacco's was not. The university paid a portion of Polacco's salary, and the balance came from grants that Polacco obtained from outside sources, including a prestigious grant from the National Science Foundation. After Polacco had been with the university for about ten years, the Department of Biochemistry announced that due to budgetary considerations it would no longer pay a portion of Polacco's salary. Polacco accused the department of engaging in sex discrimination, and she sued the university for violation of Title VII.

At the trial, the jury heard evidence that at the time that budgetary problems were said to underlie the reduction in Polacco's salary, the Department of Biochemistry had offered to hire a male professor at a salary twice the size of hers; when he declined to accept the offer, the department failed to reallocate any portion of those funds to pay Polacco's salary. Polacco claimed that this was discriminatory and that as the wife of a faculty member, she was consistently treated as a second-class citizen by the department. The jury agreed with those assessments and granted her substantial damages.

Polacco's lawsuit succeeded because she was able to show that the Department of Biochemistry treated her differently than it treated men. The inference the jury could, and probably did, draw from the department's behavior is that if Polacco had been born male, her salary would have remained intact.[10]

Disparate treatment of male and female workers may occur with respect to any aspect of the employment relationship. Linda Rodhe can testify to that. Rodhe was employed as a secretary by K. O. Steel Castings, Inc., in San Antonio, Texas. For some time, she had been engaged in a romantic relationship with a company foreman, Arnulfo Lopez. Management knew of the relationship, and apparently it had not been the cause of any problems. Those circumstances changed when Lopez struck Rodhe during an argument one evening in her apartment, and the following day she informed the company's personnel director that she was unable to report for work because of the injuries she had sustained. She returned to work the day after, only to be assaulted by Lopez again, this time on company premises. The company's president and vice president were on a business trip, but when they returned a few days later, one of their first orders of business was to resolve the matter between Rodhe and Lopez. Their solution was to fire Rodhe. Lopez was not released or even disciplined.

Even if company executives believed that both Rodhe and Lopez were guilty of offensive behavior—although no evidence was offered showing that Rodhe was at fault—they failed to consider their offenses in the same light. If company officials felt that they confronted a serious disruptive situation, why not dismiss both Rodhe and Lopez? Instead, they fired only one of the workers, the female rather than the male. But no legitimate, nondiscriminatory reason justified different treatment. Only gender could have been the basis for the disparity in treatment.[11]

Elements of disparate treatment were present in some of the cases already reviewed. As an example, it played a significant role in Mary Ann Luciano's case against the Olsten Corporation (see chapter 1).[12] The evidence in that case showed that women generally were not promoted to management positions. The existence of a glass ceiling is a form of disparate treatment. Men are not confronted with glass ceilings; they simply do not encounter artificial barriers to advancement. While Olsten's female employees faced significant restrictions on promotion to upper-level management, male employees—even those with poor performance records—were regularly promoted to those positions. At the same time that Luciano was dismissed, supposedly because her position had been eliminated, Olsten created new positions for male employees who faced the elimination of their jobs. Disparate treatment of Olsten's female workers was rampant.

Over the long history of disparate treatment at MIT, male faculty were paid more than female faculty, male professors were allotted more research money than female professors, female faculty members were barred from department head positions and rarely appointed to important committee seats, women were assigned less office space than men, and fewer awards were granted to women, even though they attained professional status equal to their male colleagues (see chapter 2). In such circumstances, disparate treatment of women was an everyday event.

Discrimination against women in the workplace assumes many forms, probably as many forms as there are employers, but as we proceed to examine cases of discrimination against specific groups—older women, women of color, women in the professions, pregnant women, and women with children—we will find that these cases, for the most part, fall within one of the three categories of sex discrimination just reviewed.

Six

Discrimination against Older Women

The provisions of the Age Discrimination in Employment Act make it unlawful for employers to discriminate on the basis of age against any worker age forty and over.[1] In the business world, middle age arrives earlier for women than for men, and women are considered "old" at a younger age than men.[2] Men generally first experience the effects of age-discriminatory practices and policies in their mid-fifties, while women commonly first become aware of age-biased employment decisions that adversely affect their work lives in their mid- to late forties. The appearance of middle age in a woman is often looked upon as either a disqualification for further advancement or a reason for her dismissal. Gray hair may be appropriate for male CEOs and other highly placed male executives, but not for older female workers.

Middle-aged and older women comprise a steadily increasing share of the workforce. Sex- and age discrimination claims asserted by women in these age groups generally relate to one of two workplace events—a failure to promote or an untimely dismissal. The typical failure-to-promote case involves an older woman passed over in favor of a younger man. The typical termination case involves the discharge of an older woman—purportedly justified on the ground of poor performance, despite many years of satisfactory performance evaluations—in favor of the retention of a less qualified younger man.

Data assembled by the Equal Employment Opportunity Commission show that women between the ages of forty and forty-nine are more likely than women in other age groups to file claims alleging *both* age and sex discrimination.[3] Women over the age of fifty, on the other hand, are more apt to claim that their workplace adversities result solely from age discrimination. The combination of age and sex discrimination in the claims of the group forty to forty-nine reflects the preferences of some employers for attractive female employees, and they equate attractiveness with youth; as a female worker approaches middle age, she is more likely to be discarded by employers holding that view. When an employer holds its women workers, but not its male workers, to a standard of youthful attractiveness, it is guilty of both age and sex discrimination.

A case in point is Carolyn Proffitt's. After several years of employment as a salesperson for Anacomp, Inc., Proffitt was terminated, despite in the preceding year having exceeded 100 percent of her sales quota. One of the reasons given for terminating the forty-one-year-old Proffitt was that women do well in sales only if they are sexually attractive, and because Proffitt's supervisor felt she no longer met that criterion, he predicted she would not do well in the future. After Anacomp terminated Proffitt, it transferred her accounts to a thirty-four-year-old female trainee whom management apparently found sexually attractive. After Proffitt filed claims of sex and age discrimination, the court denied Anacomp's motion to dismiss her suit, thus leading to its settlement.[4]

Women who serve as waitresses and flight attendants and in other positions that require direct contact with the public are frequently held to a standard of attractiveness that employers do not apply to men. Although clearly discriminatory, such a standard is nonetheless widely used, even in instances where a worker's appearance has no relationship to her job functions. Catherine Malarkey, who began working for Texaco as a grade six secretary at age thirty, already had an impressive background, having served as a secretary to a high-ranking executive in another large corporation. By all accounts, she was a commendable employee at Texaco, rising quickly through the secretarial ranks and attaining a grade twelve position within ten years. At that point, Malarkey took a six-month unpaid leave of absence to care for an ailing family member. When she returned from her leave, no grade twelve secretarial positions were available. Texaco, however, offered her an administrative position in its employment office, and Malarkey accepted it.

About a year later, Malarkey prepared a memorandum to her supervisor questioning Texaco's employment practices, alluding to possible acts of age- and sex-discriminatory conduct. Malarkey informed her supervisor that she found it very difficult to place older women in secretarial positions at Texaco, since male supervisors generally agreed to hire only young, physically attractive women. After she wrote her memo, Malarkey was demoted from grade twelve to grade eleven and forced out of the employment office.[5]

Texaco executives are not alone in preferring young and attractive female secretaries. Although sex discrimination in employment has been barred by federal law since 1964 and age discrimination since 1967, the practice of refusing to hire older women for secretarial positions not only persists, but continues to be widespread. Statistical data may be lacking to substantiate this reality, but businessmen are well aware of it, and the honest businessman, if confronted, will confirm it.

Some employers bar older women from promotion to higher positions, while others subject them to on-the-job adverse treatment calculated to force them into early retirement. Edyna Sischo-Nownejad, who served on the art department faculty of Merced Community College in California, is a case in point. The college generally based the assignment and scheduling of courses on the input of its faculty members, who customarily were consulted for their course preferences as well as with regard to their need for course materials and supplies. Senior faculty members who had developed courses were normally selected to teach them. For many years, the college followed these practices in connection with all faculty members other than Sischo-Nownejad, one of the oldest members of the art department faculty and its only woman. The college declined to consult with Sischo-Nownejad with regard to the courses she was designated to teach, it assigned courses to her she would rather not have taught, and it failed to select her to teach the courses she had developed. Although other faculty members received all the supplies they requested, she received none. If all this were not enough, for three years she was singled out among the art department faculty to have her classes closely monitored by her fellow male teachers.

For six years, the art department faculty subjected Sischo-Nownejad to biased age and gender comments. They referred to her as "an old warhorse," and to her students as "little old ladies." Her division chairperson sarcastically referred to her as a "women's libber" and on at least two occasions urged her to retire.

Eventually, Sischo-Nownejad filed charges, alleging that the college had discriminated against her on the basis of her sex and age. The college asked the court to dismiss her case, but the court refused, ruling that Sischo-Nownejad had proffered sufficient evidence of both sex and age discrimination to allow her to proceed. As the only female and one of the oldest art department faculty members, she had been subjected to treatment that differed substantially from that accorded all other faculty members. At the same time that her superiors forced less favorable working conditions on her, they made her the butt of stereotypical ageist and sexist comments. Sischo-Nownejad presented a strong case of sex as well as age discrimination.[6]

Fifty-eight percent of sex and age discrimination cases filed by older women involve discharges.[7] Typically, an employer attempts to justify the discharge of an older woman on the ground of "poor performance," even though she may have performed adequately in her position for many years. Joan Palmiero's case is typical.

Palmiero worked as a manufacturing supervisor for Weston Controls, a division of Schlumberger, Ltd. Weston terminated the fifty-four-year-old Palmiero after she had served the company for thirty years. When she asked her supervisors the reason for her dismissal, she was informed that the reassignment of her duties was in the best interests of the company. Palmiero later learned that two male workers, both much younger than she, had assumed her duties. Palmiero then sued Weston for both age and sex discrimination. At the trial, Weston's executives testified to a number of issues that proved damaging to the company's position that sex and age had played no role in the decision to terminate Palmiero. They testified that at the time of Palmiero's dismissal they were involved in replenishing Weston's work force, and in that regard, for reasons they failed to explain, they had maintained statistics on the average age of the workers on staff. In the hiring of new personnel, they had been directed by Schlumberger to recruit individuals "fresh out of college." Their goal was to keep the organization "lean and mean," and Palmiero's male replacements were described as "young comers." This testimony left little doubt that age and sex discrimination paved the way for Palmiero's departure, and the jury awarded her more than half a million dollars in damages.[8]

What Palmiero experienced as a supervisor, Verna Turner encountered as a laborer in a blue-collar position. Turner worked for Independent Stave Company (ISC), a manufacturer of wooden barrels. ISC purchased white oak logs, debarked them, and then formed them into barrel staves and headings. ISC hired Turner to work in its mill in Bunker, Missouri, as "strip catcher, stacker, and second edger." Turner, however, was unable to keep up with the mill's production demands, and ISC reassigned her to "grader," a position she filled successfully.

Several years later, when ISC confronted a diminished demand for bourbon barrels, one of its major products, ISC executives decided to combine some of the Bunker mill positions to reduce operating costs. It combined the jobs of grader and stacker and assigned the new position to Turner, but again she was unable to keep up with production. Not long after, ISC halted operations at the Bunker mill, shut it down, and laid off nine of the mill's thirteen workers, including Turner. At the time the mill ceased operations, Turner was the only woman employed at the mill and, at the age of fifty-four, was next to the oldest of its workers. About seven months later, ISC recalled all the workers who had been laid off except for Turner, who was notified that she had been permanently laid off because the position of grader had been eliminated.

After the mill reopened, ISC combined the positions of grader and stacker, and several men, each younger than Turner, attempted to perform the operations of the combined positions. Like Turner, none could keep up with production. Ultimately, ISC separated the positions of grader and stacker, as they had been when Turner held the grader position, but Turner was not recalled to fill the reconstituted grader position. Turner then filed suit for age and sex discrimination.

Turner's case was tried without a jury, and the court found in her favor, ruling that she had met her burden of proving that sex and age had been determining factors in ISC's decision not to recall her after the mill reopened. The court was persuaded by the fact that Turner was the only female worker employed at the mill, that she was the oldest worker but one, and that she had satisfactorily filled the grader position for several years. The court expressed the opinion that, except for her age and sex, ISC would have recalled Turner to fill the grader position.[9]

Although the replacement of an older woman by a younger man frequently establishes the basis for an age and sex discrimination suit, sometimes an employer's discriminatory conduct is not as clearly apparent as in the cases just reviewed. In fact, the circumstances some older women encounter simply do not fit into the types of sex discrimination claims normally pursued under Title VII or age discrimination claims commonly alleged under the Age Discrimination in Employment Act (ADEA). Ordinarily, an older woman alleging sex and age discrimination pleads separate claims, sex discrimination under Title VII and age discrimination under the ADEA, hoping to prevail in one if not both claims. But, on occasion, an older woman is confronted with a form of discrimination that differs from that commonly suffered by women pleading separate sex and age claims. Mary Arnett found herself in those circumstances.

After working twelve years with the Defense Industrial Supply Center (DISC) as a computer specialist/instructor, forty-nine-year-old Arnett sought to move on to a higher position in the company. When she filed an application in response to a job announcement for an equal employment specialist position, she was notified that her experience was insufficient to qualify her for the job. About a month later, a similar position became available, and Arnett again applied. This time, the personnel office found that both Arnett and a younger woman met the qualifications for the job. DISC selected the younger woman—more than twenty years Arnett's junior.

A short time later, DISC announced the availability of another equal employment specialist position, and Arnett and six other workers applied. Again, DISC chose not to select Arnett but instead assigned the position to a much younger worker.

Arnett then commenced an action in the federal court, alleging both age and sex discrimination. She claimed that DISC had rejected her applications because she was a woman and was over forty, and that the selection decisions pertaining to both positions had been infected with sex as well as age bias. The evidence gathered in support of her case showed that every woman ever selected for the position of equal employment specialist had been under the age of forty, and every man selected for that position had been over forty. Every female candidate over the age of forty had been rejected in favor of either a younger woman or an older man.

These circumstances presented a dilemma for Arnett and her attorneys. If Arnett were to pursue her sex discrimination claim against DISC, her case would be subject to dismissal, because women, albeit they were all under forty, had been selected for the employment specialist positions. This suggested that no sex discrimination had been involved. On the other hand, if she were to pursue her age discrimination claim, it also would be subject to dismissal, since men over forty had been successful candidates for these positions. These circumstances suggested that DISC was not guilty of age discrimination. It was only because Arnett was a woman *and* over forty—that is, she was an "older woman"—that she had been rejected for these positions. But neither Title VII nor the ADEA specifically grants protection from discrimination against older women. The ADEA affords protection against discriminatory acts directed at workers age forty and older, and Title VII bars discrimination against women. If Arnett's claim that she was discriminated against because she was an older woman were analyzed as two separate claims, one under Title VII and one under the ADEA, neither claim could survive.

In order to succeed, Arnett had to convince the court that she was entitled to relief as an older woman, either under Title VII or under the ADEA. Arnett focused on Title VII. She alleged that the discrimination she experienced was separate and distinct from that generally experienced by women. Arnett argued that even though Title VII does not specifically grant its protections to the subgroup "older women," a worker is not required to prove that her employer discriminated against *all* women. Rather, an employer may be guilty of sex discrimination even if some female employees are not adversely affected by its policies and practices. In her case, Arnett alleged that DISC discriminated against only a segment of its female staff: women over forty. Ultimately, the court was persuaded that Arnett could proceed with this sex discrimination claim under Title VII, a claim based on the premise that DISC discriminated against a specified group of its female employees—not against all of its female workers, but only against those who were older.[10]

Courts classify this type of case as a "sex plus" case or, more specifically, as in a case such as Arnett's, as a "sex plus age" case. The "sex plus" doctrine refers to discriminatory conduct based on sex plus another characteristic, such as age, race, or national origin (see chapter 7). The doctrine permits a worker to limit her claim to discrimination levied against a subclass of women, rather than women in general. The Supreme Court's ruling in the *Martin Marietta* case provided the basis for permitting Arnett to plead and prove a "sex plus age" case. In that case, the Court had recognized that a discrimination claim may be based on discriminatory conduct practiced against a limited group or subclass of women (see chapter 4). Even though Martin Marietta had not discriminated against women in general, the Court ruled that its policy of refusing to hire a subclass of women—those with preschool children—was discriminatory.

Margaret Good also was successful in relying upon this approach in proving she had been discriminated against as an older woman. After U.S. West Communications discharged her and then replaced her with a forty-two-year-old man, Good, who was forty-five at the time, alleged that U.S. West was guilty of sex and age discrimination. Although the difference in Good's age and that of her replacement was insufficient to establish a viable claim if only her age were considered, the court ruled that if Good could prove that her age, when combined with her sex, formed a substantial and motivating factor in U.S. West's decision to terminate her, she could prevail under the "sex plus age" doctrine. Thus, as in the *Arnett* case, the court permitted Good to proceed with her suit based upon a combination of factors—sex and age.[11]

While some courts have permitted older women to rely on the *Martin Marietta* rationale to sue their employers as "older women," other courts have limited the application of this rationale or have rejected it outright. Caryl Sherman alleged a "sex plus age" claim against American Cyanamid after it dismissed her from a sales representative position following fifteen years of employment. Sherman claimed that American Cyanamid had terminated her only because she was an older woman. The court agreed that the "sex plus age" doctrine could be asserted in the circumstances Sherman faced, but it then proceeded to undermine her case by requiring her to prove that as an older woman she was treated differently and less favorably than older men employed by the company. In other words, unless Sherman could show that a similarly situated group of older male workers employed by American Cyanamid was treated more favorably than she, her case was subject to dismissal.

It made no difference to the court that Sherman could prove that younger women or younger men were treated more advantageously than older female workers. The court thus severely limited the application of the "sex plus age" doctrine.[12]

An additional hurdle faced Bessie Thompson after she sued the Mississippi State Personnel Board when it denied her a promotion to a supervisory position. The court rejected her allegations that the board discriminated against her as an older woman, dismissing as irrelevant statistical data showing that fewer older women than older men were promoted to supervisory positions. According to the court, since neither Title VII nor the ADEA specifically provides protection for a subset of older women, Thompson could succeed only if her sex-discrimination and her age discrimination claims were analyzed separately. The court required her to prove that as a woman she had been subjected to acts of sex discrimination that culminated in a denial of a promotion to a supervisory position. If she wished also to show that her age was a factor in the decision, she would be required to prove, separate and apart from all other proof, that as a person over forty, she had been subjected to acts of age discrimination. In other words, the court totally rejected the "sex plus age" doctrine.[13] In courtrooms where this position has been adopted, an older woman will inevitably lose whenever the defendant employer is able to demonstrate that either younger women or older men have not been discriminated against.

Because of the difficulties some courts have with the "sex plus age" doctrine, older women often opt, circumstances permitting, to plead separate sex and age discrimination claims. A typical case involved Joan McFadden-Peel and her employer, Staten Island Cable (SIC). McFadden-Peel held the post of director of administration, one of four SIC senior management positions. When ownership of the company changed hands, a new general manager was appointed to head the company's operations. On his first day on the job, he notified McFadden-Peel that her position was to be eliminated, resulting in her termination. He also created a new position—vice president of marketing—but refused to consider McFadden-Peel for the position, even though she had handled all marketing responsibilities for the company during the previous two years. After McFadden-Peel departed the company at the age of fifty-three, she sued SIC for sex and age discrimination.

McFadden-Peel relied upon the following facts to support her sex discrimination claim:

1. She was the only worker whose position was eliminated at the time of the change in company ownership.
2. Although her position was eliminated, her functions were not. Instead, they were distributed between two positions, both held by men.

3. The remaining members of the previous management team—both men—
retained their positions.
4. New management expressed concern that McFadden-Peel would have difficulty in adapting to the new corporate culture, but no such concern was
expressed about her two male colleagues.
5. Many of the unsuccessful female applicants for the newly created vice
president of marketing position had more impressive credentials than the
successful male candidate's.
6. A pattern of sexism existed in the cable industry. Indeed, at the time of
her termination, McFadden-Peel was the highest-ranked female cable executive in New York City, and the only female executive in her fifties.

In alleging a separate age discrimination claim, she relied upon the following facts:

1. As a woman of fifty-three, she was the only worker whose position was
eliminated when ownership of the company changed.
2. Although her position was eliminated, her functions were not. Instead, they
were distributed between two positions, both held by men ten to fifteen
years younger than she.
3. The remaining members of the previous management team—both men
in their forties—retained their positions.
4. New management expressed concern that McFadden-Peel would have difficulty in adapting to the new corporate culture, but no such concern was
expressed in that connection with regard to her two younger male
colleagues.
5. The manager of human resources, a male and the oldest of SIC's workers, was offered a retirement package within months of McFadden-Peel's
discharge.
6. A representative of the new owner was reported by the *New Yorker* magazine to have stated "that older people have difficulty adapting to the new
interactive technology."

SIC asked the court to dismiss McFadden-Peel's sex and age allegations,
but the court refused, ruling that McFadden-Peel had submitted sufficient supporting evidence to permit her to proceed to trial on both claims. Since
McFadden-Peel did not claim that she was discriminated against as an "older
woman," the court analyzed her sex and age claims separately.[14] Interestingly,
if McFadden-Peel had asserted an "older woman" claim, all but two of her allegations of sex discrimination (items 5 and 6) and all but two of her allegations of age discrimination (items 5 and 6) would have supported it.

Although McFadden-Peel was successful in separately alleging claims of sex and age discrimination, on occasion this approach leads to disaster, as it did for Brenda Smith when she sued her employer, the Berry Company, for sex and age discrimination. The Berry Company, a subsidiary of BellSouth, sold advertisements for the *Yellow Pages*. During her eleven years with the company, Smith was very productive and enjoyed an excellent relationship with her co-workers and supervisors. Eventually, she was promoted to account manager, and while she held that position was one of the company's leading salespersons, winning numerous awards for her work. During the last two years of her employment, however, her relationship with her supervisors deteriorated. Smith alleged that the demise of her successful career resulted from age and sex discriminatory conduct engaged in by her supervisors. The company, however, claimed that Smith's negative attitude and adverse reaction to the restructuring of the company's salary system were the causes of her problems.

While her relationship with the company was crumbling, Smith experienced medical problems after a skiing accident. Ultimately, she had surgery and was required to take extended medical leave. Upon her return to work, management informed her that she was to be demoted, a move that meant materially fewer responsibilities, lower status, and a substantial pay cut. Believing that she was being forced out, Smith resigned and filed discrimination charges against the company.

Smith's case was supported by a memorandum prepared some years before by the company's vice president of sales, which contained statements impugning the work habits of older workers. In addition, both her age and sex claims were bolstered by the company's decision to replace Smith while she was on medical leave with a younger male worker. The jury found in Smith's favor on both her sex and age claims and awarded her $24,000 in back pay damages, $76,000 in pain and suffering damages, and $500,000 in punitive damages, a total award of $600,000.

Following the jury verdict, the presiding judge increased the award by $24,000, because the jury had found that the age-discriminatory acts to which Smith had been subjected were "willfully" ordered by the company. However, he also overruled the jury by reducing the pain and suffering award from $76,000 to $50,000 and the punitive damages award from $500,000 to $100,000. Thus, the $600,000 jury award was reduced to $198,000. But Smith's problems had just begun.

The company appealed the outcome of the trial court proceedings, and although the appellate court agreed with the jury that Smith had prevailed on her age discrimination claim, it ruled, contrary to the jury, that Smith had failed to prove her sex discrimination claim. This ruling required a new calculation of damages. Since neither pain and suffering nor punitive damages may be recovered under the ADEA, the $50,000 and $100,000 awards were deleted from the final calculation of damages. In the end, Smith recovered only $48,000.[15]

If Smith could have structured her lawsuit pursuant to the "sex plus age" approach, she might well have recovered the amounts awarded by the jury as pain and suffering and punitive damages. Of course, it is not always possible to structure a claim in that manner. But because Berry had replaced Smith with a younger male worker while she was on leave, the kernel of a "sex plus age" claim was present had Smith and her attorneys elected to take that route.[16]

In their efforts to prove workplace discrimination, older women have available to them another litigation tool. Many sex discrimination cases are denominated by the courts as "disparate treatment" cases because they rely upon allegations that one group of workers, such as older women, are treated less favorably than other workers (see chapter 5). But disparate treatment is not the only method of proving employment discrimination. "Disparate impact," as distinguished from "disparate treatment," occurs when an employment policy or practice, appearing on its face to be nondiscriminatory, falls more harshly on one group of workers than on other workers. As an example, an older woman may allege that a particular employer policy adversely affected her and other women in her age group but had no adverse effect upon all other workers.

When the disparate-impact approach is available to an older woman, she need not prove that the employer intentionally discriminated against her. The motivations of the employer are simply irrelevant in this type of case. If the older female worker is able to establish through statistics or some other evidence that an employment policy disproportionately disadvantaged her and other older women on account of sex and age, the employer must prove that the policy was required by its business needs. But even if it can establish such a condition, the worker will nonetheless prevail if she can show that the employer had other policies available that, if used, would have resulted in more equitable treatment of older women.

A case in point is that of Ruth Blonder, a forty-six-year-old social worker, who had worked at the Evanston Hospital in Evanston, Illinois, for thirteen years when the hospital initiated a program requiring its staff, largely female, to receive rubella inoculations as a condition of continued employment. The hospital's staff of physicians, who were largely male, however, was not required to be inoculated. Blonder refused inoculation, as she had been informed that these inoculations could cause recurrent arthritic symptoms in older women and that the danger of this condition increased with age. Blonder also contended that the purpose of the policy was to protect pregnant patients, but since her job functions did not involve working with these patients, it was unnecessary for her to be inoculated. When Blonder persisted in rejecting inoculation, the hospital discharged her.

Blonder filed suit, first claiming that the rubella inoculation policy discriminated against her on the basis of sex, because only staff employees (primarily female), and not physicians (primarily male), were required to be inoculated. Second, she claimed that as an older woman she was more likely to suffer serious side effects from the inoculation, and thus she was discriminated against on account of her age. Third, Blonder alleged that the hospital's inoculation policy disparately impacted her as an older woman.

The hospital asked the court to dismiss Blonder's disparate-impact claim, but the court ruled that hers was a typical claim of this type in that she had alleged that an employment policy neutral on its face (the policy requiring rubella inoculation) fell more harshly on one group of workers (older women) than on any other. Moreover, the policy could not be justified by business necessity. The court ruled that "facially neutral employment practices, which for medical reasons fall more harshly on one group, can form the basis of a disparate impact claim." Thus, the hospital's attempt to dismiss Blonder's case was denied.[17]

In another case, an employer adopted a hiring policy that considered as relevant only the more recent employment history of a job applicant and precluded consideration of employment more than ten years prior to the application. An older female applicant challenged the policy on disparate-impact grounds. She argued that women more frequently than men interrupt their careers to fulfill child-rearing responsibilities, and when these women reenter the workplace many years later, the policy of refusing to consider employment history more than ten years in the past fell more harshly upon older women than upon men, thus denying them employment opportunities. The court concluded that the employer's "recency factor" discriminated disproportionately against older women, and thus these women had been disparately impacted.[18]

The number of older women employed in the workplace has been steadily increasing for more than twenty years, a trend projected to continue into the future. Among women forty-five to fifty-four, 7 million were in the workforce in 1980, 9.1 million in 1990, and 14 million in 1999, with 17.8 million predicted for 2008. Among women fifty-five to sixty-four, 4.7 million were in the workforce in 1980, 4.9 million in 1990, 6.2 million in 1999, with 9.8 million projected for 2008.[19] The presence of greater numbers of older women in the workplace provides more occasions for older women to be subjected to employer discriminatory policies and practices. These increasing numbers, therefore, portend a proliferation of sex- and age-discriminatory claims filed by older women.

Seven

Discrimination against Women of Color

For years before many white women left the home for the workplace, African American women worked outside the home, first as slaves and later as domestic servants. While only 37 percent of white women were paid employees as recently as 1960, 83 percent of African American women were in the workforce, nearly one-half as maids and servants.[1] Although far fewer African American women are currently employed as servants, a large number are stilled relegated to low-paying jobs.

From one perspective, African American women suffer the same types of workplace discrimination as African American men:

- Both groups are less likely than white workers to be promoted, and when they are promoted, they are more likely to have waited longer for their promotions.
- Both groups are more likely to receive lower performance evaluations.
- Both groups are paid less than their white co-workers.
- Both groups are generally excluded from executive and other high-paying positions, and few ever achieve senior management positions.

But from other perspectives, African American women are treated even more adversely than African American men. Historically, they have been paid less than either white men or white women and, as disclosed by Bureau of Census 2000 statistics, they are also paid less than African American men. The median weekly income for white men in 1999 was $638; for African American men, $488; for white women, $483; and for African American women, $409.[2]

Level of education does not change this picture. Bureau of Census 1990 data show that African American women with doctorates employed in executive, administrative, and managerial positions earned significantly less than whites as well as African American men with similar educational backgrounds and employed in similar positions. White men with doctorates earned an average of $70,414; African American men, $54,741; white women, $47,876; African American women, $44,230. Even greater variance shows up among workers with professional degrees (medicine, law, etc.): white men, $90,610; African American men, $71,114; white women, $61,995; and African American women, $54,171.[3]

Similar data show that Hispanic women are paid far less than white men and women, somewhat less than African American men and women and Hispanic men.[4]

Discrimination against women of color arises, at least in part, from the values, beliefs, and expectations of business and professional leaders, a great majority of whom are white males. Unless a woman of color can somehow fit herself into a mold firmly established in and created by a culture of white males, she is likely to be treated as an alien in the workplace.

In their book *Modern Sexism,* Nijole Benokraitis and Joe Feagin cite the example of a young female Puerto Rican medical student who was evaluated by a white male medical school professor. The professor found that the student had difficulty relating to staff and patients, that her behavior was often inappropriate, that she experienced problems in coping with authoritarian figures, and that her manner was overbearing and demanding. "Although intellectually we feel she could make a good physician, unless she is able to correct her personality deficiencies, her future as a physician remains questionable." At about the same time, the same student was evaluated by health care workers in a neighborhood clinic in which she worked. They found that she had demonstrated independence and initiative in situations where little supervision was available, and that she had a good relationship with other clinic personnel, manifesting a spirit of cooperation and flexibility while willingly accepting direction and criticism. "She demonstrates a broad intelligence, a refreshing individuality, integrity, and most of all, courage in opposing pretense and rigidity."[5]

According to Benokraitis and Feagin, the medical professor's adverse appraisal emerged from his comparison of this student with the typical medical school student, that is, one who has developed in and grown out of a "white-male subcultural mold." This comparison could only conclude in a finding that the student was basically deficient in several areas. The health care workers, on the other hand, compared the student to the sort of doctor needed in a large city neighborhood clinic and concluded that she was well adapted to that type of environment. In the world of the white male medical professor, this student was doomed to failure by her inability and, more importantly, her unwillingness to fit the white man's mold prescribed for her.[6]

The same mold has contributed to the formation of the glass ceiling, a barrier inhibiting the advancement of women to higher executive positions. But a glass ceiling can be broken. Moreover—as we expand upon the metaphor—those below the ceiling can see through it and learn by observation and in turn be observed by those situated above. African American and other women of color, however, perceive the ceiling that bars their advancement to be constructed not of glass but of concrete—a near impenetrable career, cultural, and social barrier. From beneath such a barrier, they cannot learn by observing those working above it, and, in addition, they are isolated from and invisible to corporate decision makers. When African American women strive to climb higher on the corporate ladder, they bear two burdens, discrimination by reason of their gender as well as their race. Consequently, they lag behind both white women and African American men in advancing to higher positions.[7]

On occasion, an African American woman may experience race and sex discrimination simultaneously. For example, her employer may deny her promotion to a high-level position because he is biased against African Americans and, in addition, against women working in high-level positions. If the worker then charges her employer with race and sex discrimination, each claim may have to stand on its own, supported by its own facts. In such circumstances, proof of one claim is irrelevant to proof of the other, and while one claim may succeed, the other may fail.

In a typical case of this nature, an African American woman was forced to work in an environment where she continuously was subjected to inappropriate comments and jokes about her race. Her supervisors and other workers referred to African American workers as "slaves" and repeatedly told her that "it was unfortunate she was black" and that it was "disgraceful that black women did not shave their legs." Separate and apart from these racial comments, she was told that all "women should be home and pregnant." Male supervisors treated all women in her department like servants. The facts supporting her sex discrimination claim were totally separate and apart from those supporting her race discrimination claim. Each claim stood on its own, and the court analyzed the claims separately.[8]

African American and other female workers of color also may find themselves vulnerable to sex and race bias acting in combination to create workplace problems experienced only by them, a subgroup comprised of women of color. The racism they experience is shaped in part by their gender, and the sexism they experience is shaped in part by their race.[9] But Title VII has failed at times to recognize that racism and sexism may interact to harm certain groups of women.

From its inception, Title VII has been viewed primarily as a vehicle designed to protect African American men from race discrimination and white women from sex discrimination. Thus, when an African American woman has alleged race discrimination, her claim has generally been treated as synonymous with the race discrimination claims of African American men, and when she has alleged sex discrimination, her claim has been treated as synonymous with the sex discrimination claims of white women. But, an African American woman must be allowed to allege and prove discrimination claims that correspond with her experience in the workplace, which on occasion flow from acts of race and sex discrimination occurring *in combination*.[10]

An African American woman may be denied a promotion because her employer is biased against African American women, but not against African American men or white women. It promotes African American men and white women to higher positions. Only because the worker is African American *and* a women is she subjected to discriminatory conduct. But our culture tends not to recognize African American women as a separate and distinct group, as bell hooks observed in her book *Ain't I a Woman*: "No other group in America has so had their identity socialized out of existence as have black women. We are rarely recognized as a group separate and distinct from black men, or as a present part of the larger group 'women' in this culture. . . . When black people are talked about the focus tends to be on black *men*; and when women are talked about the focus tends to be on *white* women."[11]

Early court decisions interpreting Title VII failed to recognize that the workplace experiences of African American women often reflect an interaction of sexism and racism. In 1976, five African American women sued their former employer, the St. Louis Assembly Division of the General Motors Corporation, and their former union, the United Automobile Workers, alleging that GM's seniority system and its "last hired, first fired" layoff policy, mandated by GM's collective bargaining agreement with the union, perpetuated the effect of GM's past acts of race and sex discrimination.

Before 1970, GM employed only one African American woman at its St. Louis plant. Emma DeGraffenreid had applied for employment at the Assembly Division in 1968 but had not been hired. She applied again in 1973, and this time got the job. The following year, however, she lost her job in a companywide layoff. DeGraffenreid alleged that if she had not been discriminated against at the time of her first application for employment in 1968 and instead had been hired, she would not have been laid off in 1974 pursuant to

GM's "last hired, first fired" policy. Four other African American women filed similar claims, all alleging that GM's past discriminatory conduct in failing to hire African American women had caused them to lose their positions in the 1974 layoff. The judge hearing the case, however, dismissed their claims. He first noted that the five plaintiffs were suing "on behalf of black women," and thus they were attempting to combine two legal actions—one for sex discrimination and one for race discrimination—into a "new special sub-category, namely, a combination of racial and sex-based discrimination." Further, "[t]he court notes that plaintiffs have failed to cite any decisions which have stated that black women are a special class to be protected from discrimination. The court's own research has failed to disclose such a decision. The plaintiffs are clearly entitled to a remedy if they have been discriminated against. However, they should not be allowed to combine statutory remedies to create a new 'super-remedy' which would give them relief beyond what the drafters of [Title VII] intended. Thus, this lawsuit must be examined to see if it states a cause of action for race discrimination, sex discrimination, or alternatively either, but not a combination of both." Once the court limited consideration of the case to one alleging separate claims of sex and race discrimination, it concluded that the sex claim was deficient, because GM had hired women prior to 1970, albeit all but one were white. It then ruled that the African American women could pursue their race claims against GM, but only in combination with African American men who were then engaged in suing the company for race discrimination.[12]

Thus, the court rejected the claim of discrimination based on an interaction of race and sex bias. It left the African American complainants without a remedy for discrimination directed against them simply because they were African American women. Apparently, the court believed that in enacting Title VII, Congress either failed to contemplate that African American women would be subjected to discriminatory conduct as "African American women" or failed to offer them any protection if such discrimination did occur. As University of California law professor Kimberle Crenshaw has pointed out: "The court's refusal in [the *DeGraffenreid* case] to acknowledge that Black women encounter combined race and sex discrimination implies that the boundaries of sex and race discrimination doctrine are defined respectively by white women's and Black men's experiences. Under this view, Black women are protected only to the extent that their experiences coincide with those of either group."[13]

When a court requires an African American woman's claim that alleges interactive discrimination to be analyzed first as a claim for sex discrimination and second as a claim for race discrimination, the employer may defeat the sex discrimination claim by showing that it did not discriminate against white women, and it may defeat the race discrimination claim by showing that it did not discriminate against African American men. A white man claiming discrimination would not be confronted with those circumstances. The court would not separate his claim into male and white, with African American males included in his class to determine whether he has experienced sex discrimination, and white women included in his class to determine whether he has experienced race discrimination.

Just four years after the *DeGraffenreid* case was decided, another court, examining the same issue, arrived at a radically different conclusion. Dafro Jefferies, an African American, worked for the Harris County Community Action Association in Texas, first as a secretary to the director of programs and later as a personnel interviewer. In the latter position, she applied for promotion to various positions, but on each occasion her application was rejected. Subsequently, her employer posted a notice announcing vacancies for two field representative positions, and Jefferies immediately filed applications for both. The vacant positions had previously been staffed by a white female and an African American male.

Shortly after Jefferies submitted her applications, she noticed a personnel department form indicating that the association had already hired an African American male for one of the positions. Believing herself a victim of discrimination, Jefferies filed a charge with the EEOC and later commenced a legal action against the association.

Testimony at the trial disclosed that approximately 70 percent of the association's employees were female, that women held sixteen of the thirty-six supervisory positions in the agency, and that several women occupied positions on the association's board of directors. Jefferies's undisputed testimony also established that every position for which she had applied had been filled either by a white woman or by a man, black or white.

Jefferies pursued her case along three avenues, alleging separate acts of race and sex discrimination as well as acts of discrimination based on a combination of race and sex. The court rejected Jefferies's race discrimination claim, since the person hired for one of the field representative positions was also African American. Since both the person seeking the position and the person achieving the position were of the same race, the court held that it would be implausible to view the association's decision with regard to filling that position as discriminatory. The court also rejected Jefferies's sex discrimination claim. As noted, several women served on the association's board of directors, a large number of the association's supervisory positions were held by women, and one of the field representative positions for which Jefferies had applied had been filled by a woman, all of which demonstrated that the association did not discriminate generally on the basis of sex.

With the rejection of the race and sex discrimination claims, the court was left with the decision whether to allow Jefferies to pursue her third claim. Should Jefferies be allowed to sue the association for the discriminatory acts she experienced by reason of the fact that she was an African American *and* a woman? Jefferies argued that an employer should not escape liability for acts of discrimination committed against African American women merely by demonstrating that it discriminated against neither African American men nor white women.

The court agreed, basing its decision in part upon its view of the scope of Title VII. The statute provides a remedy for employment discrimination on the basis of a worker's "race, color, religion, sex, or national origin."[14] Congress's use of the word "or," in the court's view, showed that Congress intended to prohibit employment discrimination based on any or all of the listed characteristics. Moreover, the court noted, at the time of the enactment of Title VII, the House of Representatives rejected a proposed amendment that would have limited evidence of sex discrimination to that based "solely" upon sex, thus opening the door to claims based on sex as well as on one of the other of named characteristics, such as race. Thus, the court concluded: "Black females represent a significant percentage of the active or potentially active labor force. In the absence of a clear expression by Congress that it did not intend to provide protection against discrimination directed especially toward black women as a class separate and distinct from the class of women and the class of blacks, we cannot condone a result which leaves black women without a viable Title VII remedy. If both black men and white women are considered to be within the same protected class as black females for purposes [of proving discrimination,] no remedy will exist for discrimination which is directed only toward black females."[15]

That an African American male was granted promotion to the position for which Jefferies had applied was not relevant to her claim, because he was not a member of the class of workers that included Jefferies. The court allowed Jefferies to prove that the association's reasons for not promoting her to the field representative positions were discriminatory by showing that persons outside her class—African American men and white women—were treated more advantageously than she was as an African American woman. Thus, the court recognized African American women as a distinct subgroup and granted them protection from acts of discrimination barred by Title VII. As an African American woman, Jefferies stood in a class separate and apart from African American men and white women. In contrast to *DeGraffenreid*, *Jefferies* holds that discrimination against African American women may exist in the absence of discrimination against African American men or white women. This decision provides a rational basis for protecting workers who experience discrimination as a combination of factors, such as sex and race.

Since *Jefferies*, the courts have generally followed the rationale of that court rather than that advanced in *DeGraffenreid*. June Graham's legal action against Bendix Corporation proved successful when the court in which her action was pending adopted the *Jefferies* rationale. Graham, an African American female, claimed that Bendix treated her and other African American women differently than other workers. She was continuously singled out for critical and job-threatening performance reviews, often scheduled upon her return to work from authorized absences for illness and other matters. At the trial, Graham's supervisor testified that he maintained special time records for her, although he did not keep such records for any other workers in his department. He frequently filed absence reports that criticized Graham, even on the occasion she was absent to attend her child's funeral. On the other hand, white male or female workers were not faulted for frequent absences. Indeed, the only two workers criticized for absences were Graham and another African American woman in the same department. The evidence clearly showed that African American women were treated more severely in the matter of attendance than all other workers.

The court ruled that Graham, as an African American woman, was protected against discrimination based on a combination of race and sex, and an employer who singles out African American females for less favorable treatment cannot defeat a charge of discrimination merely by showing that its white female workers or its African American male workers are not similarly subjected to such unfavorable treatment. Thus, the court affirmed the proposition that African American women who experience adverse treatment, separate and apart from that experienced by African American men on the one hand and white women on the other, are protected by the provisions of Title VII.[16]

More recently, this Title VII protection has been extended to other women of color. Professor Maivan Lam, a woman of Vietnamese descent, sued the University of Hawaii's Richardson School of Law, alleging that when she applied for the position of director of the law school's Pacific Asian legal studies program, she was discriminated against on the basis of her race, sex, and national origin. Born in Vietnam, Lam was fluent in several languages, including French, English, Vietnamese, and Thai. After college, she earned a master's degree in Southeast Asian studies at Yale and later was awarded a Ford Foundation fellowship. After several years as a full-time mother, Lam taught anthropology courses at Hawaii Loa College and then obtained a second master's degree from Yale. Lam then changed direction and attended the Richardson School of Law. After graduation from law school, she taught at Hawaii Loa College, lectured at the University of Hawaii, and presented guest lectures at the law school.

Lam and approximately one hundred others applied for the position of director of the Pacific Asian legal studies program. A search committee designated to review the credentials of the applicants recommended ten finalists for review by the full faculty, Lam among them. Five of the ten were women and three were Asians, two of whom were women. The candidate list was eventually reduced to four, but a consensus did not form around any one of the candidates, and the faculty voted to cancel its search to find an appropriate person to fill the position.

When Lam was not awarded the directorship position, she claimed she had been discriminated against as an Asian woman. The law school, however, argued that its dean had supported the application of an Asian male for the position, and that the search committee subsequently had offered another position to one of the white female candidates for the director's job. These two factors, the law school insisted, showed a lack of bias toward Asians as well as women. The court, however, criticized the law school's approach to the issue. An analysis of alleged acts of race discrimination separate and apart from alleged acts of sex discrimination was not warranted, since the two "cannot be neatly reduced to distinct components." Any attempt to bisect a person's identity at the intersection of race and sex ignores, if not distorts, the nature of the person's experiences.

Like other subclasses, Asian women may be subjected to a set of assumptions directed at neither Asian men nor white women. In consequence, they may be targets of discrimination even when those groups are not. Indicating its agreement with the *Jefferies* approach to the issue, the court stated in *Lam*: "[W]e agree with the *Jefferies* court that when a plaintiff is claiming race *and* sex bias, it is necessary to determine whether the employer discriminates on the basis of that *combination* of factors, not just whether it discriminates against people of the same race or of the same sex" (emphasis in the court's opinion).[17]

An economy that employs workers of all races and colors, male and female, requires a body of law capable of acknowledging and responding to workplace experiences that may be unique to particular groups of workers. Fortunately, as the cases just reviewed demonstrate, the employment discrimination laws have been developed to a degree that they are now capable of affording protection to specific groups of workers, thus eliminating workplace disadvantages that only those groups encounter.

As a consequence of still another development in the enforcement of Title VII prohibitions against workplace discrimination, African American and other women of color are now able to aggregate evidence of racial and sexual bias to show that an employer permitted a work environment hostile and discriminatory to women of color to exist in its workplace. Even though this evidence may be inadequate to establish separate and distinct race- and sex discrimination claims, it may nevertheless be sufficient to show that a pervasive discriminatory atmosphere corrupted the workplace for women of color. Marguerite Hicks was employed in such a workplace at Gates Rubber Company.

Hicks worked at Gates Rubber as one of thirty security guards, the sole African American woman and one of only two African Americans. She charged Gates with both sexual and racial harassment. Gates workers testified at the trial that their work environment was permeated with racial slurs and jokes. At least one supervisor referred to African American workers as "niggers" and "coons," and on one occasion, the same supervisor referred to Hicks as a "lazy nigger." Another supervisor referred to her as "Buffalo Butt." In addition to evidence demonstrating the existence of racial harassment in the workplace, Hicks also offered the court evidence that she was sexually harassed by at least two of her supervisors.

In spite of this evidence, the trial court rejected Hicks's race and sex discrimination claims on the ground that the evidence was insufficient to establish either. On appeal, the appellate court ordered the trial court to reconsider the case from a *Jefferies* point of view to determine whether evidence of race bias and sex bias, when aggregated, was sufficient to demonstrate the existence of a discriminatory workplace in which both racial and sexual bias existed in combination. The appellate court stated that Hicks, as an African American woman, should be allowed to rely upon the intersectional character of her alleged sex and race bias claims by establishing a pattern of discriminatory harassment.[18] As one law commentator expressed it, the appellate court, in effect, authorized Hicks to proceed with her discrimination suit on the ground that Gates permitted "racialized sexual hostility" or "sexualized racial hostility" to exist in its workplace.[19] In other words, the appellate court ruled that evidence of racial bias may assist in establishing a sexually hostile work environment, and evidence of sexual bias may assist in establishing a racially hostile work environment.

After *Hicks*, some courts expanded the scope of evidence that a plaintiff may rely on to prove the existence of a discriminatory or hostile work environment. Even evidence of racial and sexual conduct directed against workers other than the plaintiff, as well as racial and sexual conduct she neither witnessed nor knew of, may be offered to prove the hostility of the work environment in which the plaintiff worked. This expansive view of evidence relevant to a hostile work environment claim was adopted by the court in Yvette Cruz's race and sex harassment case against her employer, Coach Stores.

Cruz, a Hispanic, worked at Coach as a secretary. She depicted Coach's human resources manager as notorious for his discriminatory attitude toward minorities, which he expressed in racial and ethnic slurs. He frequently referred to Hispanics as "spics" and African Americans as "niggers," and stated that "they are only capable of sweeping the floor at McDonald's." Other Coach workers testified to similar remarks made by the manager when Cruz was not present and thus not the target of his racial epithets. Cruz also testified to instances of daily acts of sexual harassment by the same manager. He remarked that women "should be barefoot and pregnant" and repeatedly stood very close to female workers when talking to them, ogling them and causing them to feel very uncomfortable. When Cruz informed the manager that she found his behavior objectionable, he only laughed or ignored her.

Following a male worker's crude sexual comment about Cruz's appearance and the altercation that ensued, Coach fired Cruz. Cruz then charged Coach with maintaining a race- and sex-based hostile work environment, but the trial court rejected her claim on the ground that the admissible evidence demonstrated only "vague and unspecified" instances of inappropriate sexual behavior and only a single instance of racial conduct. Thus, the court ruled, she had failed to submit sufficient evidence to establish the level of pervasive hostility necessary to support a hostile-workplace claim. The appellate court that later reviewed this decision did not agree.

In reversing the decision of the lower court, the reviewing court held that Cruz was required to prove that Coach's workplace was "permeated with discriminatory intimidation, ridicule and insult" sufficiently severe or pervasive to alter the conditions of her employment. Whether the workplace harassment was severe or pervasive depended on all of the circumstances, and in examining all of these circumstances, the lower court should have considered incidences of racial and sexual harassment directed against other workers as well as those levied against Cruz. The court expanded the scope of admissible evidence when it ruled: "Nor must offensive remarks or behavior be directed at individuals who are members of the plaintiff's own protected class. Remarks targeting members of other minorities, for example, may contribute to the overall hostility of the working environment for a minority employee." The court observed that Cruz's hostile-workplace claim found additional support in the interplay between the racial and sexual harassment she experienced. Because the evidence disclosed both race-based and sex-based workplace hostility, the manager's racial harassment may well have exacerbated the effect of his sexual harassment, and his sexual harassment may have exacerbated the effect of his racial harassment.[20]

The appellate court approved the concept that sexual and racial comments and conduct all contribute to the perception that an employer's workplace is hostile and discriminatory. If an employer permits racial epithets to pervade its workplace, it is likely to condone the presence of offensive sexual conduct as well. Thus, in advancing an expansive rather than a restrictive view of the relevancy of the evidence tending to prove a hostile and discriminatory work environment, the court provided women of color with a powerful weapon to root out workplace harassment directed at them.

In light of the progressive views the courts have advanced in extending the protections of Title VII to African American and other women of color, these women should be encouraged to charge their employers with race- and sex-based discrimination whenever the circumstances warrant.

Eight

Discrimination against Women in the Professions

More than thirty-five years after the enactment of Title VII, one would not expect discrimination against women in the professions to continue as a serious workplace problem. Yet discrimination against them remains as prevalent as discrimination against women in other segments of the workforce.

Early in the nineteenth century, law schools generally excluded two groups of applicants—felons and females. Among the many reasons advanced for the rejection of women "were the dangers of unchaperoned intellectual intercourse in the libraries, and the diversion of male attention in the classroom."[1] Even late in the century, women were still barred from practicing law in many states. As one judge pontificated while endeavoring to justify his decision to deny the admission of female candidates to the Wisconsin bar, "The peculiar qualities of womanhood, its gentle graces, its quick sensibility, its tender susceptibility," were surely not qualifications for "forensic strife."[2]

As late as the middle of the twentieth century, female attorneys were openly discriminated against. As noted earlier, when Supreme Court justice Sandra Day O'Connor graduated near the top of her Stanford Law School class, the only offer of employment she received was for the position of legal secretary. As recently as 1965, major Wall Street law firms could point to only three female partners in their midst.[3]

The legal profession has also long denied equal status to minorities. Of the forty thousand law firm partners listed in the 1997–98 *National Directory of Legal Employers*, only 1 percent were African American, and all minorities comprised less than 3 percent.[4] A survey conducted in 1999 by the *American Bar*

Association Journal and *National Bar Association Magazine* revealed that 75 percent of the black lawyers participating in the survey believed that law firms engage in tokenism rather than in genuine diversity and equality in advancing blacks to partnerships. Sixty-seven percent of black lawyers believed that minority female lawyers are treated less fairly than white female lawyers.[5] Nonetheless, women, black and white, in ever increasing numbers, have entered this hostile environment. In 1975, 23 percent of the nation's law school students were women; by 1992, the number had risen to 42 percent, by 1996 to 44 percent, and by 1999 to 46 percent.[6] The entering class in 2001 was comprised of more women than men.[7]

Although obstacles to women entering the profession have gradually diminished, barriers still keep them from advancing to higher positions. In this regard, the law profession differs little from others: Women are underrepresented in the top positions and overrepresented in those at the bottom.

When Candace Krugman Beinecke was named chair of Hughes Hubbard & Reed in 1999, she became the first woman ever to head a major New York City law firm. At the time, only two other large firms in the country were led by women. Although nearly half the students then sitting in law school classrooms were female, only 15 percent of the partners in law firms of 140 or more lawyers were women. Obviously, no direct correlation exists between the increased numbers of women in the profession and their ascension to positions of power.[8]

Women teaching in law schools face similar conditions. In 1999, they accounted for only 20 percent of the full professorships in the country's law schools and for 10 percent of law school deans.[9] Moreover, at the eleven most selective law schools in 1997, only 18.6 percent of the faculty was female; at the fifteen least selective law schools, the number was 24.9 percent. Harvard Law School's faculty that year was only 15 percent female.[10]

The number of women holding general counsel positions in Fortune 500 firms increased from six in the late 1980s to forty-four in 1999. Still, only 9 percent of top corporate legal positions are filled by women. Only 16 percent of corporate legal departments of between fifty-one and one hundred lawyers are directed by women, while more than one-half of the legal departments with twenty-five and fewer lawyers are headed by females.[11]

Clearly, the legal profession has its own glass ceiling. Myriad factors have led to its continued existence, but one appears to stand out: Young male attorneys have always been encouraged to focus on career development, while female lawyers are expected to focus on home and family, as well as on their careers. Thus, the law firm role of the male lawyer differs significantly from that of the female attorney, and the contribution to the firm made by the single-focused male lawyer carries the greater value. Thus, more law firm partnerships go to men than to women.

In 1989, the Association of the Bar of the City of New York created a committee to study, monitor, and then address issues confronting the city's women lawyers. The committee focused first on the issues thought to be affecting the advancement of women in the city's largest law firms. Committee members assumed that a glass ceiling either existed or was perceived to exist in these firms, and they undertook to determine why. They concentrated on two issues. First, since both family and career are established during the years immediately following graduation from law school, to what extent do a woman's family responsibilities constitute a hindrance to law firm advancement? Second, do glass ceilings exist at various points in a female attorney's career?

The committee selected Cynthia Fuchs Epstein, a professor of sociology at City University and author of a work on the difficulties confronting women in the legal profession, entitled *Women in Law,* to design a study to explore these issues. Over the next several years, Epstein studied eight large city firms and the positioning of women lawyers in them. She presented her report to the committee in 1995.[12]

Epstein's study showed a steady upward trend in the proportion of women hired by New York City law firms, to the point where their numbers were nearly equal to men. An upward trend in the number of female lawyers elevated to partner also occurred, but not at an equal rate. Although the proportion of female lawyers at these firms increased from 26 to 40 percent from 1980 through 1994, the proportion of female partners never exceeded 12 percent. Epstein concluded that sex stereotyping and the perception of differences in motivation between men and women constituted serious obstacles to women's mobility in these firms.

Many of the female lawyers reported to Epstein that after giving birth to a child they were denied the more coveted work and case assignments. Moreover, an expectation seemed to form in the firm that now that they were mothers they would withdraw from the partnership track, and this attitude tended to discourage women's full participation and commitment to their firms. Women, moreover, were often categorized as "outsiders" and perceived to be less committed to the firm. Sex stereotyping and the treatment of women as a category rather than as individuals provided serious obstacles to advancement. Some women, however, lowered their partnership aspirations when they found the pressure of work too difficult to reconcile with family responsibilities.

Although motherhood was usually considered a deterrent to career mobility, three-quarters of the women who did achieve partnership status were married with children. Epstein also observed that female lawyers were working in all specialties of the law instead of clustering in a few as in the past. Few women, however, headed practice groups or held management positions in their firms.

Epstein also reported that women faced prejudices emanating from stereotypical assumptions that often led to the selective assignment of women in connection with certain of the firm's matters. Women lawyers also confronted a "double-bind." If they did not exhibit behavior based on male models, they were branded as not tough enough or insufficiently aggressive, but if they were perceived as tough and aggressive, they were regarded as impaired women who acted like men. This "damned if you do, damned if you don't" attitude acted as a significant deterrent to the acceptance of women for partnership.

As committee members had anticipated, Epstein confirmed the existence of a number of glass ceilings that barred or limited the advancement of women at different career levels. Some of these ceilings were imposed by senior partners who issued the standards that structured their firms and who were responsible for decisions regarding promotion and the paths leading to it. Some glass ceilings were the product of conscious decision making, and others of general firm practices that adversely affected women. Glass ceilings, in some instances, were imposed by women themselves, based on pressures internal to their firms, as well as on pressures emanating from their familial responsibilities.

The law firms Epstein studied generally fell into two categories: the firm with established traditions in which partners were committed to replicating the firm as they knew it, and the market-driven firm where the financial bottom line effectively determined the firm's structuring. In the latter, decisions relating to partnership revolved around profitability; therefore, the ability to develop business was thought to be a sufficient, if not the only, reason for promotion.

Women were disadvantaged in both types of firms. The traditional firms replicated themselves as white male institutions. In the market-driven firms, expectations for business development were largely based on subjective criteria susceptible to the influence of stereotypes relating to the roles, motivations, and preferences of women.

Epstein's study demonstrated conclusively that Title VII has not eliminated sex discrimination from the legal profession. The statute's strict equal-opportunity policy fails to take into account that most female lawyers are mothers, and that working mothers are required by the profession to accede to a male model of competition at a time in their lives when it is not possible for them to compete on that basis. In addition, although Title VII has been generally successful in rooting out overt acts of workplace sex discrimination, it has more often failed to provide female lawyers with adequate protection from more subtle acts of discrimination, usually based on false stereotypical assumptions about female workers and women in general.

Title VII has given female attorneys little protection from discriminatory denials of partnership status, as Nancy Ezold learned when her firm denied her a partnership. Ezold sued Wolf, Block, Schorr and Solis-Cohen, a Philadelphia law firm, alleging that the firm intentionally discriminated against her because of her sex when it decided not to admit her to partnership.

Wolf, Block had hired Ezold as an associate on a partnership track. Before entering law school, Ezold had accumulated thirteen years of administrative and legislative experience, first as an assistant to Maine's senator Edmund Muskie, later as a contract administrator for the Model Cities Program, and finally as an administrator in the Office of a Special Prosecutor of the Pennsylvania Department of Justice. She had graduated from the Villanova University School of Law in the top third of her class and had then worked at two small law firms in Philadelphia. After Wolf, Block hired Ezold, it assigned her to its litigation department, where she worked for the next six years.

Throughout her tenure with the firm, Ezold's performance was reviewed regularly, as was that of each of Wolf, Block's associates, in accordance with commonly accepted standards of legal performance, such as legal analysis and research, negotiation, and advocacy skills, and in accordance with ten categories of personal characteristics, such as reliability, attitude, and the ability to work independently. These evaluations were recorded on standard forms that were later used by the firm's partners in deciding whether to offer partnership status to an associate.

Ezold received positive evaluations from nearly all the partners for whom she had done any substantial amount of work, but two of her later evaluations questioned her ability to analyze legal issues. Subsequently, the firm's partners voted to deny Ezold promotion to partner. Ezold then resigned and sued Wolf, Block for sex discrimination.

After the trial court reviewed the evidence, including the associate evaluation forms, it determined that Ezold had been held to a higher standard of performance than the firm's male associates, and that she was at least as capable, if not more so, than the male associates who had been offered partnership positions. Wolf, Block, the court ruled, was not entitled under the law to apply its promotion standards more severely to female associates, and it concluded that the firm's differential treatment of female lawyers constituted discriminatory conduct—the real reason for Ezold's rejection for partnership.

Ezold's victory was short-lived, as the appellate court reversed the trial court's decision. The appellate court ruled that Wolf, Block's partners were entitled to exercise their business judgment in deciding whether Ezold possessed the legal analytical skills sufficient to meet the firm's standards. It rejected as "immaterial" the trial court's finding that Ezold excelled in other areas, and it held that the trial court should not have interfered with Wolf, Block's evaluation process: "Wolf's articulated reason for refusing to offer Ezold a partnership was its belief, *based on a subtle and subjective consensus among the partners*, that she did not possess sufficient legal analytic ability to handle complex litigation. . . . We have cautioned courts on several occasions to avoid unnecessary intrusion into subjective promotion decisions" (emphasis added).[13]

Only five of Wolf, Block's 107 partners were women. Thus, when the appellate court gave its approval to the firm's denial of partnership to Ezold, a denial based on a "subtle and subjective consensus among the partners," the court was relying upon a "consensus" fashioned primarily by men. In these circumstances, female candidates for partnership are required to fit a cast or model subjectively formulated by men; in essence, the court ruled that even though this model may disadvantage female candidates for partnership, it is not a matter of concern for the court, which must avoid intruding upon the subjective evaluative process designed by the male members of the firm.

The Ezold case reflects the difficulties women lawyers meet when they contest decisions denying them partnership status. It is next to impossible to win such a case without evidence of overt and blatant acts of sex-discriminatory conduct, which usually is not available. In the view of many lawyers, the appellate court's opinion in this case "cemented the glass ceiling in place" in the legal profession.[14]

A glass ceiling also exists in our colleges and universities. The American Association of University Professors (AAUP) reported in 1998 that the gap in salaries between male and female faculty members widened between 1975 and 1998, even though greater numbers of women moved into the profession during that period. Although some of the salary differences may be explained by seniority as well as by life-style choices of women with family responsibilities, gender bias continues to generate substantial disparities in university salaries. Further, women, more often than men, are forced to accept appointments in lower-paying institutions. Accordingly, women are more likely to hold positions in community colleges than in research universities. The largest salary disadvantages reflect the relegation of women to less remunerative positions.[15]

Disparities in rank and tenure also persist. Although women are more likely to hold professorial positions, disproportionate numbers continue to work as lecturers and instructors. Even among women professors, relatively few are elevated to full professorship. The increasing numbers of women entering the profession have not culminated in any improvement in the positions they are assigned. In fact, the proportion of women who achieve tenure is declining. A glass ceiling is fully in place in academia.[16]

Despite disparities in salary, rank, and tenure, female participation in the profession has continued to increase. The expansion of college and university faculties is largely attributable to increasing numbers of women in the profession; the number of men entering academia is barely sufficient to sustain current participation rates. The AAUP reported that the female share of college and university faculty positions had increased from 23 percent in 1975 to 34 percent in 1998.[17] It appears likely that more women will aspire to professorial positions as ever increasing numbers of women earn Ph.D. degrees. Of the more than 42,000 research doctorates granted by U.S. universities in 1997, more than 40 percent were awarded to women.[18]

With more women entering the professorial ranks, the problems experienced at MIT (see chapter 2) are likely to occur in educational institutions with increasing frequency. A case in point is Christine Sweeney's. Sweeney earned a bachelor of education degree at Keene State College, a small liberal arts college that is part of the University of New Hampshire. She later acquired master's and Ph.D. degrees at Catholic University. After teaching for three years at Emmanuel College, Sweeney was appointed associate professor of education at Keene State. Three years later, she sought promotion to full professor.

Sweeney's department chair had recommended her for promotion, but an all-male Faculty Evaluation Advisory Committee unanimously voted against the promotion, and, subsequently, her dean concurred with that decision. Shortly thereafter, Sweeney charged the school with sex discrimination. Pending the trial of her lawsuit, Sweeney again sought promotion, again the all-male faculty committee voted against her, and again the dean concurred. The president of the college told Sweeney that she lacked the qualifications required for promotion, that she held narrow, rigid, and old-fashioned views, that she tended to personalize professional matters, and that she emphasized to her students the importance of maintaining her classroom window shades at an even height.

A few months after the president's criticisms, Sweeney tried for full professor a third time and succeeded. Thus, the issues in her discrimination suit were limited to whether the college had discriminated against her on her first two attempts.

Sweeney submitted statistical evidence supporting her claim that sex bias undermined her first two attempts at promotion, and that a glass ceiling had barred her and other women from moving up. Only four women in the entire history of Keene State had achieved the rank of full professor, while in the seven years before Sweeney filed her sex discrimination suit, the number of male full professors had increased from ten to twenty-three. In fact, more men held full-professor positions than instructor positions, despite the school's insistence that entry to full-professor rank was a significant achievement reserved for the excellent few. Sweeney also showed that each of the four women who achieved full professorship had first attained a Ph.D., while several male professors had not. The court held that this evidence supported a finding that Keene State applied a double standard in promotion decisions.[19]

The court could have relied on other evidence that also indicated that Keene State had engaged in sex-discriminatory conduct. The reasons given Sweeney for denying her a promotion on her first two attempts were pretexts. If Sweeney was unqualified for promotion, as the president alleged, because of her narrow and old-fashioned views (including her views on window shades), what explanation did Keene State have for promoting her a few months later? Why was Sweeney deemed unqualified on the first two occasions but qualified on the third? The position taken by the school to justify the promotion denial was simply not believable. In these circumstances, courts frequently rule that if the reason given by the employer for its actions is not credible, then the court may assume that the employer proffered a false reason to cover up or mask its true reason, namely, that it had engaged in discriminatory conduct.

One aspect of academia's glass ceiling that has been the subject of much litigation, beginning soon after the inception of Title VII, is the failure to grant tenure to women on the same terms it is granted to men. This is an area of the law of sex discrimination that the courts are reluctant to enter, and when they do, they rarely overturn a tenure decision. When four women assistant professors at Cornell University alleged they had been denied tenure because of their gender, the court listed six reasons why contested tenure decisions must be set apart from other types of Title VII claims:

- Tenure contracts, unlike the ordinary employer-employee relationship, entail lifetime commitments and collegial relationships.
- Tenure decisions are generally noncompetitive in the sense that a decision to grant or not grant tenure to a particular person does not necessarily affect the future of other tenure candidates.
- A tenure decision is usually highly decentralized in that the decision is made at a departmental level by many persons rather than by a single person or small group of individuals, as in other employment decisions.
- The number of factors considered in a tenure decision is quite extensive.
- Tenure decisions are often a source of great disagreement, as strongly held views are common.

- Tenure decisions involve conflicting views of scholars working in specialized academic fields. The courts cannot hope to master these areas of academic scholarship, even though they may need to do so to resolve differences in these scholars' opinions.[20]

Although tenure decisions are not exempt from Title VII review, the reluctance of the courts to consider them has led to a judicial attitude that requires the submission of particularly strong evidence of discriminatory conduct for the claimant to have any reasonable hope of success.

In denial-of-tenure cases, the plaintiff often relies upon evidence that demonstrates that her college or university held her to a stricter standard of performance than that required of male faculty members. Although, as noted, the litigation success rate among tenure claimants has not been great, Connie Rae Kunda was an exception.

Kunda was an instructor in the Department of Physical Education at Muhlenberg College in Allentown, Pennsylvania. At the time of her hiring, she had a bachelor's degree in physical education, and although she had not earned a master's degree, college administrators had not advised her that one would be required for advancement at Muhlenberg. Five years later Muhlenberg rejected her for promotion to assistant professor. Nothing was said to Kunda indicating that the college had denied her the promotion because she lacked a master's degree, nor was she told that a master's degree was mandatory for promotion or for tenure consideration. Two years later, the college's Faculty Personnel and Policies Committee unanimously recommended Kunda for promotion to assistant professor, but the dean of the college disagreed: "I cannot recommend that she be promoted because she holds only a Bachelor's degree. If she held a Master's degree I would certainly recommend her promotion on the strength of the known excellence of her work at the College. She is an outstanding teacher in her area, has made fine contributions within the Physical Education Department, and has been a dedicated and loyal member of the faculty." The following year, the committee again unanimously recommended her promotion and, in addition, urged that she be granted tenure. Again, the dean rejected the recommendations. Kunda then sued the college for sex discrimination.

Kunda first brought to the court's attention particulars pertaining to the promotions of other faculty members in the physical education department, some of whom had not earned master's degrees. In fact, the department chair had been promoted to full professor although he held only a bachelor's degree. Kunda then submitted evidence demonstrating the differences in the counseling the college extended to male members of the physical education department and that extended to Kunda during the process leading to the tenure decision. Male candidates were advised that a master's degree would strengthen an application for tenure. On one occasion, the dean initiated a meeting with one of the male faculty members, a candidate for tenure at about the same time as Kunda, and specifically advised him that he should obtain a master's degree. The dean also encouraged two other men in the department to obtain master's degrees. Kunda, however, never received similar counseling. She was not made aware of the importance of a master's degree to the tenure process. This evidence clearly showed that the college favored male faculty members over Kunda. She had been subjected to disparate treatment; the college treated female faculty less advantageously than male faculty.

Kunda also submitted evidence of procedural irregularities in the tenure approval process. First, the dean spoke against Kunda's tenure candidacy at a meeting of the Faculty Personnel Policies Committee, although in the past he had declined to appear at committee meetings that considered matters pertaining to tenure or promotion. Second, earlier in the process, the dean had failed to advise the committee that Kunda was a candidate for promotion, and thus on that occasion her application was not acted upon. With evidence of this type at hand, together with evidence of disparate treatment, the court had little difficulty in concluding that Kunda had been a victim of sex discrimination.[21]

Sex discrimination is not limited to the legal profession and academia. We have already seen an example of the type of discriminatory conduct women experience in the accounting profession (see the discussion of Ann Hopkins's sex discrimination case against Price Waterhouse in chapter 5). In another case, after Brenda Smart obtained a bachelor's degree in economics, she worked as an analyst for Columbia Gas System Service Corporation in Wilmington, Delaware. Smart, under the supervision of the assistant controller, prepared cash-flow forecasts and analyzed SEC reports and regulatory disclosures. When she expressed interest in a newly created senior analyst position, she received conflicting advice; one supervisor told her she would need a bachelor's degree in accounting, while another advised her that her degree in economics was sufficient. To be on the safe side, Smart began taking evening accounting courses at the University of Delaware.

After some delay, Columbia Gas decided to fill the senior analyst position, and the task of selecting the person to fill that position fell principally to Donato Furlano, Smart's direct supervisor. Subsequently, on three separate occasions, Furlano offered the position to a male employee, each of whom rejected the offer. The personnel department then assembled a list of employees who appeared to meet the minimum qualifications for the position, and Smart and four other women were on the list. Furlano rejected out of hand all of the women on the list, and then offered the position to a newly hired male worker who was not on the list. Furlano's choice for the position had an accounting degree and five years of accounting experience.

When Smart later charged Columbia Gas with sex discrimination, company officials claimed that Smart was not promoted to the senior analyst position because she lacked accounting experience and the requisite analytical skills, though they admitted that with appropriate training, she would have been capable of performing the duties of the position even without an accounting degree.

Smart claimed that she was as qualified as the male employee selected, that the company had failed to consider any women for the position, and that Columbia Gas's method of promoting employees to middle- and upper-management positions favored men. The trial court found that the five women that Furlano had rejected out of hand were at least as qualified, if not more so, as the male candidates that he had not rejected, and that Smart was as qualified as the worker chosen by Furlano. At the conclusion of the trial, the court ruled that gender had been a determinative factor in the decision not to promote Smart, and thus it awarded judgment in her favor.[22]

Physicians rarely appear as claimants in sex discrimination cases, in part because many doctors are self-employed or practice as members of small medical teams. But discrimination against women exists in medicine just as in the other professions. The *New England Journal of Medicine* recently reported that female doctors are more likely than their male peers to teach at medical schools but are less likely to be promoted to senior medical positions: Women are 26 percent less likely than men to be promoted from junior faculty positions to associate professor, and still fewer advance from associate to full professor.[23]

Jean Jew's case reflects these conditions. Jew obtained her medical degree from Tulane University, and later the University of Iowa's College of Medicine appointed her an associate professor in its Department of Anatomy, headed by Terrence Williams. Previously, Williams had been at Tulane University, where Jew had conducted research under his supervision. Throughout her employment at the University of Iowa, Jew worked closely with Williams as a research collaborator, and they coauthored several articles for scientific publications. The professional relationship between Jew and Williams was close, and she was a friend of his wife, also a professor at the College of Medicine.

Not long after Jew's appointment to the Department of Anatomy, rumors began to circulate suggesting that a sexual relationship existed between Jew and Williams. The ongoing rumors accused her of using her sex as a tool for advancement in the department. Thereafter, sexually suggestive cartoons and sex-based graffiti referring to Jew appeared on the wall of the men's room and at other places in the department. One of the male faculty members repeatedly speculated aloud about a sexual relationship between Jew and Williams, and he told faculty, graduate students, and staff that Jew had been observed having sexual intercourse with Williams in his office, that she was a "slut," and that she had received preferential treatment based on her sexual relationship with Williams. Another male doctor referred to Jew as a "slut," a "bitch," and a "whore."

Jew complained to the dean of the College of Medicine, advising him of the conduct of the male doctors in her department, and charged the college with ignoring the existence of a pattern of sexual harassment intended to discredit her professional and personal reputation. College officials advised her that nothing could be done, that a single woman commonly encountered these kinds of difficulties in a small-town, goldfish-bowl type of environment.

Jew continued to author and coauthor with Williams a number of articles that were published in prominent medical journals. She received two grants from the National Institute of Health and another from the National Science Foundation. In due course, the medical school considered her for promotion from associate professor to full professor. In accordance with established procedures, school administrators placed the proposed promotion before the entire faculty of the Department of Anatomy for approval or rejection.

The same faculty members who had verbally harassed Jew were among those called upon to evaluate her work and vote on her promotion. Two of the doctors who voted against her promotion were those who had called her a "slut" and a "whore." Another doctor who voted no commented that Jew had received many more advantages than he. All the voting faculty had heard the rumors, and, not surprisingly, they voted against her promotion. Those who voted no gave as their reason their belief that Jew had not established her "independence" in the areas of research and publication.

When Jew later sued the university for sex discrimination, the court, citing the conduct she had endured, ruled in her favor: "The ongoing rumors, which were false, accused her of physically using her sex as a tool for gaining favor, influence and power with the Head of the Department, a man, and suggested that her professional accomplishments rested on sexual achievements rather than achievements of merit. . . . The sexual relationship rumors, of course, also implicated Dr. Williams. . . . Unlike the import of the rumors with respect to Dr. Jew, however, there was no suggestion that Dr. Williams was using a sexual relationship to gain favor, influence and power." The court held that Jew's rejection for promotion flowed directly from the harassing and discriminatory conduct of the male doctors in her department and directed the university to promote Jew to full professor.[24]

Female lawyers, university professors, accountants, and doctors continue to be victimized by sex-discriminatory conduct, as are women in all the professions—even in the world of astronomy. For more than a century, women have earned at least 10 percent of the doctorates awarded in astronomy, and women currently account for 25 percent of these degrees. At a meeting of the American Astronomical Society in early 2000, researchers presented the results of a survey on the status of women in the profession: Women at the highest levels of the profession remain a rarity. Only 5 percent of the country's professors of astronomy are female. Among the elite universities, more male than female graduate students win postdoctoral appointments to the schools from which they received their graduate degrees. For women in the field of astronomy, the glass ceiling reaches to the sky.[25]

Nine

Discrimination against Pregnant Women

Not long after congressional enactment of Title VII, pregnant workers began to file claims alleging sex discrimination. The statute provided that it was unlawful for an employer to discriminate against a woman *because of sex*, but it was silent with regard to pregnancy.[1] Thus the courts were confronted with the question whether "because of sex" included "because of pregnancy." The early pregnancy cases concluded with victories for the complainants,[2] but the Supreme Court, rarely a leader in matters relating to civil rights in employment, declared in a case involving the General Electric Company that discrimination against pregnant women was not barred by Title VII.

After General Electric adopted a disability plan that afforded its employees sickness and injury benefits but excluded benefits for disabilities arising from pregnancy, a group of female workers brought a class action against the company, claiming that the exclusion of pregnancy from the terms of the plan amounted to an act of sex discrimination in violation of Title VII. The trial court agreed, declaring that discrimination against pregnant women is a form of sex discrimination, and thus the exclusion of pregnancy from the plan was discriminatory. But the Supreme Court thought otherwise. The Court, speaking through Justice Rehnquist, first noted that pregnancy is merely a physical condition, and an employer is free to include or exclude disability coverage for pregnancy just as for any other physical condition. In Justice Rehnquist's view, the GE plan did not afford coverage for any disability or illness that excluded either women or men. "There is no risk from which men are protected and women are not. Likewise, there is no risk from which women are protected and men are not." Since the plan did not exclude anyone from coverage because of gender, it complied with Title VII. For that reason, the Supreme Court rejected the lower courts' position that discrimination based on pregnancy was a form of sex discrimination.[3]

Congress reacted to the Supreme Court ruling by enacting the Pregnancy Discrimination Act (PDA), which amended Title VII by defining discrimination against pregnant women as a form of sex discrimination: "The terms 'because of sex' or 'on the basis of sex' include . . . because of or on the basis of pregnancy, childbirth, or related medical conditions; and women affected by pregnancy, childbirth, or related medical conditions shall be treated the same for all employment-related purposes . . . as other persons not so affected but similar in their ability to work."[4]

Congress designed the PDA specifically to address a commonly accepted but false stereotype that women are less desirable employees because they are or may become pregnant. In rejecting this stereotype, Congress declared that pregnancy must be treated like any other temporary disability. The decision to work or not to work during pregnancy must be reserved to each woman to make for herself. But in providing these protections, Congress also made it clear that employers are not required to provide pregnant women with any form of special treatment—employers are merely required to treat pregnant women in the same manner as they treat all other employees.[5]

After the Pregnancy Discrimination Act passed, the Equal Employment Opportunity Commission adopted regulations defining its scope with greater specificity.

- An employer may not refuse to hire a woman who is pregnant, so long as she is able to perform the major functions necessary to the job. Any written or unwritten employer policy that excludes female employees from employment because of pregnancy, childbirth, or related medical conditions constitutes a violation of Title VII.
- An employer is required to treat a pregnant employee temporarily unable to perform the functions of her job as a consequence of her pregnancy in the same manner it treats other temporarily disabled employees, by providing modified job functions, alternative assignments, or disability leaves.
- An employee must be permitted to work at all times during her pregnancy so long as she is capable of performing her job functions.
- Unless a pregnant employee has informed her employer that she does not intend to return to work after giving birth, the employer must hold her job open for her return on the same basis as for other employees who are on sick or disability leave.

- An employer may not adopt a rule that would prohibit a female employee from returning to work for any predetermined period of time after giving birth to a child.
- Employer policies relating to seniority, vacation benefits, pay increases, and other employee benefits for pregnant workers must be the same as policies relating to employees absent for other medical reasons.
- Health, disability insurance, and sick leave plans made available to workers by an employer must treat all disabilities caused by pregnancy, childbirth, or related medical conditions in the same manner as disabilities caused by other medical conditions.[6]

The basic principle underlying the PDA requires an employer to treat pregnant workers in the same manner as it treats other workers temporarily disabled, that is, on the basis of their ability or inability to do their jobs. If other employees on disability leave are entitled to return to their jobs when they are again able to work, then women also are entitled to return to their jobs after a maternity leave absence. But the PDA does not obligate employers to grant preferential treatment to pregnant women, as Mirtha Urbano discovered.

Urbano worked for Continental Airlines as a ticketing sales agent, assisting customers with their ticket purchases and baggage. When she became pregnant and began to suffer low-back pain, her physician ordered her to refrain during the balance of her pregnancy from lifting anything heavier than twenty pounds. Urbano then applied to Continental for reassignment to a light-duty position that would not require her to lift passenger baggage. Continental denied her request. Its policy was to grant reassignments to light-duty positions only to employees who had suffered on-the-job injuries. Workers with nonoccupational injuries or illnesses did not have the right to reassignment but were assigned to light-duty positions in accordance with seniority. In those circumstances, Urbano was unable to obtain a reassignment, and she was forced to use her accrued sick leave and, ultimately, to take unpaid medical leave during the remainder of her pregnancy. Urbano then sued Continental for pregnancy discrimination.

Continental treated Urbano in the same manner as it treated other workers suffering from nonoccupational injuries and illnesses. Light-duty positions were at a premium; each of the forty-eight workers granted light-duty assignment during the year previous to Urbano's application for reassignment had suffered an on-the-job injury. Continental denied Urbano's application for a light-duty assignment only because she had not suffered a work-related injury, as it was entitled to do as long as it treated nonpregnant workers in a similar manner. Since the PDA does not impose any duty on an employer to treat pregnant employees better than other employees, Urbano's discrimination claim was dismissed.[7]

An employer may treat pregnant employees not only as well, but also as badly as it treats other employees. Holly-Anne Geier's is a case in point. Geier, a sales representative for Medtronic, Inc., was something less than a model employee. Her supervisors had given her several warning notices and, on one occasion, had placed her on probation. Geier became pregnant, and although soon after she was confined to bed due to pregnancy-related problems, her supervisor called her at home once or twice a day, demanding that she continue to call her sales accounts, and threatening to relieve her of her position if she declined. Geier complied, working from her bed. When Geier was later hospitalized, her supervisor continued to harangue her about remaining in communication with her accounts. Geier then miscarried. While she was recovering at home, her supervisor directed her to get out of bed and start calling her accounts if she wanted to keep her job. Geier returned to work less than a week later.

As Geier's performance deficiencies continued, her supervisor again placed her on probation, and when her performance failed to improve, he dismissed her. Geier then sued the company for pregnancy discrimination, but she faced a difficult evidentiary hurdle. She had to prove that the treatment she had been subjected to differed from that meted out to nonpregnant workers. However, she was unable to establish that her supervisor's haranguing telephone calls were motivated by her pregnancy rather than by her absence from the workplace. The PDA requires an employer to ignore an employee's pregnancy, but it does not require it to ignore her absence from work, unless it also ignores similar absences of nonpregnant workers. Evidence of the supervisor's boorish behavior, in and of itself, did not establish discriminatory intent, as he may have acted similarly with any employee absent from the office, pregnant or not. Without evidence that her employer treated bedridden pregnant employees differently than bedridden nonpregnant employees, Geier's case could not succeed.

The outrageous character of the supervisor's conduct makes it hard to accept this outcome, but Geier's case illuminates the underlying philosophy of the PDA—pregnancy discrimination exists only in situations where pregnant women are treated less favorably than nonpregnant employees working in similar circumstances. Holly-Anne Geier was treated badly, but not unlawfully.[8]

The major hurdle facing a woman who claims pregnancy discrimination is that she must prove that *on account of her pregnancy* her employer treated her differently and less favorably than other employees, that it failed to deal with the disability associated with pregnancy in the same manner it dealt with other temporary disabilities. A California hotel made it easy for a group of female housekeepers to clear that hurdle when it admitted that it customarily fired all housekeepers when they became pregnant but did not terminate other employees temporarily disabled.[9] Most employers are not so accommodating as to admit their discriminatory practices. Frequently, the evidence necessary to establish a pregnancy discrimination claim is not readily available to the complainant.

One method of establishing a pregnancy claim is to show that the employer, while acting adversely to the interests of a pregnant worker, failed to follow its own policies and procedures. On the last day of her maternity leave, Margaret McLemore was notified by her employer, Continuity Programs, that due to a business downturn the company could no longer afford to pay her salary, and she was terminated. Continuity's maternity leave policy stated, as with the case of leave taken by other workers, that the company would attempt to place a woman returning from maternity leave in the position she held before she left work to give birth. In the event a position was unavailable for a woman returning from maternity leave, the policy afforded her a preference for the next available position for which she was qualified. A short time after McLemore was dismissed, Continuity filled three positions for which she was qualified. In each instance, however, Continuity failed to notify her of the vacancy and thus failed to follow its own policy, denying McLemore the benefits that the company provided nonpregnant employees returning from disability leaves, and this fact supported McLemore's claim that she had been discriminated against because of her pregnancy.[10]

Although women generally establish their claims of pregnancy discrimination by demonstrating that pregnant workers are treated less advantageously than nonpregnant workers, a woman may also prove her claim by showing that she was treated adversely once she informed her employer of her pregnancy. Instead of comparing her treatment as a pregnant employee with the treatment afforded nonpregnant employees, she compares her treatment as a pregnant employee with the treatment she experienced before she became pregnant, as was the case with Caroline Sanford.

Yenkin-Majestic Paint Corporation hired Sanford to work in its operations division, performing secretarial duties as well as other tasks related to the work done by chemists in the company's paint laboratory. Some of her work was highly technical, as she was required to complete material safety data reports and to type paint formulas and other documents containing technical data. A significant portion of Sanford's job functions involved the work she performed for the laboratory chemists.

About six months after she was hired, Sanford informed her supervisor she was pregnant. Four days later, her supervisor, for the first time, criticized her performance, claiming she often overstayed her lunch hour and abused her personal telephone privileges. Not long after, the company was reorganized; the operations division in which Sanford worked was dissolved and a technical division was created. A newly hired manager of the technical division asked the company to assign him a secretary with a technical background and experience with paint laboratory functions and who was familiar with chemical terminology. Although Sanford clearly met those criteria, the new manager was advised that the company did not currently employ any secretaries with that type of experience. Subsequently, Sanford was fired, purportedly because of lack of work, even though she remained involved in ongoing projects and was fully occupied until the day of her termination. On the day of Sanford's discharge, the company began interviewing candidates for the new technical secretarial position. The person hired possessed only a cursory knowledge of technical paint data, and after she resigned a few months later, the company replaced her with a worker who had no training or experience with paint or chemicals.

Once she announced her pregnancy, Sanford's world was turned upside down. The manner in which she was treated after the announcement of her pregnancy was wholly dissimilar from her earlier treatment. Her supervisor criticized her performance, the company ignored the expertise she had gained working for the laboratory chemists, and although she was constantly busy, she was terminated for lack of work. The EEOC sued Yenkin-Majestic on Sanford's behalf, alleging that the company's actions that followed Sanford's announcement of her pregnancy violated the Pregnancy Discrimination Act. After a trial, the court agreed with the EEOC and entered judgment against Yenkin-Majestic and in favor of Sanford.[11]

On occasion, comments by management or supervisory personnel may lend support to a pregnancy discrimination claim. After a waitress announced her pregnancy, her working hours were reduced because, as her manager explained, "it doesn't look right" to have someone pregnant waiting on tables. The same manager later commented to another employee that "it looks tacky" for a pregnant woman to wait on tables. After the EEOC sued on the waitress's behalf, the court ordered the restaurant to reimburse her for her lost wages, and it enjoined the restaurant from committing similar violations of the PDA against its other waitresses.[12]

In another case of pregnancy discrimination, Regina Sheehan was five months pregnant with her third child when she was fired by her employer, Donlen Corporation, which led Sheehan to assert a legal claim under the Pregnancy Discrimination Act. Sheehan's first and second pregnancies also occurred while she was working for Donlen. Upon her return to work after her second maternity leave, Sheehan was assigned a greatly increased workload. She jokingly commented to her supervisor, "Maybe I should go home and have another baby." Her supervisor responded, "If you have another baby, I'll invite you to stay home." A year later, when notified of the third pregnancy, the supervisor said, "Oh my God, she's pregnant again," and a short time later she informed Sheehan, "You're not coming back after this baby." Three months later, Sheehan's department head informed her that she was to be dismissed and commented, "Hopefully, this will give you some time to spend at home with your children." Until then, the department head had fired only one other worker. She too was pregnant.[13]

The remarks of the supervisor and the department head, both of whom participated in the decision to discharge Sheehan, provided the court with direct evidence of discrimination, and the jury awarded Sheehan $117,000 in damages. On appeal, Donlen argued that inasmuch as the department head did not explicitly say that Sheehan's termination was ordered on account of her pregnancy, his statement did not rise to the level of direct evidence of discrimination. The appellate court rejected Donlen's position, noting that remarks that reflected a propensity to evaluate an employee on the basis of an illegal criterion constitute direct evidence of discrimination. In this case, pregnancy was the illegal criterion that Donlen used to determine whether Sheehan's employment would continue or not.[14]

After nearly twenty-five years of experience with the PDA, employers are far more likely to conceal rather than disclose any discriminatory predilections they may harbor against pregnant women. As a consequence, they are far less likely to engage in discussions with their workers that reveal those predilections. Since direct evidence of pregnancy discrimination similar to that in the *Sheehan* case is less available to pregnant workers, they must rely on other types of evidence to establish their claims. Currently, the most common approach to proving pregnancy discrimination is through indirect or circumstantial evidence, which was the route taken by Sondra Tamimi, a desk clerk at a Howard Johnson Motor Lodge in Montgomery, Alabama. When she was hired, her supervisor informed her that she had to comply with a dress code, but he did not advise her that she had to use makeup while working behind the front desk. This was important for Tamimi, since, for religious reasons, she did not use makeup. Although she was the only member of the staff without makeup at the front desk, management did not complain. However, two days after Tamimi announced her pregnancy, management initiated a new dress code that required all employees at the front desk to wear makeup. When Tamimi refused to comply, she was fired.

Management's discontent with Tamimi's appearance began on the day it became aware of her pregnancy. It then inaugurated a new dress code that affected only Tamimi, as all other female workers already used makeup. When Tamimi sued for pregnancy discrimination, the court ruled that management knew that on account of religious reasons, Tamimi would refuse to use makeup, and thus it adopted a course of action that could culminate only in her discharge. The dress code was implemented for the purpose of getting rid of the pregnant Tamimi.

Although Tamimi did not have any direct evidence of discrimination, she was able to offer the court indirect evidence of management's discriminatory intent—indirect evidence demonstrating that the mandatory makeup rule was conceived, implemented, and applied to Tamimi only because she was pregnant. Hence, the court awarded judgment in her favor.[15]

Discrimination against pregnant women may occur at any point in the employment relationship, from hiring to firing. After working for about six months as a clothing clerk at a Wal-Mart store in Green Valley, Arizona, Jamey Stern decided to resign and enroll in courses at a local community college. Shortly after her resignation, Stern learned she was pregnant. She decided to postpone her education and reapply for employment with Wal-Mart. At her interview, Wal-Mart's personnel manager discussed three positions Stern might fill, and they agreed on one of them. When Stern disclosed her pregnancy during the course of the interview, the personnel manager asked her if she had any concerns about working while pregnant. Stern responded that she was confident she could fill the position without difficulty. At the conclusion of the interview, Stern was informed that, as the final step in the hiring process, she would be required to take a drug test administered by one of the store's assistant managers.

When the drug test was not immediately scheduled, Stern telephoned the store. On each occasion that she called to schedule the test, she was told that the assistant manager was unavailable. Ultimately, the assistant manager informed Stern that due to her pregnancy, Wal-Mart had decided not to hire her. Questioned further, she advised Stern that the decision had been made on the basis of Stern's statement at her interview that she would be unable to lift boxes. Stern denied making such a statement. She then filed a pregnancy discrimination charge with the Equal Employment Opportunity Commission, who sued Wal-Mart on her behalf.

At the trial, Wal-Mart painted a new picture of Stern's interview. The personnel manager testified that Stern failed to disclose her pregnancy during the initial interview, and that Wal-Mart first learned of her condition when she was questioned by the assistant manager. The assistant manager testified that Stern had told her she was concerned about her pregnancy and her ability to perform the job functions that would be assigned to her. The assistant manager also testified that she had documented her discussion with Stern by preparing an Interview Comment Sheet, which, according to Wal-Mart procedures, should have been retained in Stern's application file. The EEOC reviewed the files of fifty other job applicants interviewed by Wal-Mart at about the same time that Stern's application was rejected, and each of those files contained an Interview Comment Sheet, but Stern's file did not.

Two other elements of indirect evidence materially undermined Wal-Mart's defense. First, the personnel manager testified that she had seen the Interview Comment Sheet prepared by the assistant manager but that it had not been completed. Second, Wal-Mart initially told the EEOC that it had decided not to hire Stern because she had stated in her application that she would be unable to work more than two days per week. Stern's application contained no such statement. With this evidence in hand, the jury decided that Wal-Mart had engaged in intentional discrimination against Stern on account of her pregnancy, and it returned a verdict in her favor.[16]

When applying for a position, a pregnant woman should always disclose her condition to her prospective employer. A rejected job applicant cannot successfully sue an employer for pregnancy discrimination unless she is able to prove that the employer was aware of her pregnancy and on that account rejected her. Then again, a job applicant's failure to reveal her pregnancy may lead to other unhappy events, as Margaret Ahmad found when she applied to the Loyal American Life Insurance Company to fill the position of medical claims examiner. She was told that the company's training process for this position usually lasted five to six months, but in view of her prior experience, it could be shortened. Her first day on the job, Ahmad informed Loyal personnel she was four months pregnant. The company advised Ahmad that the timing of her anticipated maternity leave would significantly interfere with her training, and under the circumstances, Loyal could not employ her. Ahmad then sued Loyal for pregnancy discrimination, but the court dismissed her claim. The evidence failed to establish that the company denied Ahmad employment on account of her pregnancy. Rather, the evidence revealed that Loyal withdrew its offer of employment only because Ahmad's maternity leave would have adversely affected her training and thus materially reduce her value to the company. Since these circumstances constituted a legitimate business reason for rejecting Ahmad, the court refused to hold Loyal liable for pregnancy discrimination.[17]

Pregnant workers frequently find that once their employers learn of their pregnancies, promotions previously promised them are instead granted to other employees. In one case, a female worker, after receiving favorable performance evaluations, was offered promotion to a supervisory position. At the time, no other employees were even considered for the position. However, when her employer learned that the worker was pregnant, it withdrew the offer and awarded the supervisory position to a male worker instead.[18] Failures to promote, undesirable transfers, and objectionable job assignments, unfortunately, commonly occur following the announcement of a pregnancy. Suzanne Goss's career abruptly ended after she announced her pregnancy.

Goss was a highly successful sales representative for Exxon Office Systems in Montgomery County, Pennsylvania. Her future appeared bright, as Exxon had assigned her to one of the company's most desirable sales territories and had given her responsibility for several major accounts. But when she became pregnant, her sales manager expressed doubt about her ability to combine motherhood and career. Goss, however, assured him that she planned to be a working mother and saw nothing inconsistent in having a family and pursuing a career. Shortly thereafter, the issue became moot, as Goss suffered a miscarriage.

A few months later, Goss again became pregnant. Her supervisor again closely questioned her about the dual responsibilities of career and motherhood. Afterward, he verbally abused her, criticized her performance, and threatened to relieve her of one of her major accounts. A few weeks later, Goss again miscarried. When Goss returned to work, her supervisor informed her that he had transferred her to another sales territory, one that Exxon sales people considered most undesirable. When Goss objected to her transfer, she was told to accept it or resign. Goss chose the latter and sued Exxon for pregnancy discrimination.

After a trial without a jury, the court ruled that Goss's pregnancies and her expressed desire to combine motherhood with her sales career were determining factors in Exxon's decision to transfer her to a less desirable sales territory. The court ordered Exxon to reimburse Goss for the monetary losses she suffered as a consequence of its violations of Title VII.[19]

In another case, an employer told one of its workers that "it could easily get away with discharging a pregnant employee by stating that her position was eliminated."[20] Many employers have used this tactic, but not all of them have succeeded. Mary Quaratino began her employment with Tiffany's Fifth Avenue jewelry store in Manhattan as a second assistant account executive. After several promotions, Tiffany designated her manager of corporate sales support and administration. In that position, she received a favorable performance evaluation, but at its conclusion, her supervisor asked, "Are you really serious about your career, or are you just going to go home and get pregnant?" Unknown to her supervisor, Quaratino was then three months pregnant.

She did not disclose her pregnancy until a month after the evaluation. Her supervisor reacted with an expletive. He avoided speaking to her during the following week, became highly critical of her performance, and sent her a memo accusing her of consistent tardiness. Even after Quaratino demonstrated to him that five of the six instances of alleged tardiness were based on inaccurate information, her supervisor refused to withdraw his criticism.

After Quaratino gave birth to her child, Tiffany notified her that her position had been eliminated in a reorganization of the department she had worked in before her maternity leave. She was the only person terminated in the reorganization.

After Quaratino sued Tiffany for pregnancy discrimination, she learned that before she had gone on maternity leave, Tiffany had hired a single woman without children to fill her position. Tiffany, however, argued that it had not hired the new employee to replace Quaratino, but rather it had transferred Quaratino's responsibilities to a newly created higher-level managerial position and had then assigned the new employee to that position.[21]

Did Tiffany embark on an elaborate scheme to make it appear that Quaratino's position had been eliminated, thus justifying her termination while she was on maternity leave? Did Tiffany restructure Quaratino's job responsibilities to implement a discriminatory purpose? Or was the transfer of Quaratino's job responsibilities to a newly created managerial position a business decision uncorrupted by unlawful bias? These are the types of issues a woman may confront when she claims her employer was motivated to eliminate her position due to her pregnancy. Quaratino and Tiffany settled their dispute, and thus the court was relieved of answering these questions. Based on the evidence on the record, however, it appears that Quaratino might very well have succeeded in proving her case.

In addition to pregnancy, the Pregnancy Discrimination Act bars discrimination "on the basis of . . . childbirth, or related medical conditions." What are related medical conditions? Does the PDA afford protection to a woman fired on the ground that her infertility treatments interfered with the performance of her job responsibilities? The argument has been made that the inability of a woman to become pregnant is not a pregnancy-related condition. A broader interpretation of the statute, however, would afford its protections to any condition related to the potential for pregnancy. The courts have generally held that adverse acts directed against a female worker who intends to become or is trying to become pregnant constitute a form of discrimination barred by the statute.[22] Yet breastfeeding and other child-rearing concerns that arise after a pregnancy are not considered conditions related to pregnancy within the meaning of the PDA.[23] Similarly, claims of discrimination based on one's new-parent status—or, as sometimes defined, on being a "new mom"—are not valid under the provisions of the PDA.[24]

Because the statute has been broadly interpreted by the courts, its basic coverage has been extended to women who choose to terminate their pregnancies. Thus, no employer may refuse to hire, fire, or otherwise treat a woman adversely simply because she has exercised her right to have an abortion.[25] Conversely, an employer may not discriminate against a woman who refuses to have an abortion.[26]

One need only read the daily newspapers to realize that employer discrimination against pregnant women continues unabated. When a television actress became pregnant, the producer of her show fired her on the ground she would then be unable to play the role of a nonpregnant woman. A jury awarded the actress $5.8 million in damages.[27] More than two hundred teachers and students rallied outside an Elmont, New York, school board meeting in support of a teacher who alleged she had been denied tenure after she became pregnant.[28] In another suit, a secretary who claimed that a New York assemblywoman fired her for having a baby agreed to a settlement of $95,000.[29]

The number of pregnancy discrimination claims filed with the EEOC between 1992 and 2000 increased by nearly 25 percent.[30] Even these figures understate the problem. The full extent of the discrimination practiced against pregnant women cannot be judged by counting claims filed, since many, if not most, mothers are reluctant to initiate legal proceedings while caring for a newborn child. As a result, we may never learn the full extent of workplace discrimination that confronts pregnant women.

Ten

Discrimination against Women with Children

Since women first entered the U.S. workplace, employers have treated women with children differently from other employees. In 1908, when the Supreme Court gave its approval to an Oregon statute limiting the working hours of women (see chapter 3), its comments on motherhood and women's place in the workplace epitomized stereotypes then commonly held: "[Public opinion has produced] a widespread belief that woman's physical structure and the functions she performs in consequence thereof, justify special legislation restricting or qualifying the conditions under which she should be permitted to toil. . . . That woman's physical structure and the performance of maternal functions place her at a disadvantage in the struggle for subsistence is obvious. This is especially true when the burdens of motherhood are upon her."[1] Nearly a century later, such sex stereotypes remain prevalent, albeit modified in form. Working mothers remain subject to significant restrictions on advancement to higher positions in the workplace.

Shortly after World War II, for example, the Edwin L. Wiegand Company in Pennsylvania initiated a policy of discharging female employees upon marriage and of refusing to hire women who were married. The policy was necessary, according to Wiegand's management, to provide jobs for male "bread winners" returning from the war.[2] At the time, the policy was lawful, and it remained lawful until July 2, 1965, the effective date of Title VII.

The EEOC later adopted regulations providing workplace protection specifically for married women: "The Commission has determined that an employer's rule which forbids or restricts the employment of married women and which is not applicable to married men is discrimination based on sex prohibited by Title VII of the Civil Rights Act."[3] An employer policy or practice, even if not directed against all female employees, is nevertheless discriminatory if a subgroup, such as married women, is singled out for treatment different from that extended to male employees. Similarly, an employer may not select unmarried women with children for adverse treatment.

Over the past four decades, the number of married women with children employed outside the home has increased significantly. In 1960, approximately 6.6 million married women with children were employed in the workplace, and by 1997, this number had grown nearly threefold to 18.2 million. The workplace participation of women with very young children has also greatly increased. In 1960, the labor force participation rate of married women with children under six years of age was 18.6 percent, but by 1997, it had increased to 63.6 percent. In that year, 77.6 percent of married women with children between the ages of six and seventeen were gainfully employed.[4] Statistical studies forecast the continued presence of working women with children in the workplace, even while at home they continue to be the major child-care givers.

With this marked growth in the employment of married women with children has come an increased reliance of working mothers upon Title VII protections against workplace discriminatory policies and practices. In Hot Springs, Arkansas, Martha Coble applied for the position of director of the school district's new teachers' center, designed to improve teacher skills, revise curricula, and experiment with new teaching methods and materials. In her thirteen years with the school district, she had accumulated a wide variety of classroom experience and was certified as an elementary school teacher, an elementary school principal, an elementary school supervisor, and a curriculum specialist for grades kindergarten through high school. Bill Nipper, the other applicant for the director's position, was similarly qualified. After the school district superintendent interviewed each candidate, he selected Nipper. Coble then charged the superintendent and the school district with sex discrimination.

At the trial, Coble argued that her status as a working mother had been the primary reason for the superintendent's decision not to select her as the director of the teachers' center. Coble testified that during her interview, the superintendent noted her absences attributable to the illnesses of her children, questioned her about her children's ages, and asked her whether, in light of her family obligations, she could handle the long hours the director's position demanded. When the superintendent later notified Coble that he had selected Nipper for the position, he noted that although Coble was as qualified as Nipper, she had a family and he did not. Thus, it was clear that the superintendent's choice was influenced by his assumption that Coble's family responsibilities would interfere with her performance.

The superintendent rebutted none of this evidence, and the court concluded that his decision to reject Coble was largely based on the false premise that a mother's performance of child-care responsibilities necessarily interferes with her workplace functions. The court's ruling was buttressed by the failure of the school district to offer any evidence demonstrating that marital or parental status had been a factor in filling other administrative positions presumably as demanding as the director's position, and most of those positions had been filled by men with children. Clearly, women with children, as compared with men with children, faced substantial barriers to advancement in the Hot Springs school district.[5]

Joann Trezza, also a working mother, was an attorney in the legal department of Hartford, Inc., an insurance company with offices in New York City. Working alongside Trezza in the department was a female attorney, unmarried and without children. When an opening occurred for a management position in the legal department of one of Hartford's suburban offices, the unmarried attorney was appointed to the position, even though Trezza was senior to her. When Trezza asked why Hartford had not considered her for the post, the managing attorney of the legal department told her that it was assumed that because she had a family she would not be interested in the position.

A year or so later, Trezza was in line for promotion to an assistant managing attorney position, but Hartford again rejected her in favor of a female attorney who was unmarried and childless. At the time, Hartford also elevated a male attorney, married with children, to an assistant manager post. After Trezza complained to one of Hartford's senior vice presidents that she felt she had been denied the promotion solely because she was a married woman with children, Hartford finally ordered her advancement to an assistant managing attorney position.

Four years later, the managing attorney of the legal department decided to retire. Since Trezza was then the second most senior attorney in the office and had consistently earned excellent performance evaluations, she believed she was the logical choice to be the retiree's successor. Rather than naming Trezza, however, Hartford appointed a thirty-eight-year-old female attorney with no children. The appointee had considerably less experience than Trezza, had never practiced law in New York, and, in fact, was not admitted to practice law in the state. Trezza sued Hartford for sex discrimination.

When Hartford asked the court to dismiss Trezza's case, her attorneys submitted an abundance of evidence supporting her claim that during the course of her employment Hartford had discriminated against her merely because she was a married woman with children and that male employees with children were not similarly treated. First, they showed that only seven of the forty-six managing attorneys employed by Hartford nationwide were women, and of these seven, four were employed in East Coast offices, and none of the four had school-age children. On the other hand, many of the men serving in managing attorney positions had children. Second, on three occasions Trezza's supervisor disparagingly commented on "the incompetence and laziness of women who [were] working mothers." In addition, on another occasion, a senior vice president of the company declared that it was his opinion that working mothers cannot simultaneously be both good mothers and good workers, remarking to Trezza, "I don't see how you can do either job well." Based on this evidence, the court denied Hartford's motion to dismiss Trezza's claims, and thus they were required to proceed to a trial of the ultimate issue—did Hartford discriminate against Trezza because she was a working mother?[6] A trial was avoided, however, when Hartford agreed to resolve Trezza's claims. If the matter had not been settled prior to the trial, it appears highly likely that Trezza would have prevailed.

Both Coble and Trezza submitted evidence that their employers favored their male employees who had children over female employees with children. This type of evidence is typical of sex discrimination cases based on allegations of disparate treatment, that is, men and women similarly situated are not similarly treated. What would have been the result in these cases if evidence of disparate treatment had not been available? We turn to Andrea Bass's sex discrimination claim against Chemical Bank for the answer.

Bass's responsibilities as assistant vice president and product manager at the bank included the development of marketing plans for new cash management products. Given her success in this position, Bass anticipated promotion to vice president. Chemical, however, declined to promote her. Subsequently, Bass gave birth to her first child, and on her return from maternity leave, Chemical relieved her of certain of her responsibilities, making it less likely she would be promoted. Three years later, after Bass had her second child, Chemical reassigned virtually all of her remaining responsibilities as product manager. Not long after, Chemical promoted a single woman with no children to the vice presidency position that Bass had long anticipated being awarded. At this juncture, Bass sued Chemical for sex discrimination, claiming she had been denied promotion only because of her status as a working mother.

Bass was passed over for promotion in favor of another woman, not a man. She was unable to produce any evidence comparing the treatment afforded her by Chemical with its treatment of married men with children. Thus, the basic piece of evidence that would have established discriminatory conduct was missing; Bass could not prove that Chemical's decision to deny her promotion to vice president was based on gender. The most that Bass could show was that she was discriminated against because of her parental status, but that type of discrimination is not prohibited by Title VII.

Coble, on the other hand, demonstrated that she was discriminated against not only because she was a parent, but also because she was a woman. Trezza's initial concerns with the failure of her company to promote her were based on allegations that women without children were being favored over her, but ultimately she also produced evidence that the company's failures to promote her were based on her gender as well as her parental status. Missing from Bass's claim was any evidence that she was discriminated against because she was a woman, and thus her claim was doomed to failure.[7]

Melissa Fuller's sex discrimination case against GTE Corporation was similarly deficient. Fuller claimed that GTE discriminated against her because of her status as a mother of young children. She alleged that her department supervisor continuously made negative comments about her children, suggesting that Fuller needed to get her priorities straight, as her job came before her family. On one occasion, the supervisor suggested a pet carrier as a cage for Fuller's children. Despite this apparent animus toward working mothers, thirty-five of the forty-four employees subordinate to the department supervisor were women, twenty-two with children. Of the nine males in the department, only one had children. The court dismissed Fuller's case because she had failed to prove that she was treated differently from men, and more specifically, she failed to show that she was treated differently from male workers with children.[8]

Some working mothers, among them Susan McGrenaghan, have attempted to extend the scope of the protections of Title VII to smaller subgroups of married women with children. McGrenaghan charged the St. Denis School in Philadelphia with having discriminated against her because she was the mother of a disabled child. After the birth of her son, the school transformed McGrenaghan's full-time teaching position to one requiring her to work a half day as a teacher and a half day as a resource aide. This constituted a demotion, as it involved significantly diminished job responsibilities. McGrenaghan alleged that the reduction in her job responsibilities was based on unfounded stereotypes concerning the adequacy of the work performance of mothers having disabled children, and that a similar employment decision would not have been made either for a woman without a disabled child or for a father of a disabled child. In support of her claim, McGrenaghan offered evidence that she was replaced in her full-time teaching position by a less qualified woman who was not the mother of a disabled child. She also introduced testimony that the principal of the school had expressed animus against working mothers of disabled children. Even though McGrenaghan's claim extended only to a very small subclass of women, the court ruled that she had a valid Title VII claim.[9]

The court in this case adopted a broader view of Title VII proscriptions. The school argued that it could not be held liable for sex discrimination because McGrenaghan had failed to produce any evidence that she was treated less favorably or differently on the basis of her gender as she failed to prove that she was treated differently from its male employees. Moreover, her replacement was a woman. This argument tracked that asserted in the Bass case. In rejecting the school's position, the court relied on the "sex plus" doctrine. McGrenaghan was a member of a subclass of women who have children with disabilities, and she alleged that her job transfer was based on unfounded stereotypes concerning mothers of disabled children, that a similar decision would not have been made of a woman without a disabled child or of a father with a disabled child. She also charged the school with discriminatory animus against working mothers with disabled children. These allegations, according to the court, were sufficient to establish a valid Title VII claim.

We turn now to a different type of sex discrimination often encountered by women with children. Title VII provides for a strict equal employment opportunity policy for women; women must be treated no less favorably than similarly situated men. But enforcement of this policy does not inevitably lead to equality. Although men are now more likely than in the past to assume a larger share of family and child-rearing responsibilities, women remain the primary caregivers in the home. Many working mothers must fulfill their family responsibilities while employed in a work environment designed by men with far fewer family obligations. Since men have traditionally relied on their wives to take on most child-rearing and other family responsibilities, they could structure a work environment that demanded nearly total commitment to the job, ignoring in greater part the impact such commitment had on their families. But a married woman with children cannot adequately fulfill her responsibilities at home while working in such an environment. Thus, providing women with treatment equal to that extended to male workers fails to produce equality: A strict equal opportunity policy holds mothers to a male model of competition in which they cannot equally compete.[10]

The failure of employers to afford workplace equality for working mothers appears under many guises, one of which condemns women who leave the workplace for relatively long periods of time to raise their children. Men who have made their jobs the central priority in their lives often find it difficult to accept on equal terms co-workers who have not. These men—and on occasion, even some women—are unwilling to accommodate working mothers who, because of their responsibilities to their children, cannot and will not be guided by such priorities. The refusal to accommodate working mothers is an attitude that too often culminates in job-related decisions adverse to them.

The courts have struggled with these workplace problems. On some occasions, courts have viewed charges of workplace inequality from the perspective of a working mother, but on other occasions, they have been blind to that perspective, regarding it as irrelevant or inappropriate to determining whether workplace discrimination exists.

When women return to the workplace after a lapse of several years, they often discover that their employers perceive them differently from workers without career interruptions. After Arlene Coopersmith graduated from law school, she practiced law for about four years before giving birth to her first child. Except for some part-time work, for the next fifteen years she was primarily engaged in raising her children, and she returned to full-time employment only after her youngest child turned twelve. After working in nonattorney positions for a few years, Coopersmith applied for an attorney-advisor position with the Veterans Administration in Washington, D.C. The VA rejected her application, primarily on the ground that she could not point to any recent legal experience relevant to the type of work she would be required to perform if the VA hired her.

Coopersmith then charged the VA with sex discrimination, arguing that its preference for applicants with recent legal experience discriminated against women. She contended that since women are more likely than men to interrupt their careers to raise children, they would less likely have recent legal experience. When Coopersmith's charges of discrimination reached the court, her attorneys submitted statistical data showing that a large portion of women in the general labor force interrupts employment for child rearing. Based on these data, they argued that many women would be rejected for positions that called for recent experience. The court rejected this statistical evidence because it failed to demonstrate that female attorneys, as distinguished from female workers in general, similarly interrupt their legal careers. In effect, the court said that Coopersmith was comparing apples with oranges, and that the statistical data failed to support her position.

But even if Coopersmith had submitted statistical evidence demonstrating that female attorneys also interrupt their careers to raise their children, the court stated, it would have rejected those statistics since they would fail to disclose whether male attorneys temporarily leave their practices to fulfill family responsibilities. From the court's perspective, Coopersmith had not submitted data that would permit a comparison of the treatment extended to women with children with that extended to men with children. In the court's view,

Coopersmith had failed to demonstrate that the VA's preference for applicants with recent experience disadvantaged female more than male applicants. Although Coopersmith's case was weak, it is nonetheless clear that the court assumed a very narrow and restrictive view of the measure of proof necessary to establish her case.[11] A similar viewpoint led to the demise of Cynthia Fisher's claims against Vassar College.

In her sex discrimination case, Fisher claimed she was denied tenure when Vassar discriminated against her because of her absence from academia for eight years while she was raising her young children. She won a resounding victory in the trial court, only to encounter defeat on appeal.

At the time of the trial, Fisher was married with two adult daughters. She held a bachelor's degree from the University of Wisconsin and a master's degree and a Ph.D. from Rutgers University. She had also engaged in postdoctoral studies at Rutgers Medical School, and after the eight-year hiatus, had taught biology at Marist College. At that point, Vassar hired Fisher as a member of its Biology Department faculty. After teaching nine years at Vassar, Fisher was denied tenure; that was when she sued the college for sex discrimination.

In the thirty years prior to Fisher's tenure review, no married woman had ever achieved tenure at Vassar in the hard-science departments, that is, in biology, mathematics, physics, chemistry, geology, and computer science. All women tenured in the hard-science departments during that thirty-year period had been unmarried when they were hired and still unmarried when they were granted tenure. Evidence submitted to the trial court showed that while married women in the hard sciences were discouraged from advancing to tenure, single women without children were not. In fact, at the time of Fisher's denial of tenure, Pinina Norrod, an unmarried female, was granted tenure. But while Norrod had not taken any breaks from her career, the Department of Biology professors reviewing Fisher's credentials and qualifications for tenure were very much aware that she had interrupted her career to raise her children. During the tenure review process, the Biology Department focused on this hiatus in Fisher's career, criticizing her for being "out of the field for [eight] years" and being "out of date."[12] The "out of date" reference, which implied that Fisher's scholarship was obsolete as a result of the time spent at home with her children, did not square with the facts. While Fisher was caring for her children, she kept abreast of developments in her field. At the time of her tenure review, seven of Fisher's papers had been accepted for publication in prestigious journals, and she also had written a book that was later published. Her record of publication was superior to that of three male assistant professors who had just been granted tenure. In addition, she had received several grants that would not have been awarded if her knowledge of her field were deficient or out of date.

In examining the evidence submitted in support of Fisher's claim, the trial court focused its attention on Vassar's grant of tenure to the unmarried Norrod, who, unlike Fisher, had not experienced a break in her career. Norrod had taught in the Biology Department six fewer years than Fisher, had a much lighter teaching load, and was considered for tenure after she had served as an assistant professor for two years, while the normal period of service was seven years.

Ultimately, the court ruled that the Biology Department's apparent obsession with a married woman's family choices reflected its acceptance of the stereotype that a married woman with child-rearing responsibilities cannot be a productive member of its faculty: "The persistent fixation of the Biology Department's senior faculty on a married woman's pre-Vassar family choices reflects the acceptance of a stereotype and bias; that a married woman with an active and on-going family life cannot be a productive scientist and, therefore, is not one despite much evidence to the contrary." The court ruled, despite Vassar's protest that it had historically advanced the cause of women, that the college had consistently demonstrated prejudice toward its married female faculty members, and it awarded Fisher damages in the sum of $627,000.[13]

On the appeal of the trial court's ruling, the appellate court noted that the trial evidence supported an inference that Fisher's eight-year absence from academia had diminished her chances for tenure, and if the Vassar professors and administrators involved in the tenure process equated that absence with child rearing, then a sex-based animus may have underlain the entire process. But for such a claim to succeed, the appellate court ruled, Fisher would have to submit evidence comparing the tenure experience of women who had taken extended leaves of absence from work with the tenure experience of men who had taken such leaves. That is to say, Fisher would have to prove that women who left the workplace to fulfill child-rearing responsibilities were treated differently from, and less favorably than, men who took extended leaves of absence, and that these men were more likely to be granted tenure than the women. This type of statistical data, however, was unavailable to Fisher or, for that matter, anyone else. Nevertheless, from the perspective of the appellate court, her claim had to be rejected.[14]

This narrow-minded and parochial approach to the issue was highly criticized by three dissenting judges: "[T]he predominant reason that working women take absences from work is to bear and raise children; there is no persuasively comparable reason for absences among working men, and it is fatuous . . . to suggest that Dr. Fisher is to be faulted for not producing evidence of the tenure experiences of men who took absences. . . . With rare exception, men do not take extended absences from work to raise children (or for any other reason). . . . [The trial court] was entirely correct: the Biology Department's 'persistent fixation on [Dr. Fisher's] pre-Vassar family choices reflects the acceptance of a stereotype and bias.'"[15] It was clear to the dissenting judges that the majority's position called for an exercise in futility.

Vassar was entitled to deny Fisher tenure if her extended absence had left her deficient in knowledge of the developments in the field of biology. But, her publications and grant awards demonstrated the timeliness of her knowledge. The trial court was entirely justified in considering the Biology Department's adverse views of Fisher's hiatus as constituting evidence of bias against married women. Unfortunately, the appellate court's position prevailed.

Despite the generally unfavorable reception given by the courts to cases that raise these issues, some employers have altered their position regarding the workplace role of working mothers. In recognition that women with children confront problems in the workplace unique to them, some employers have initiated special career paths, commonly called "mommy tracks," designed specifically to accommodate working mothers. Flex-time, part-time, extended maternity leaves, and job sharing are some of the workplace variations that typical mommy-track plans offer. Many women, however, object to special career paths designed solely for working mothers. Acceptance of the mommy track as a normal workplace fixture is in effect an acknowledgment that women with children require special consideration to succeed. Opponents of the mommy track fear that its existence will only buttress the stereotype that working mothers, regardless of the efforts they exert on behalf of their employers, are less committed to their jobs and their employers. Others fear that women who accept the mommy track remove themselves from the center of activity; they become second-string players, confining themselves to positions of lesser power. Indeed, some of my fellow lawyers have confirmed those fears, noting a recent trend among employers to withhold promotions from mommy-track participants.

The elimination of the workplace problems that working mothers have long experienced does not appear to be close at hand. Sex bias will continue to corrupt the workplace whenever employers question the appropriateness of the presence of working mothers. Unhappily, the courts give increasing evidence that their views of the protections provided by Title VII for working women with children may not be sufficiently expansive to bring about meaningful change.

Eleven

Sex Discrimination at Various Stages of the Employment Relationship

An employer's discriminatory sex bias may motivate it to act adversely to a female worker's interests at any time between her interview as a job applicant and her termination following long-term employment.

Hiring

Before Title VII, newspaper advertisements for job openings were gender oriented. It was a common practice to list help-wanted ads in columns headed "Male" or "Female." Other advertisements specified a preference for one sex or the other: "Excellent opportunity for a young and attractive woman"; "Male office clerks wanted." We rarely, if ever, see this type of advertisement today. Now employers generally have no knowledge of an applicant's sex until a resume or the applicant appears in its offices.

In one case, a female applicant for an entry-level position was asked about her marital status, the number of her children, whether they were legitimate, her child care arrangements, and her future childbearing plans. No evidence was offered by the employer to suggest that male job applicants were similarly questioned. Under EEOC regulations, questions of this type violate Title VII.[1] An employer may not have in place two interview policies for job applicants—one for men and one for women—without violating Title VII.[2]

Madison County, New York, officials asked equally repugnant questions of job applicant Maureen Barbano (see chapter 5). One of the county officials participating in Barbano's interview asked about her plans for raising a family. As he explained it, he did not want the county to hire a woman who would later become pregnant and then resign. He also interrogated her about her husband's attitude toward the type of work she would be required to perform if hired. The court labeled these questions discriminatory. Inquiries about pregnancy, family planning, and Barbano's husband's attitudes were totally unrelated to any qualifications for the position.[3]

A job interviewer's questions concerning an applicant's family responsibilities may be proper where a real potential exists for conflict between those responsibilities and the duties of the position in question. As an example, a female applicant for a paramedic position that entailed twenty-four-hour shifts was asked about her arrangements for the care of her children while she was on duty. In these circumstances, this may have been a reasonable and nondiscriminatory question, as long as it was asked of both male and female applicants.[4]

Discrimination in the hiring process occurs in other forms. Some employers regularly assign women to lower-paying jobs delineated as "women's work," generally on the basis of the stereotype that these jobs are the "proper" place for women. Such stereotypes create a segregated workforce, with men holding the better-paying positions and mostly women filling certain lower-paying jobs (see chapter 2), including bookkeeper, payroll clerk, telephone operator, bank teller, child-care worker, cleaner and servant, nursing aide and orderly, dental assistant, and dietitian. Some women, of course, voluntarily select these types of jobs, but discriminatory hiring practices also account for the recruitment and assignment of many women to these positions.

Compensation

Pay inequity for women has long been a common practice. Women, on occasion, have asserted unequal-pay claims under the umbrella of Title VII protections. To succeed, a complainant must first demonstrate that she is paid less than a man performing similar work. The two jobs in question must be such as to permit the court to determine that the two workers are "similarly situated." The complainant then must prove that her employer's decision to pay her less than her similarly situated male co-worker was an act of *intentional* discrimination. This is a burden of proof not readily sustained.

The continuing existence of disparities in compensation between men and women has been a central issue in the battle to attain workplace equality for women. Even before the enactment of Title VII, Congress passed and President John Kennedy signed into law the Equal Pay Act of 1963 (EPA), legislation designed to assist women in achieving "equal pay for equal work."[5] The Supreme Court later commented that Congress's purpose in enacting the EPA was to remedy what was perceived to be a serious and continuous problem of discrimination against women—the fact that the wage structure of many segments of U.S. industry was based on "an ancient but outmoded belief that a man, because of his role in society, should be paid more than a woman even though his duties are the same."[6]

An employer violates the EPA if it pays a man more than a woman who performs a job requiring the skill, effort, and responsibility equal to that of the man's job, and the two jobs are performed under similar working conditions. Unlike Title VII, the EPA complainant is not required to prove that her employer intended to discriminate against her by paying her less. The mere fact that a compensation disparity exists is sufficient to prove her case, unless the employer is able to justify a pay differential by reason of the existence of seniority, merit, or an incentive system, or as a result of some factor other than gender. It appears, therefore, that a woman complaining of a compensation disparity should be able to establish her case with ease. In practice, however, proving an equal-pay case is far more difficult than Congress originally intended.

A woman seeking recourse under the statute need not prove that she is paid less for performing a job that is *identical* to that of a more highly paid male worker, but she must establish that the two jobs are equal or, as some courts have described it, are "substantially similar." EPA cases are frequently lost because female complainants are unable to prove that their jobs require skill, effort, and responsibility equal, or substantially similar, to those of the more highly compensated male. If the two jobs are unequal in any one of those respects, the court must reject the complainant's claim, and—because of the difficulties experienced by women in demonstrating that the positions in question are equal or substantially similar—the EPA thus has provided little protection for the vast majority of women asserting pay equity claims.

To understand how the courts have applied the Equal Pay Act to pay discrimination claims, we will examine several cases. Dr. Marjorie McMillan was director of the radiology department, one of seven veterinary departments, at Angell Memorial Animal Hospital in Massachusetts. When a local newspaper published a letter relating to the hospital's finances, it listed the salaries of various employees, and McMillan discovered a disparity between her salary and that of the other department directors: She was earning $58,000 a year, while her male counterparts' annual salaries ranged from $73,000 to $80,000. With this information in hand, McMillan sued the hospital for pay discrimination in violation of the EPA.

At the trial, McMillan offered evidence comparing the skills, effort, and responsibilities of her position, as the director of the radiology department, with those of the male department directors who were more highly compensated, and she demonstrated that the job requirements for each of the department heads were basically the same. Her proof satisfied the demands of the Equal

Pay Act, and the jury's award of substantial damages in McMillan's favor was later affirmed on appeal.[7]

In a less successful case, Cherry Houck, a professor at Virginia Polytechnic Institute, sued VPI for violation of the Equal Pay Act. In contrast to the approach taken by McMillan, Houck failed to identify specifically the male colleagues she claimed were paid more than she. She merely testified that in her department, men generally received higher pay than she, even though their jobs were basically the same as hers. Because she failed to compare her job with that of any particular male in her department, the court was unable to determine whether she was in fact paid less for substantially similar work. Houck's case was fatally flawed.[8]

In an Equal Pay Act case, the complainant and her attorney must take care to select the right job for comparison with the complainant's. Josephine Cherrey, an "inside sales clerk" for the Thompson Steel Company in Sparrows Point, Maryland, alleged that Thompson violated the EPA since it paid her, on average, $14,000 a year less than it paid two male employees who she claimed performed substantially the same work as she. Before analyzing the facts in the case, the court established a framework to determine whether the jobs to be compared actually required the same skill, effort, and responsibility. The court stated that if the jobs had a common "core of tasks," the inquiry would then turn on whether differing or additional tasks required greater skill or effort or entailed greater responsibilities for the workers in the positions being compared. The court used this framework to measure the degree of similarity between Cherrey's job and the two other jobs in the inside sales department she claimed were comparable.

Clearly, some overlap existed in the three positions. The employees in all three positions handled customer sales and complaints, and all three worked to expedite sales and quote price and delivery terms to customers. However, significant differences also were present. One of the positions that Cherrey used for comparison was that of her supervisor. But he regularly conferred with upper management and Cherrey did not. Both comparison employees performed functions that Cherrey was not required to perform, such as market research and the development of sales strategies. In the court's view, the differences in the requirements of the three positions outweighed the common "core of tasks," thus rendering the positions unequal in terms of skill, effort, and responsibility. This evidence was more than sufficient to defeat Cherrey's claim.[9]

Prior to the enactment of Title VII and the EPA, women were paid only 60 percent of the wages paid to men. By 1997, they were earning 74 percent of their male colleagues' compensation.[10] The gains in compensation for women have been consistent, but small. The failure of the EPA and Title VII to deal more effectively with the pay equity problem has fomented interest in amending the statutes, especially the Equal Pay Act, to ease the required burden of proof. Critics of the EPA have long recommended changing "equal skill, effort, and responsibility" to "comparable skill, effort, and responsibility." In fact, the first drafts of the EPA submitted to and considered by Congress used the term "comparable" rather than "equal." If that language had been retained, the burden of proof would be a less formidable barrier to female complainants pursuing pay equity cases. Based on the history of case failures, an amendment of the statute appears to be in order.

Promotion

Historically, courts have been reluctant to enter into employer-employee frays involving promotions. Even where the presence of flawed promotion procedures is apparent, a court may hesitate to overrule management's decision to deny promotion to an employee, as that decision may have been based on bad judgment rather than discrimination, and bad judgment, in and of itself, will never rise to the level of unlawfulness. "The law forbids invidious distinctions, not mistakes."[11] Unless a worker's qualifications, when compared with those of the worker who has been awarded the promotion, are so far superior that the employer's reasons for the promotion must be viewed as a subterfuge or pretext for discrimination, the worker generally will not prevail, except in instances where she is able to submit independent evidence of a discriminatory motive. Nearly all promotion cases, therefore, turn less on a comparison of a worker's qualifications than on the weight of the evidence demonstrating an invidious employer motive. This approach to promotion cases is well illustrated in Jane Flucker's sex discrimination case against Fox Chapel Area School District in Pennsylvania.

Flucker, an English teacher, complained that she had not been interviewed for promotion to a middle school position. The school district argued that an interview was unnecessary, as the selection committee was aware of her work and had viewed her performance evaluations. The judge that heard Flucker's case stated that if the decision had been left to him, Flucker would have been selected for the promotion: "As a graduate of Smith College, with over three years' experience in the Princeton, New Jersey high school, with a face out of Botticelli and the charm of Southern speech, how could she possibly lose out in competition with a graduate of West Liberty State College . . . who . . . had taught 'Mass Media, Revolutionary Lit., Myths & Legends'?"

But the mere fact that Flucker was better qualified than the successful male candidate did not necessarily prove sex discrimination. Although the failure of the selection committee to choose the better-qualified teacher for the promotion may be considered evidence of a discriminatory motive, in this case the court felt that the evidence was insufficient to establish sex discrimination. The court was not prepared to declare that Flucker's qualifications for the position were so far superior to those of the other candidate that the school district's reasons for not promoting her necessarily had to be considered as pretextual. Thus, to prevail, Flucker had to offer the court evidence establishing more than just the shortcomings of the school district's promotion procedures. She had to offer convincing proof that the real reason for the selection of the successful candidate was his gender. But Flucker was unable to offer any such corroborative evidence, and thus the court dismissed her case.[12] As another judge expressed it, without corroborating evidence of a discriminatory intent, "We must accept the harsh fact that numerous individual mistakes are inevitable in the day-to-day administration of our affairs."[13]

Some employers appear oblivious to the negative appearance they present to anyone reviewing their promotion procedures; their overt behavior supplies the corroborating evidence missing in the Flucker case. In one case, the State of Hawaii created a new civil service position entitled "deputy state librarian" and advertised for applicants who held master's degrees in library science and, in addition, had at least five years of library service. Seventeen female applicants with either master's or doctoral degrees in library science and the requisite experience were rejected in favor of a male applicant with a bachelor's degree in political science who had never worked in a library. After state officials hired the male applicant, they developed a new job description whose substantially reduced job qualifications fit the background the male applicant brought to the job.[14] In another case, an employer asked its male workers whether they were interested in advancement to a vacant position, while it concealed the vacancy from its female employees, most of whom had greater experience than the men.[15] In still another case, on twenty-three separate occasions, an employer refused to consider a female managerial employee for promotion, and in all twenty-three instances, it awarded promotions to males, some of whom were totally unqualified for promotion.[16] Courts have little difficulty in awarding substantial damage awards to claimants subjected to outrageous acts of discrimination such as these.

Corroborative evidence of an employer's discriminatory motivation sometimes surfaces in the form of indiscreet remarks made during the promotion process. When a female member of a small-town Louisiana police force sought advancement to a superintendent's position, the male town official charged with making the selection for promotion was heard to say: "Ain't no bitch gonna get this job. My man's already picked out and that's the way it's going to be."

As further proof of the town official's animus toward women, evidence was offered disclosing that he relieved the female members of the police force from duty during a hurricane emergency because, in his opinion, the female officers should remain at home, since "somebody's got to make the beds and cook the food and, you know, do the things [that] men can't do."[17] Although it is not likely that many women will encounter this type of blatantly expressed sex bias, all women should remain alert to verbal expressions that may reveal an employer's discriminatory motive.

As in the case of new hires, inappropriate questions asked of a candidate for promotion may disclose an underlying bias. In one instance, a selection committee asked a female promotion candidate a series of gender-based questions: Would she be happy working with men? Did she work well with men? Was she willing to travel with men? What type of arrangements would she make for her children when she traveled? The selection committee, however, declined to put these inquiries to male candidates. Clearly, the selection committee exhibited an unlawful bias against women.[18]

Even the U.S. government has been guilty of unlawfully denying promotions to women. Angie Gobert, a female Native American, worked for the Minerals Management Services (MMS), a division of the U.S. Department of the Interior, as a GS–12 petroleum engineer. She had a great deal of experience in matters relating to oil-spill prevention and cleanup, and on occasion had served as a spokesperson for MMS in its dealings with other governmental agencies and with industry. When MMS issued a vacancy announcement for a GS–13 petroleum engineer position, Gobert applied for the position and, along with seven other applicants, was declared qualified for the promotion. MMS then selected a male candidate, who rejected the promotion, as he felt he was better qualified for another position that was about to become vacant. After Gobert complained that she had not been selected, MMS changed course and decided not to fill the opening.

Shortly after, MMS issued another vacancy announcement, purportedly for a newly created GS–13 position entitled "oil spill program administrator." Although the job carried a different title, the vacancy announcement was nothing more than a re-advertisement of the previous GS–13 position, with no significant differences in job responsibilities. Both positions focused on oil-spill prevention and cleanup, as well as on the responsibility to serve as an agency spokesperson in these matters. Gobert again applied and MMS once again found her qualified. However, MMS awarded the position to a male applicant who did not hold a college degree and was not a petroleum engineer. Although the responsibilities of the position had remained unchanged, the qualifications for the position had been altered to permit the selection of the male who ultimately was chosen. When Gobert sued MMS for sex discrimination, the court agreed that the entire promotion process had been contrived to permit the selection of the less qualified male candidate and thus deprive Gobert of the promotion, and it concluded that MMS had unlawfully discriminated against her on account of her gender.[19]

Private industry has acted with equal boldness in denying promotions to female workers. Svenska Handelsbanken, an international banking corporation with headquarters in Stockholm, Sweden, maintained a branch office in New York City ("SH-NY"). When the New York branch hired Victoria Greenbaum for a position in its treasury department, it promised her the title of vice president after her first annual review. Over the next several years, Greenbaum received the highest possible performance reviews and her supervisor repeatedly recommended her for promotion, but the bank denied her a vice presidency. After each denial, bank personnel offered a different explanation to support the decision that Greenbaum's promotion was inappropriate at that particular time.

Ultimately, Greenbaum sued SH-NY for sex discrimination, and at the trial she demonstrated she had been consistently recommended and repeatedly rejected for promotion, while similarly recommended men were routinely promoted. This evidence strongly suggested that when it came to a woman, the bank departed from its ordinary promotion practices and procedures. In the absence of some other explanation for this series of events, this kind of departure from internal office procedures is often sufficient to support a finding of discrimination. But Greenbaum had additional evidence of discrimination to offer the court.

SH-NY officials testified that the bank relied upon two principal criteria for promotion to vice president: first, whether the employee could perform appropriately as a role model for the bank, and second, whether the bank would be "comfortable" with that individual's role as a representative of the bank. In applying these criteria, bank managers tended to use the word "aggressive" to describe a form of excellence when applied to male candidates for promotion, but as a ground for disqualification when applied to female candidates. Other testimony disclosed that a member of senior management had referred to a female worker as a "tough broad," openly stating that he did not want any "tough broads" working at SH-NY. This evidence strongly suggested that Greenbaum was denied the title of vice president, at least in part, because SH-NY applied promotion standards that were inappropriately stereotypical and gender biased. At the conclusion of the trial, the jury awarded Greenbaum $320,000 in compensatory damages and more than $1.25 million in punitive damages.[20]

Loralei Sones-Morgan and Pamela Hurst worked as rental representatives at the Hertz Corporation facility in Memphis, Tennessee. The line of career progression at Hertz extended from rental representative to station manager to senior station manager. On four occasions, Sones-Morgan and Hurst applied for promotion to vacant station manager positions, and on each occasion Hertz awarded the promotion to a man. When Sones-Morgan and Hurst charged Hertz with sex discrimination, they offered evidence showing that Hertz had a long history of discriminatory conduct in refusing to promote women to managerial positions. Because a cadre of male management preferred men rather than women as managers, they promoted only men to station manager positions. With this sort of evidence, the court was not hesitant to issue its ruling in favor of the two complainants.[21]

Demotion

Workers demoted by their employers less frequently sue for sex discrimination. As Gail Derr learned, a victory in a demotion case may present all the attributes of a defeat. Derr worked for Gulf Oil Corporation as an associate lease analyst, a career ladder position leading to a lease analyst post. Derr's supervisor was grooming her to fill such a position, and one was about to become vacant as a result of an older worker's retirement. Rather than allow Derr's promotion to proceed, however, Gulf management demoted her to an accounting clerk's job, thus making it impossible for her to advance to the lease analyst position. After Gulf demoted her, Derr resigned.

When Derr sued for sex discrimination, she submitted evidence showing that a bias against women existed among certain members of Gulf's management. One of Derr's managers had criticized her for endeavoring to achieve her career goals with two small children at home, also commenting that problems arise when a woman has too much education. The court ruled that Derr's demotion had been motivated by sex bias, and it ordered Gulf to reimburse her for her damages. Derr's damages were computed by determining the difference in compensation between what she earned as a clerk and what she would have earned in a lease analyst position had she been promoted (see chapter 19). Because Derr resigned immediately after her demotion, the difference was zero. Those were the damages the court awarded.[22]

It is not uncommon in demotion cases for the recovery of damages to be small. In some instances, a worker may be demoted to a lower position while her compensation remains unchanged, thus severely limiting the damages that may be recovered. The amount of a damage award in a demotion case often cannot justify the effort expended and the expense incurred in litigating the case.

Transfer

Intracompany transfers have been the subject of sex discrimination litigation in two sets of circumstances. The first involves an employer who, because of a discriminatory bias, refuses to grant a female employee a desirable transfer. The second pertains to an employer who unlawfully imposes upon a female worker an undesirable transfer—either a transfer that removes an opportunity for promotion or other benefits or a transfer to a distant locality.

For example, on two occasions, a female postal carrier applied for transfer to a clerk's position, and each time her request was denied; instead, the postmaster assigned the positions to male postal carriers. The court later determined, based on the postmaster's changing and inconsistent testimony, that he had failed to offer a legitimate reason for denying the transfer requests of the female applicant, and that the inconsistent explanations were merely pretexts to cover up his discriminatory conduct.[23]

In another case, a court was asked to determine whether the transfer of a teacher from a middle school to an elementary school constituted an undesirable move. Carmen Rodriguez had earned master's and doctoral degrees at Columbia University, where she had focused her studies on art programs for the middle school student. After she had taught art for twenty years in a middle school in Eastchester, New York, the school district decided to transfer Rodriguez, a move she found wholly undesirable and did not want to accept.

Due to declining student enrollment, the Eastchester school district decided to terminate the art teacher with the least seniority in the district. The teacher selected had taught in one of the district's elementary schools, and school administrators decided that the terminated teacher should be replaced with one of the art teachers assigned to the middle school. In addition to Rodriguez, the school district employed two art teachers in the middle school, both male and neither with Rodriguez's teaching credentials. Still, the school district selected Rodriguez for transfer. When she protested that one of the male art teachers would be better suited for the assignment, her principal responded, "They wouldn't have a male grade school art teacher." Indeed, in the previous twenty-two years, there had never been a male art teacher assigned to the Eastchester elementary schools. Pouring oil on the fire, the school district then filled Rodriguez's middle school position with a male high school art teacher with half her teaching experience in the district.

When her continuing protests failed to persuade the school district to alter its position, Rodriguez filed suit, alleging that the transfer was discriminatory, and that it constituted for her a professional setback and a stigma on her career. Later in the litigation, Rodriguez offered evidence showing that the art programs at the elementary school level were so profoundly different from those in the middle school as to render useless her twenty years' study and experience in developing programs for middle school children. Clearly, for Rodriguez, this was an undesirable transfer.

Rodriguez also submitted evidence demonstrating that female teachers in the Eastchester system were relegated to lower grade levels. Even with this evidence, Rodriguez's case was dismissed at the trial court level, but the appellate court reversed the dismissal: "In her complaint, Dr. Rodriguez alleges that there has never been a male grade school art teacher in the Eastchester schools. . . . If substantiated, . . . these allegations would prove nothing less than segregation, depriving female teachers of the opportunity to instruct older, more advanced pupils. Regardless of whether a higher wage-rate is at issue, female teachers have the statutory right to compete on an equal basis with their male counterparts throughout the entire school system. While this sort of sex stereotyping may once have been a virtually unquestioned feature of our national life, it will no longer be tolerated."[24]

Working Conditions

Only a few years ago, when a young lawyer wearing pants stood up in a courtroom to address the court, the judge reprimanded her and directed her in the future to dress more appropriately in his courtroom. "But Judge," she responded, "defendant's counsel is wearing pants." Defendant's counsel was male.[25]

Some types of discrimination against women occurred more commonly in the early days of Title VII. Dress codes, height and weight standards, and grooming requirements that discriminated against women were made mandatory by employers. In one case, an employer was found guilty of sex discrimination when it required a young female office-building lobby attendant, as a condition of her employment, to wear a revealing and sexually provocative uniform.[26] This type of discrimination appears less commonly in today's workplace. Discrimination against women in connection with current workplace conditions is generally subtle, not readily detected, and sometimes impossible to prove in a court of law. Few cases involving sex discrimination and working conditions appear in recent court records.

Corporate Reorganizations

As is the case with middle-aged and older workers, women are frequently targeted for termination or other adverse treatment in corporate reorganizations. In some instances, employers have implemented corporate reorganizations primarily to deplete their workforce of female workers. A case in point involved a newly assigned plant manager who reorganized his employer's administrative structure, changing it from a traditional supervisory staff model to an administrative format that depended upon team leaders for supervisory guidance. Before the reorganization, twenty-five management and professional employees worked at the plant—twenty-one men and four women. After the new plant manager eliminated eight of these positions in the reorganization, all the women had been removed from their jobs, leaving only men in the plant's management and professional staff positions. The plant manager then selected two team leaders, both of whom were men.

Two of the women affected by the reorganization filed charges of sex discrimination against the company, alleging that the plant manager had initiated the team leader concept with the intention of removing all the women from supervisory positions. They further argued that even if the plant manager had adopted the team leader concept for gender-neutral reasons, he had nonetheless targeted women in the reorganization for removal from supervisory positions. The court ruled that the charges were valid and held the company accountable for the women's damages, while enjoining the company and its officials from further discriminatory conduct.[27]

In an even more egregiously conceived plan of reorganization, the president of a company decided to reduce permanently the number of women on the company's production staff. To achieve that goal, he implemented what appeared to be a gender-neutral plan of reorganization. He ordered ten men and eleven women laid off, and during the next nine months, none of them was recalled to work and no new employees were hired. After nine months, however, when the workers' collective bargaining right of recall had expired, the company began hiring new workers, and the vacancies created by the layoffs were all filled by men. Over the next four and one-half years, the company hired sixty-four new production workers, sixty-three of whom were men. When one of the laid-off female workers filed sex discrimination charges, the court awarded her more than $833,000 in punitive damages.[28]

Termination

Some workers are formally terminated; others are forced to resign. When a worker, forced to labor under conditions so intolerable as to require her, or any reasonable worker, to abandon her position, she is considered to have been "constructively discharged." The distinction between a resignation and a constructive discharge is a significant factor in determining the amount of damages a victim of sex discrimination is entitled to recover. The sex discrimination claimant who resigns may be deprived of a full recovery of her damages in cases where the constructively discharged complainant will not (see chapter 15).

Whether a particular set of working conditions is intolerable is an issue often litigated. Claims of constructive discharge have generally failed in cases based on pay inequality and denial of a promotion, as the courts rarely find that disparities in compensation or refusals to promote create circumstances that a reasonable person would consider "intolerable."[29] Rather, the courts generally limit the application of the term "intolerable" to workplace conditions that fall far outside the scope of the ordinary.

In one case, when a worker requested a transfer to another location, her employer at first denied her request, claiming that no positions were then open at that location. Later, it attempted to accommodate the worker by offering her the option of choosing transfer to one of several positions, but apparently none of these positions was to her liking, and so she resigned. The court held that these circumstances failed to rise to the level of a constructive discharge.[30]

In another case involving a transfer, an employer ordered a female worker transferred to a distant facility that was scheduled to be closed within the year. If the worker had accepted the transfer, she would have had to remove her son from school and relocate her family, only to face job elimination when the facility closed. When the worker resigned to seek another position in her locality, a trial court ruled that she had been constructively discharged. But when the court's decision was appealed, an appellate court ruled that although the complainant surely confronted a painful choice, the exercise of that choice did not render her situation intolerable, and thus she was not constructively discharged.[31]

In contrast, Stella Chertkova filed a successful claim against Connecticut General Life Insurance Company, for whom she had worked for several years in various computer-related positions. Immediately following a change in her department chief, two supervisory employees began a campaign of harassment calculated to force Chertkova from her job. They placed her on probation and ordered her to improve her performance in such areas as "active listening skills." One of her supervisors held "coaching sessions" by calling her into his office and screaming at her, criticizing her performance. At one session, he threatened her: "What do you hope for? Do you think you are going to outlive us? There is no chance. You are not going to be here." Subsequently, they again placed her on probation. When she successfully completed her period of probation, her supervisor informed her that during the ensuing two years she would be subject to immediate dismissal if she failed to maintain satisfactory performance standards in all areas of her position, including her communication skills. Yet when Chertkova asked to attend a course on communication skills offered to all department employees, her supervisor denied the request.

Later, when Chertkova discovered that her supervisor was soliciting other company employees for negative information about her, she suffered a mental breakdown and was unable to continue on the job. These circumstances, the court ruled, were sufficient to establish a constructive discharge.[32]

It is difficult to give guidance in this area. What one judge considers intolerable, another declares tolerable. Each case stands on its own facts, and each set of facts is viewed from a different judicial perspective. But as a general rule, the greater the variance between an employer's conduct and that which is generally accepted as normal behavior, the more likely a worker will be successful in persuading a court that she has been subjected to a constructive discharge.

All kinds of issues arise when a worker is terminated. In one case, an employer claimed that it terminated a woman's job because she was difficult to work with, but the court was convinced that the employer's difficulties with the worker arose only after it had discriminated against her. "[N]othing in the law says that a person suffering discrimination must stand mute in the face of invidious treatment."[33] An employer cannot consider as a basis for termination a worker's forceful response to discriminatory conduct. Personality dysfunction induced by a hostile work environment does not justify the discharge of a worker who negatively reacts to that environment.[34]

As in the past, employers intent upon acting adversely to the interests of female workers will strive to conceal their unlawful conduct under an appearance of propriety and lawfulness. Women, as in the past, will strive to unmask and expose such conduct to reveal its true nature.

Twelve

Increased Incidence of Sexual Harassment in the Workplace

The sexual harassment of a woman by a man higher on the corporate ladder conveys the message that she is primarily perceived, not as a workplace colleague and a valuable asset, but rather as a sexual object. The sexual harassment of women expresses the age-old belief that women should be sexually available to men, and it simultaneously reminds women that they are neither respected nor viewed as workplace equals.[1]

Because sexual-harassing acts generally evolve from unequal status between a man and a woman, the harassment of a female worker usually involves a power relationship affecting the terms and conditions of the woman's employment. Since such acts generally culminate in a hostile and offensive work environment, the harassed woman must live and work under abusive and antagonistic conditions every working day. Women, therefore, perceive sexual harassment as a reflection of a status that emphasizes their sex roles over their work roles and thus threatens their livelihood.[2] One writer argues that our culture "identifies women not with minds but with bodies . . . [and] the more beautiful the woman, the more sensuous her body, the less likely she is to be credited with a mind."[3]

Catharine A. MacKinnon, the first to argue that workplace sexual harassment constitutes a major problem for women, stated in her seminal book *Sexual Harassment of Working Women* that "[s]exual harassment is seen to be one dynamic which reinforces and expresses women's traditional and inferior role in the labor workplace." From these circumstances, MacKinnon concluded and was one of the first to contend that sexual harassment in the workplace is a form of sex discrimination.[4] The courts, at first, were divided on this issue, but most did not agree with MacKinnon.

In 1976, in one of the earliest sexual-harassment cases decided after the advent of Title VII, the complainant alleged that her supervisor had retaliated against her when she refused his request for an "after hours affair." The District of Columbia federal court held that the substance of the complainant's allegations centered on her claim that she was discriminated against, not because she was a woman, but because she had declined to engage in a sexual affair with her supervisor. According to the court, this was not sex discrimination: "This is a controversy underpinned by the subtleties of an inharmonious personal relationship. Regardless of how inexcusable the conduct of plaintiff's supervisor might have been, it does not evidence an arbitrary barrier to continued employment based on plaintiff's sex."[5]

Less than a year later, an Arizona federal court arrived at a similar conclusion. That court ordered the dismissal of the legal claims of two women who alleged they had been verbally and physically harassed by their supervisor and that his sexual harassment continued unabated until they were compelled to resign. The court ruled that although Title VII clearly bars discrimination against a woman by her employer, nothing appears in the statute to apply to sexual advances of a supervisor in its employ: "In the present case, [the supervisor's] conduct appears to be nothing more than a personal proclivity, peculiarity, or mannerism. By his alleged sexual advances, [he] was satisfying a personal urge. Certainly no employer policy is here involved. . . . Nothing in the complaint alleges nor can it be construed that the conduct complained of was company directed policy which deprived women of employment opportunities." The court also expressed its concern that a ruling that such activity was actionable under Title VII would culminate in a federal lawsuit "every time a worker made amorous or sexually oriented advances toward another." In such circumstances, the court opined, the only sure way an employer could avoid such charges would to be to hire only employees who were asexual.[6] A judge in another case remarked that if sexual harassment was covered by Title VII, "we would need 4000 federal trial judges instead of 400."[7] If the rationale underlying these decisions had prevailed, no working woman would ever have successfully prosecuted a sexual-harassment claim under Title VII. Fortunately, not all courts were as myopic.

One year later, a District of Columbia federal appellate court reversed course and held that women subjected to acts of sexual harassment are discriminated against, not because of their refusal to engage in sexual acts demanded by a supervisor as the first court had held, but simply because they are women: "But for her womanhood . . . her participation in sexual activity would never have been solicited. To say, then, that she was victimized in her employment simply because she declined the invitation is to ignore the asserted fact that she was invited only because she was a woman."[8] Soon after, another federal appellate court ruled that if a supervisor, with the knowledge of his employer, makes sexual demands of a subordinate female employee and conditions her employment status on a favorable response to those demands, he and his employer act in violation of Title VII.[9]

Following these cases, the EEOC jumped into the act and issued guidelines based on the assumption that sexually harassing conduct constituted a violation of Title VII. There the matter stood until 1986, when Mechelle Vinson's sexual-harassment case against Meritor Savings Bank reached the Supreme Court. This was the high court's first opportunity to rule on issues involving allegations of sexual harassment in the workplace.

Vinson had worked for the bank for four years, first as teller, next as head teller, and then as assistant branch manager. Throughout the term of her employment, she worked under the supervision of Sidney Taylor. After Vinson was fired for taking excessive sick leave, she brought a legal action against the bank and Taylor, claiming that during her four years of employment, Taylor had continuously subjected her to acts of sexual harassment.

Vinson alleged that soon after she began working at the bank, Taylor suggested to her that they have sexual relations. At first she refused, but when he persisted, she eventually agreed out of fear of losing her position. Thereafter, Taylor made repeated demands for sex, both during and after business hours, and they had intercourse on numerous occasions. Vinson also alleged that Taylor fondled her in the presence of other employees, followed her into the restroom, exposed himself to her, and even raped her on more than one occasion. Because she feared Taylor and was concerned for her job, Vinson neither reported Taylor's harassment to any of his supervisors nor attempted to use the bank's grievance procedures.

Vinson's case presented the Supreme Court with three basic issues for resolution:

- Is sexual harassment a form of sex discrimination barred by Title VII?
- Is an employer liable to a female worker for an offensive working environment created by her supervisor's acts of sexual misconduct?
- Does a Title VII violation occur when a sexual relationship between an employee and her supervisor is "voluntary"?

The Court's responses to these questions proved to be of paramount importance in the development of the law barring sexual harassment in the workplace.

In holding that a woman may establish a Title VII violation by proving that her supervisor sexually harassed her, the Court quoted from an earlier appellate court opinion: "Sexual harassment which creates a hostile or offensive environment for one sex is every bit the arbitrary barrier to sexual equality at the workplace that racial harassment is to racial equality. Surely, a requirement that a man or woman run a gauntlet of sexual abuse in return for the privilege of being allowed to work and make a living can be as demeaning and disconcerting as the harshest of racial epithets."[10]

For sexually harassing conduct to violate Title VII, however, it must be sufficiently severe or pervasive to alter the terms and conditions of the harassed woman's employment, thus creating a hostile and abusive work environment. Without question, Taylor's conduct, as alleged, was sufficiently severe to alter the terms and conditions of Vinson's employment, and his behavior created an abusive and hostile environment in which she was compelled to work. Thus Vinson's allegations of Taylor's harassing conduct, if proved, were sufficient to establish a claim of sexual harassment under Title VII.

On the issue of the bank's responsibility and liability for Taylor's conduct, the bank argued that it could not be held legally liable for Taylor's behavior because it was unaware that he had engaged in the sexual harassment of Vinson. Vinson's attorneys, on the other hand, maintained that since Taylor had been placed in a supervisory role over Vinson, the bank was liable for Taylor's misconduct even if it had no knowledge of the harassment. They maintained that when Vinson received direction from Taylor, she in effect received direction from the bank. That is to say, when Taylor acted in his supervisory capacity, he acted as the representative or agent of the bank, and since the bank is legally liable for the actions of its representatives and agents, it was liable for Taylor's acts of sexual harassment.

The Supreme Court essentially agreed with Vinson's attorneys. Since supervisors are delegated authority by their employer, they generally act as agents of that employer whenever they exercise that authority, and thus the employer is liable for any misuse of authority. Circumstances may arise, however, where supervisors may not be acting as agents of their employer. In each case, therefore, the court must determine whether—in light of the facts in that particular case—the harassing supervisor actually acted as an agent of the employer, thus rendering it liable for the harassment.

On the issue of Vinson's voluntarily consenting to a sexual relationship with Taylor, the Court pointed out that the correct inquiry is not whether Vinson's participation in sexual intercourse with Taylor was voluntary, but rather whether Taylor's conduct was "unwelcome" to her. The fact that Vinson was not forced to participate against her will in a sexual relationship with Taylor is not a valid defense to her sexual-harassment claim. However, one of the elements of proof borne by a complainant in a sexual-harassment suit may be sustained only with persuasive evidence that the harassing conduct was unwelcome to her. Since that issue had not been considered by the lower court, Vinson's case was remanded for further proceedings. Before those proceedings were conducted, however, Vinson and the bank agreed to a settlement of the case.[11]

To make sense of sexual-harassment cases, we must understand that the law perceives sexual harassment as taking two forms. First, it is the abusive treatment of a female employee that would not occur but for the fact that she is a woman, and it usually entails demands for sexual favors either in return for employment benefits or under threat of some adverse employment action. This type of sexual harassment is referred to as "quid pro quo" harassment. Under guidelines adopted by the EEOC, quid pro quo sexual harassment exists when "submission to [sexual] conduct is made either explicitly or implicitly a term or condition of an individual's employment [or when] submission or rejection of such conduct by an individual is used as the basis for employment decisions affecting such individual."[12]

The second form of sexual harassment occurs when an employer encourages or tolerates the existence in its workplace of an environment fraught with sexual innuendo and intimidation or other form of harassing conduct sufficiently severe or pervasive to alter the terms and conditions of a woman's employment. This type of sexual harassment is referred to as "hostile work environment" harassment.

As the next three chapters attest, most recent sexual-harassment cases involve hostile work environments. A sexually hostile environment is one that is both objectively and subjectively hostile: objectively, in that any reasonable person would find it hostile or abusive, and subjectively, in that the victim of the harassment also perceives it to be so. Whether a work environment is sufficiently hostile or abusive to support a sexual-harassment claim is determined by viewing all the circumstances, including

- the frequency of the acts of sexual harassment
- the severity of the offensive conduct
- whether the offensive conduct was physically threatening or verbal
- whether the victim was humiliated by reason of the conduct
- whether the harasser was a co-worker or a supervisor
- whether other workers joined in the harassment
- whether the harassment was directed at more than one individual
- whether the harassment unreasonably interfered with the victim's work performance, thus altering the terms and conditions of her employment

Title VII does not prohibit all sex-related conduct at the work site. Genuine differences in the ways men and women routinely interact fail to rise to the level of sexual harassment. Flirtation, teasing, off-hand comments, isolated incidents, and vulgar language that is trivial and annoying are generally insufficiently serious to support a sexual-harassment charge.[13]

The incidence of legal claims alleging sexual-harassing conduct in the workplace has increased substantially since October 1991. At that time, the Senate conducted confirmation hearings in connection with President George Bush's nomination of Clarence Thomas to serve as a justice of the Supreme Court. While viewing the televised hearings conducted with regard to the nomination, the nation heard law professor Anita Hill's vivid testimony describing the sexual harassment she experienced when Thomas was her supervisor at the EEOC. The hearings greatly increased public awareness of the existence of sexual harassment in the workplace. The number of sexual-harassment charges filed with the EEOC rose from 728 during the last three months of 1990 to 1,244 during the same three-month period in 1991, a 71 percent increase.[14] The tally of harassment charge filings increased from 6,883 in 1991 to 10,532 in 1992 and continued to rise each year until 1997, when they numbered 15,889. Thereafter, the annual number of filings has remained approximately the same: 15,618 in 1998, 15,222 in 1999, 15,836 in 2000, and 15,475 in 2001.[15]

But even these figures fail to disclose the full extent of workplace harassment of women. Like other forms of sexual victimization, such as rape and domestic violence, sexual harassment is generally underreported. Several studies have shown that its occurrence in the workplace is far more common than annual EEOC charge filings reflect.[16] One survey reported that 60 percent of women in management positions have experienced some form of sexual harassment during their work lives, but only 14 percent of these women reported the harassment, and less than 1 percent filed a charge or began legal action.[17] If all of these women had formally charged their employers with sexual harassment, the annual EEOC filings would number in the millions.

Women who decide to turn to the law are often richly rewarded, as juries have displayed no reluctance to award sexually harassed women huge damages verdicts. A female police officer employed by the Village of Sleepy Hollow, New York, was awarded $2.2 million after a jury heard testimony that she had been sexually harassed by her training officer, and later retaliated against by the police chief and the village mayor.[18] A jury awarded a sexually harassed legal secretary compensatory damages of $50,000 and punitive damages of $7.1 million even though she had worked for the defendant law firm for less than two months.[19] Still another jury awarded a female worker employed by a Daimler Chrysler factory $21 million for acts of sexual harassment she had been subjected to over a period of years.[20] Even though trial or appellate courts often reduce such huge jury awards (see chapter 18), the recovery of damages in cases of this type still often runs into the millions.

Sexual-harassment cases also are settled outside of court for immense sums. In one case, a family-owned importing firm in New Rochelle, New York, agreed to pay $2.6 million to 104 of its women workers who were sexually harassed by the seventy-nine-year-old owner and president of the company.[21] The EEOC reached a major settlement with the Ford Motor Company that awarded nearly $8 million in damages to female workers who were sexually and racially harassed.[22] After the Mitsubishi Company was accused of ignoring—and even encouraging—the sexual harassment of women workers in its automobile assembly plant, it agreed to pay $34 million to the harassed women. This settlement followed upon an earlier settlement of a private lawsuit for $10 million.[23]

Before exploring the legal issues that commonly arise in these cases, we will look at some illustrations of the types of sexual harassment that women continuously encounter in their workplaces, beginning with some examples of harassment due to hostile work environments. Connie Blackmon, a security guard for Pinkerton Security, was the only female on a five-member team that worked the night shift at a Firestone plant. From the time Blackmon was first assigned to the team until she was terminated, her four co-workers engaged in constant, graphic sexual conversations in her presence. They used lurid language to comment on the bodies of female employees and described sex acts they would like to perform with them. They graphically portrayed their sexual conquests and fantasies to each other and used vulgar language in referring to sex acts and the female anatomy.

When Blackmon complained to her shift superintendent, he asked her if the source of her complaint lay in the fact that "she was not getting any sex." She continued to complain, advancing up the company's chain of command, and ultimately her complaints reached Pinkerton's district manager, who agreed to conduct an investigation. His investigation, however, rather than centering on the particulars of Blackmon's complaints, focused on Blackmon herself. He obtained a written statement from one of her fellow employees averring that Blackmon used foul and abusive language. He then asked the male team members to make a written record of all conversations with Blackmon and encouraged them to make certain that this record was not supportive of Blackmon's complaints. Obviously, the district manager's intent was to show Blackmon's active participation in the conduct she had complained of, or even to show that she was the cause of it. Attacking the victim of sexual harassment is a typical employer strategy, and the best way to attack her is to find or create a basis for her dismissal.

Blackmon's supervisors scheduled her to attend a training session, but the date of the session coincided with a previously arranged parent-teacher meeting pertaining to her son. Blackmon obtained permission from her supervisor to attend a later training session so she could go to the parent-teacher meeting. Later, Pinkerton's district director accused Blackmon of having deliberately ignored a scheduled training session and ordered her dismissal. After she was fired, Blackmon charged Pinkerton with retaliation for her complaints about the sexually harassing conduct of her team members.

When Blackmon sued Pinkerton, a jury awarded her $75,000 in damages for emotional distress suffered as a consequence of the harassment, and $100,000 in punitive damages.[24] Without doubt, Blackmon had been forced to work in a hostile and a sexually offensive environment, and thus the damage awards were wholly warranted. Employers often retaliate against a worker who complains of sexual harassment, and jurors who hear evidence of retaliatory conduct, as they did in this case, are apt to award damages to punish such conduct.

Women who read this book can only hope and pray they will never be forced to work in an environment as despicable and degraded as that encountered by Cynthia Stoll at the Sacramento post office. What follows is not for those with weak stomachs.

Stoll, a single mother of three boys, worked for six years as a letter-sorting machine operator before literally fleeing her workplace to escape multiple acts of sexual harassment she had been persistently subjected to by a network of male workers. An untold number of co-workers and supervisors asked her to perform oral sex for them, asked her to wear lacy black underwear, bumped up against her from behind and rubbed their penises into her backside as she was sorting mail, followed her into the women's bathroom, asked her to go on vacation with them, fondled her body, and generally stalked her throughout the post office.

Stoll's supervisor intimidated her by refusing to permit her to visit the restroom except when she was on a scheduled break. On one occasion, Stoll's request to leave her workstation to go to the women's room was denied, although she was menstruating heavily. She was forced to remain at her post bleeding all over herself and eventually ran to the nurse's office covered in menstrual blood.

Stoll, described as "fairly shy," was easily intimidated by her supervisor, who seemed to take sadistic pleasure in screaming at and tormenting her. Another supervisor intervened on her behalf and then demanded sexual services from her. Stoll rejected these advances and tried to avoid him; he then raped her.

Ultimately, she had to resign to escape this daily denigration and unrestrained vulgarity.

After Stoll resigned, she suffered a severe depression and on four occasions attempted suicide. A psychiatrist testified that Stoll was scarred for life, would never again be able to work, and probably would continue to try to commit suicide. At that point in Stoll's treatment, the psychiatrist was only trying to keep her alive.

An EEOC administrative law judge later ruled that Stoll had been the victim of both quid pro quo and hostile-environment sexual harassment. What judge could rule otherwise? Other women may survive corrupt work environments with less severe psychological damage, but hostile environments inflict acute psychological pain and suffering on nearly all women who are compelled to work in them.[25]

Women at the Eveleth Taconite Company in Minnesota filed a class action lawsuit against the company, alleging that it tolerated a work environment sexually hostile to and abusive of women. The women offered evidence demonstrating a long-existing pattern of sexual hostility. As an example, the women testified that the company permitted sexually explicit graffiti, pictures, and posters to be placed on its office walls, in lunchroom areas and tool rooms, and in elevators and women's restrooms; similar materials were posted on the company's locked bulletin boards and distributed in interoffice mail. In addition, women were subjected to incidents of unwanted kissing, touching, pinching, and grabbing. Everyday workplace language reflected a male-oriented and an anti-female tone. Offensive comments, such as "women should remain home with their children" and "women deprive men of their jobs," were common in conversations initiated by male workers.

The court found that at Eveleth Taconite sexual harassment amounted to "standard operating procedure." First-line supervisors were well aware of the harassing behavior of nonsupervisory personnel, and in fact, some of the supervisors participated in the harassment. The company was male dominated in terms of power, position, and atmosphere. Male-focused attention on sex and references to women as sexual objects created a sexualized work environment, and the presence of graffiti and other sexual materials, together with the general sex-oriented conduct of the male workers, reinforced stereotypical attitudes toward women. The court ruled that the company had engaged in a pattern and practice of maintaining a sexually hostile work environment and ordered it to pay damages to its female employees.[26]

Not all sexual-harassment cases end in success for the victim. Patricia Brooks worked as telephone dispatcher for the City of San Mateo in California.

Brooks and Steven Selvaggio, the senior dispatcher, ran the city's communications center on the evening shift, monitoring 911 calls. One evening, Selvaggio approached Brooks as she was taking an emergency call and placed
his hand on her stomach. Brooks demanded that he stop touching her and
pushed him away. Selvaggio forced his hand underneath her sweater and bra
and fondled her breast. Brooks forcefully removed his hand and again pushed
him away. Selvaggio then approached Brooks as if to fondle her again, but at
that point another dispatcher arrived in the office, and Selvaggio backed off.
Brooks immediately reported the incident to her supervisor. When the city initiated termination proceedings against Selvaggio, he resigned, and he later
served 120 days in jail for sexual assault.

Despite the city's prompt remedial action, Brooks did not readily recover
from the incident. She immediately arranged for a leave of absence and placed
herself under the care of a psychologist but was unable to return to her job
for six months. Brooks alleged that upon her return, she was ostracized by
male workers, mistreated by her supervisors, and later given an unwarranted
negative performance evaluation. She resigned and filed suit against the city.

Brooks claimed that a sexually pervasive work environment was the underlying cause of her need for psychological treatment. But for a work environment to be legally hostile, the complainant must prove that it is both objectively
and subjectively hostile. The court will consider the environment objectively
hostile if a reasonable person would find it offensive or abusive, and it will find
it subjectively hostile if the victim of the harassment also perceives it to be hostile. Although Brooks proved that she viewed the environment to be wholly
hostile, the question remained whether she could prove that a reasonable person would similarly perceive it.

Selvaggio was Brooks's co-worker, not her supervisor. While a series of sexually harassing acts—or even a single act—by a worker's supervisor may create
a hostile environment resulting in altered terms and conditions of employment
for the victim, an isolated incident of harassment by a co-worker ordinarily fails
to alter the employment relationship. This is especially the case if the employer
takes appropriate corrective action, as the city did in this case, to prevent any
further acts of harassment. Because Brooks was unable to establish that a reasonable person would perceive her work environment as hostile, the court dismissed her case.[27] As a general rule, a single incident of co-worker sexual
harassment will not support a hostile work environment claim unless the incident is so severe as to inalterably cause a material change in the terms and
conditions of employment of the woman who experiences such conduct.

Unlike the *Brooks* case, the typical sexual-harassment case involves multiple
acts of harassment. Unlike the *Blackmon* case, most sexual-harassment cases

involve acts of harassment committed by a single worker rather than by a group of workers. This is particularly true in cases of sexual harassment of white-collar workers, and almost always the case when professional women and women working in managerial positions in the business world are sexually harassed.

One of my clients, a young woman recently graduated from a small western college, arrived in New York City hoping to advance her career in corporate finance. A medium-size investment banking firm hired her as an assistant to one of its managing directors. The firm had recently expanded and had outgrown its office space, so that nearly every worker had to share an office. My client and the managing director shared a very small office, his desk located to the rear of the office and hers a few feet in front of his. She could not help but hear every word of every one of his telephone conversations, whether business or personal.

At first, the managing director appeared merely insensitive to the fact that the young woman seated a few feet from him could hear the sex-oriented telephone conversations he frequently engaged in with friends and business associates. Then, after a few weeks, he began to make sexual comments directly to her, and these became increasingly more frequent and offensive. He insisted upon describing the details of his extramarital affairs with various women. He identified nearly every female telephone caller as a woman with whom he was having an affair. He frequently referred to the bodies of other women, including women employed by the firm. He described in detail the bodies of women with whom he was having affairs, and told her on at least one occasion, "She looks like you." He was prone to leer at her breasts. While speaking to a friend by telephone, he referred to her as a person "who does everything I say, at least she has so far. But, we haven't had sex together, at least not yet." He often alluded to his genitals and suggested that she accompany him to the men's room. He made obscene gestures, intimating that he wanted to have sexual intercourse with her.

As the months passed, his behavior became more and more offensive and objectionable, finally passing from sexual commentary to sexual touching. On one occasion he slapped her on her buttocks and placed his arms around her shoulders, pinning her to her desk. At that point, my client broke down and sought help from other firm employees.

Evidence was lacking that anyone else in the firm had engaged in similarly objectionable conduct, and no other women working for the firm had ever complained of sexual harassment. When informed of the managing director's behavior, the firm's owners were aghast and later swore under oath that they were totally unaware that these conditions existed at their firm.

Here is a case in which a supervisory employee created an extremely hostile, abusive, and highly offensive environment that affected only a woman working under his supervision. In many respects, this case is typical of the cases that follow in the next three chapters, where we will find other instances of hostile work environments created by a male supervisor acting alone, and in many of these cases, the hostility, abuse, and offensive conduct are suffered solely by a woman working under his supervision.

Thirteen

Hostile-Environment Sexual Harassment

Whether a work environment is sufficiently hostile or offensive to support a sexual-harassment claim can be assessed only after examining all of the circumstances. While the courts will always consider as paramount the frequency, severity, and degree of pervasiveness of the harassing conduct, they will scrutinize other factors as well. Was the defendant's conduct physically threatening? Did it unreasonably interfere with the victim's work performance? Were there any other factors bearing on the degree of hostility and offensiveness of the harasser's behavior?

A lone instance of sexual harassment may appear at first glance to fail the test of frequency and degree of pervasiveness, but a single act of physical touching, or some other egregious act of harassment, may create a work environment as offensive and hostile as that resulting from a long-running pattern of harassment.

The EEOC guidelines state that sexual harassment that "has the purpose or effect of substantially interfering with an individual's work performance or creates an intimidating, hostile, or offensive working environment" constitutes a violation of Title VII. The severity and pervasiveness of the offending conduct must be viewed objectively and subjectively, that is, from the viewpoint of a reasonable person and from that of the victim of the harassment.[1]

Suppose a woman alleges that she perceived her work environment to be hostile and that a reasonable person would similarly view it. Furthermore, the totality of the circumstances appears to support her claim that she has been sexually harassed. But in spite of the abusive conduct she experienced, she

133

was able to deal with it without suffering any psychological ill affects. She is unable to prove, therefore, that the hostility and offensiveness of her work environment seriously affected her psychological well-being. Is her inability to prove psychological harm fatal to her claim? This question arose in connection with Teresa Harris's sexual-harassment claim against her employer.

Harris worked as a manager at Forklift Systems, and over several years the company's president subjected her repeatedly to offensive sexual remarks and disgusting behavior. But Harris was unable to prove that this conduct had caused her any psychological harm. Ultimately, her case reached the Supreme Court. The primary issue was whether Harris could successfully sue Forklift for hostile-environment sexual harassment in light of her inability to prove that the president's harassing conduct had psychologically damaged her.

Justice Sandra Day O'Connor succinctly imparted the Court's stance: "Title VII comes into play before the harassing conduct leads to a nervous breakdown." Although an abusive work environment may not seriously affect a worker's psychological well-being, it may nevertheless detract from her job performance, interfere with the advancement of her career, or discourage her from remaining on the job. Thus, even if the harassment produced no tangible effect upon her mental well-being, a woman may still prevail in a hostile environment case if she proves that the harassing conduct was so severe or pervasive as to create an abusive work environment that altered the terms and conditions of her employment.[2]

A victim of harassment need not endure the harasser's conduct for an extended period of time before she is entitled to the remedies provided by Title VII. This is especially the case when the objectionable behavior includes unwelcome touching. The offensiveness of the behavior is the principal factor in determining whether it is severe or pervasive enough to create an abusive work environment. As noted, even a single act may be enough.

Ordinarily, a worker has little difficulty in establishing subjective hostility. If she testifies that she found the defendant's conduct to be offensive, that generally is sufficient. On occasion, however, the credibility of the plaintiff's testimony on this issue is questioned, as was the case with Lisa Ann Burns, who worked for McGregor Electronics Industries. The evidence admitted in her sexual-harassment suit against McGregor painted a picture of a glaringly hostile work environment. The owner of the company continuously barraged her with sexual propositions, asked her to attend pornographic movies with him, suggested oral sex, and stalked her at work. The trial court, however, questioned whether Burns considered any of the owner's behavior offensive, as she had posed nude for two national motorcycle magazines. The court reasoned that a woman who would allow her nude photograph to be distributed nationally would not be offended by the type of conduct engaged in by the company's owner, and thus she had exaggerated the severity and pervasiveness of the harassment and its effect on her. An appellate court viewed the case differently. A worker's activities engaged in outside the workplace are irrelevant to whether she considered her employer's conduct offensive. Evidence of her private life cannot be used to demonstrate a woman's acquiescence to sexual advances in the workplace.[3]

The worker may confront greater difficulty in demonstrating to the court that a reasonable person would view her workplace as hostile and offensive in the same way as she views it. Since men are infrequently the victims of sexual assault, they generally view workplace sexual conduct from an entirely different perspective than women do. In some circumstances, the perspective of a reasonable man may materially diverge from the perspective of a reasonable woman. Should a man's view of workplace hostility be a factor the court considers in determining the degree of hostility in the workplace? Is the "reasonable person" test appropriate if that test is colored by a man's point of view? When Kerry Ellison sued the Internal Revenue Service for sexual harassment, the court questioned the appropriateness of applying a reasonable-person test rather than a reasonable-woman test to the circumstances of her case.

Ellison worked as a revenue agent for the IRS in its San Mateo, California, office. Sterling Gray was assigned a desk about twenty feet from hers. Revenue agents in the San Mateo office often lunched in groups, and on one occasion Ellison lunched with Gray. Ellison later claimed that subsequent to the lunch, Gray pestered her with silly questions and dawdled around her desk. About two months later, Gray asked her out for a drink after work, an invitation Ellison declined. A week later, Gray invited her to lunch, and again Ellison said no. A few days later, Gray handed her a handwritten note: "I cried over you last night and I'm totally drained today. I have never been in such constant term oil [*sic*]. Thank you for talking with me. I could not stand to feel your hatred for another day."

Ellison was so shocked and frightened upon reading the note that she ran from the office. Gray followed her into the hallway and demanded that she talk to him, but she fled the building. Ellison later reported Gray's behavior to her supervisor, who agreed that Gray was engaging in sexually harassing conduct. Rather than file a formal complaint of harassment, however, Ellison decided to handle the matter herself. She asked a male co-worker to speak to Gray and inform him that she was not interested in him and that he should leave her alone.

The following week, after Ellison had started a four-week training session in St. Louis, Gray sent her a three-page love letter. Ellison notified her supervisor, who immediately confronted Gray and directed him to cease all contact with Ellison. Gray was then transferred to an IRS office in San Francisco, but after he filed a union grievance, he was ordered transferred back to San Mateo. Before returning, Gray wrote another letter to Ellison, intimating that they had some sort of relationship. At that point, to avoid Gray on his return to the San Mateo office, Ellison asked to be transferred to another IRS office, and she followed her request with the filing of a formal complaint alleging sexual harassment.

The court that heard Ellison's case had to decide whether Gray's conduct was sufficiently severe or pervasive to have altered the conditions of Ellison's employment. The court emphasized that the victim's view of the allegedly offensive conduct must first be considered, and the nature of that perspective fully understood: "We therefore prefer to analyze harassment from the victim's perspective. A complete understanding of the victim's view requires, among other things, an analysis of the different perspectives of men and women. Conduct that many men consider unobjectionable may offend many women. . . . [M]any women share common concerns which men do not necessarily share." Men and women do not share the same perspective with regard to rape and sexual assault, for example. Since women are far more often the victims of criminal sexual assault, they are much more concerned with any form of aberrant or aggressive sexual behavior. Even when confronted with a mild form of sexual harassment, a woman may fear that a harasser's conduct is prelude to a violent assault. A man, on the other hand, who probably has never feared sexual assault, may view the same conduct without a full appreciation of the underlying threat of violence that a woman perceives. Based on this rationale, the court concluded that the severity and pervasiveness of Gray's actions should be viewed from the perspective of a reasonable woman rather than that of a reasonable person: "We adopt the perspective of a reasonable woman primarily because we believe that a sex-blind reasonable person standard tends to be male-biased and tends to systematically ignore the experiences of women."[4]

Analyzing the facts of this case from Gray's point of view, he was trying only to woo Ellison. There was no evidence that he harbored any ill will toward her, and thus from his perspective, his actions were trivial and unintimidating. Ellison, however, was shocked and frightened by Gray's conduct. The court felt that a reasonable woman would have similarly reacted and would have considered Gray's behavior to be sufficiently severe and pervasive to alter the conditions of her employment and thus create a hostile work environment.[5]

A minority of courts have adopted the reasonable-woman test, but the EEOC approach to the issue appears not to differ substantially from the *Ellison* approach. In applying the reasonable-person standard, the EEOC holds that the victim's perspective should also be considered, and all stereotypical notions of acceptable behavior should be discarded.[6] Stereotypical notions of acceptable behavior are notions advanced by men. The EEOC formula, therefore, is not far distant from the reasonable-woman test.

In a hostile work environment case, a woman may recover damages for acts of sexual harassment only if the harassment is "sufficiently severe or pervasive to alter the conditions of the victim's employment."[7] In Mechelle Vinson's case against the Meritor Savings Bank, Vinson alleged that her supervisor repeatedly demanded sex of her, both during and after business hours, fondled her in the presence of other employees, followed her into the restroom and exposed himself, and raped her on several occasions (see chapter 12). The Supreme Court ruled that Vinson's allegations, "which include not only pervasive harassment but also criminal conduct of the most serious nature are plainly sufficient to state a claim for 'hostile environment' sexual harassment."[8] As noted in the discussion of Vinson's case, flirtation, teasing, off-hand comments, vulgar language, and annoying isolated incidents are usually insufficiently serious or pervasive to support a sexual-harassment charge.[9] Many acts of sexual harassment, however, are less severe than the criminal conduct alleged by Vinson. In most cases, the severity of the harassing conduct does not rise to the level of criminality.

A case in point is Sheri Bishop's against Interim Industrial Services, in which Bishop charged her supervisor, Armando Perez, with sexual harassment. She testified that Perez asked her out on a date, but she rejected his offer. On another occasion, Perez followed her around the workplace, and on another, asked her why she did not wear looser clothing. He once asked her if she was involved with anyone and inquired as to why not. Although one of Perez's responsibilities as Bishop's supervisor was to observe her work performance, she claimed that he watched her from his office, with the lights off. The court ruled that Bishop had failed to show that Perez's conduct was severe or pervasive, categorizing it as ordinary workplace socializing and flirtation, conduct that should not be confused with sexual harassment that breeds discriminatory conditions of employment.[10] Perez's conduct was neither pervasive nor sufficiently severe to create a hostile work environment or to alter the conditions of Bishop's employment.

The conduct of one of Susan McKenzie's co-workers was somewhat more offensive than that Sheri Bishop experienced, but McKenzie's claim of sexual harassment met a similar fate. As an employee of the Illinois Department of Transportation, McKenzie was responsible for training one of her co-workers, Donald Croft, in the use of a computerized inventory system. On one occasion during a training session, McKenzie became ill and vomited. At the time,

Croft remarked to her that she had "screwed around" so much with one of her supervisors that she probably was pregnant. Sometime later, Croft telephoned McKenzie in her office and said that he had heard that coffee induces sexual arousal, and since he was about to come to her office, he wanted to know if she was drinking coffee. Shortly after, when one of the workers mentioned to Croft that he had to collect some money from McKenzie for her participation in a baseball betting pool, Croft said that he should "take it out in trade." Croft's remarks were made over a three-month period. When McKenzie sued for sexual harassment, the court held that a reasonable person would not perceive McKenzie's work environment to be hostile or abusive: "Title VII is not directed against unpleasantness per se but only . . . against discrimination in the conditions of employment. . . . Although Croft's comments were most certainly offensive, we cannot hold that the frequency or severity of the comments rose to the level of unreasonably interfering with Ms. McKenzie's working environment." Accordingly, the court dismissed McKenzie's claim.[11] A complainant requires more than three isolated instances of moderately offensive behavior to prove an alteration in the terms and conditions of her employment.

A case where the harasser's offensive behavior was described by a court as tending "toward the lower end of the spectrum" of sexually harassing conduct was brought by Brenda Borello, who worked as a bookkeeper for A. Sam & Sons Produce Company. Charles Sam, son of the president of the company, served as the company's vice president. Borello's work required her to have intermittent contact with Sam, such as delivering telephone messages and obtaining delivery authorizations. Five months into her employment, Borello left a delivery slip on Sam's desk for his authorization. The following morning, she found the slip on her desk with Sam's notation, "whore, what is the amount?" Later that day, Borello overheard a loud argument in which Sam shouted that all the women in the office were "whores and all [they] knew how to do [was] fuck." In the following week, while walking near Borello's office, Sam remarked, "Nothing but a whore, nothing but a little whore, just a whore." A week later, while Borello was waiting to punch her time card, Sam said as he passed by, "Why don't you stare at the time clock a little bit more, ya whore." About a week later, when Borello called Sam to advise him that he had telephone messages, he shouted, "Go fuck yourself!" and slammed down the receiver.

When Borello sued the company for sexual harassment, the company centered its defense on the argument that since the incidents of Sam's conduct were both sporadic and isolated they were not sufficiently severe or pervasive to result in a hostile environment. The court, however, ruled otherwise. A female worker need not be subjected to an extended period of demeaning and degrading treatment before she is entitled to the protections of Title VII. The offensiveness of the behavior complained of also is a factor to be considered, and more offensive the conduct, the fewer the number of incidents needed for it to be characterized as severe or pervasive. For the court, the five incidents represented enough harassment to constitute a hostile work environment.[12]

In another case, James Pocrnick worked for the Professional Bank as senior vice president of consumer lending and in that capacity had the authority to hire and fire employees in his department. Pocrnick first met Rhonda Mallinson-Montague when he closed a consumer loan for her at the bank. Despite Mallinson-Montague's lack of banking experience, Pocrnick offered her a loan officer position that paid a base salary plus commissions based on the number of loans closed. Although Mallinson-Montague had reservations concerning the job, she accepted the offer after Pocrnick assured her that she would be properly trained and he would provide her with sufficient leads to earn commission income.

Almost immediately after Mallinson-Montague began work at the bank, Pocrnick began to sexually harass her. On one occasion, he instructed her to meet him at a nearby park to review some business matters, and when she arrived at the park, he pressed himself against her, kissed her, and asked her if she could feel his erection. When Mallinson-Montague rebuffed these advances, Pocrnick denied her the business leads he had previously promised and began to reject loans that she had originated. Apparently, Pocrnick had induced Mallinson-Montague to accept employment at the bank primarily to carry out a sexual conquest. His acts of retaliation following Mallinson-Montague's rejection of his advances only added to the severity and pervasiveness of his harassing conduct.

Not long after, Mallinson-Montague retained an attorney who wrote to the bank's president disclosing Pocrnick's behavior, and the harassment subsequently ceased. Mallinson-Montague, however, felt her career at the bank had been compromised, and she resigned. When she later sued Pocrnick and the bank for sexual harassment, the jury quickly rendered its verdict in her favor.[13]

In a similar case, Lynn Fall worked for the South Bend branch of the University of Indiana, and David Cohen served as its chancellor. Not long after Fall was hired, Cohen sent her an e-mail message requesting her to make an appointment to see him regarding legislative issues that were important to the university. According to Fall's recollection, on the day of her meeting with Cohen, she entered his office and he closed the door behind her. After they had spent some time discussing matters then before the state legislature,

Cohen told her that he had used the e-mail message merely as a ruse to get her into his office. Fall rose from her chair to leave, but before she could make her exit, Cohen put his arms around her, started kissing her, and forced his hands down her blouse and groped her breasts. Fall eventually broke from his grasp and fled the office, proceeding directly to a restroom where she vomited.

Fall filed suit against the university. The court focused its attention on whether Cohen's single act of harassment rose to the level of severity or pervasiveness required to support a hostile-environment claim. First, the court noted Cohen's deception in luring Fall into his office, indicating that his attack upon her was calculated in advance, significantly adding to the degree of severity of his conduct. Second, the court observed that the social context in which the offensive behavior was committed was a factor to be considered. Cohen had not approached Fall in a social setting or out in the open where she could more readily have deterred or escaped his advances. Instead, Cohen's attack occurred behind closed doors within the confines of his office, concealed from public view. Third, and most important to the court, the physical nature of Cohen's harassment bore upon its severity. He grabbed Fall and kissed her while groping her breasts. Although Fall alleged only a single act of sexual harassment, the court ruled that an incident involving physical assault such as that experienced by Fall may sufficiently alter the conditions of the victim's employment and create an abusive work environment.[14]

The EEOC has adopted a similar position. Because an unwelcome physical advance can seriously corrupt the victim's work environment, the EEOC assumes that one unwelcome, intentional touching of a woman's intimate body areas is sufficiently offensive to alter her working conditions: "More so than in the case of verbal advances or remarks, a single unwelcome physical advance can seriously poison the victim's working environment. If an employee's supervisor sexually touches that employee, the Commission normally would find a violation [of Title VII]."[15] In sum, a single offensive act may be severe enough to create a hostile environment, while a variety of isolated and less offensive actions may not.

The offensive conduct that forms the basis of a sexual-harassment claim must be "unwelcome" in the sense that the victim neither solicited nor incited the conduct and, in addition, regarded it as undesirable and offensive.[16] If the complainant immediately protests the offensive behavior and advises a higher authority in the company of its occurrence, her case will be considerably strengthened, since questions regarding the welcomeness and severity of the conduct are less likely to arise in the minds of the jurors and the court. On the other hand, delay in protesting and in reporting the harassment will only create doubt. If the complainant fails to protest the harassment and undertake measures to deter its reoccurrence, jurors may ask themselves whether the conduct was truly unwelcome, undesirable, and offensive.

Unfortunately, nearly all women choose to wait before they report acts of sexual harassment. Some fear retaliation or other repercussions. Others, at least initially, believe they can resolve the situation without the intervention of third parties, and still others are too embarrassed to disclose to anyone the particulars of the harassment. Since the credibility of the complainant is almost always placed in issue in a sexual-harassment case, the defendant employer generally attempts to exploit the complainant's delay in reporting the harassment as a means of undermining and discrediting her testimony.

A victim of sexual harassment should immediately apprise the harasser that she considers his behavior reprehensible and wholly unwelcome. If she fails to protest, not only is it likely that the harassment will continue, but when the harasser eventually is called to task, he will plead innocence, claiming he understood the complainant was not offended by his conduct since she never indicated otherwise. In such instances, the female worker usually insists that the very fact that she failed to respond to the harasser's conduct sufficiently communicated to him the unwelcomeness of his behavior.

At times, a defendant's actions are so degrading that the court will assume they were unwelcome, as any reasonable person would be offended by them.[17] In other instances, defendants have successfully used the "welcomeness" issue as a defense, especially when the complainant participated in the conduct she claims to have found offensive. In one case, the court described an employer's work environment as "very distasteful" and conducive to sexual harassment. The evidence showed, however, that the harassing conduct was substantially welcomed and, in fact, encouraged by the complainant. She regularly used crude and vulgar language and initiated sexually oriented conversations with her male and female co-workers. She frequently asked male employees about their marital sex lives and made her own marital sex relationship a topic of office conversation. Under these circumstances, she could not prove that similar conduct of other workers was unwelcome to her.[18]

The unwelcomeness issue frequently arises when one of the workers involved in a consensual sexual relationship decides to end it. Feelings of betrayal may elicit unsubstantiated charges of harassment on the one hand, or acts of actual harassment on the other. Shayne Kahn worked for Objective Solutions International as a senior executive recruiter. Kahn had an exemplary work history, having been neither criticized nor disciplined at any time during her employment. Throughout her employment, she had a consensual sexual relationship with Steven Wolfe, the company's owner and president. Soon after Kahn's second anniversary with the company, Wolfe told her that because of his wife's objections, he was terminating their relationship, and said that if he could not be intimate with her, he no longer wanted her present in the office. Then he fired her.

Kahn sued Wolfe and the company for sexual harassment, but the court dismissed her claim. In view of the fact that her relationship with Wolfe had been consensual and had not been a condition of her employment, the relationship cannot be said to have been "unwelcome." Nor could she claim that her termination had arisen out of a refusal on her part to submit to sexual requests. Rather, she could allege only that she was discharged in the wake of Wolfe's decision to terminate their sexual relationship. As observed by the court, these facts cannot support a claim of quid pro quo harassment.

Kahn also pleaded a hostile work environment claim. To succeed, as the cases just reviewed make explicit, she had to prove that her workplace was filled with discriminatory or harassing conduct sufficiently severe or pervasive to alter the terms and conditions of her employment. But Kahn was unable to offer any evidence of harassing conduct arising from the sexual relationship. Participation in a consensual office affair does not amount to sexual harassment merely because the end of the employment relationship coincides with the end of the affair. Wolfe's decision to simultaneously terminate the sexual and the employment relationships may have been unchivalrous, but it was not sexually harassing conduct.[19]

On occasion, defendants offer the court evidence of a claimant's sexual history to show she could not have considered the harassing conduct unwelcome. Most courts frown upon, if not reject outright, this type of evidence. Whether a victim welcomed the harassing conduct should not turn on her private sexual behavior. A woman's workplace rights should not be affected by the life she leads outside the workplace.[20] The workplace is one part of her life; the rest of her life remains separate and wholly apart.

Fourteen
Other Forms of Sexual Harassment

In the last two chapters we reviewed quid pro quo cases, in which submission to unwelcome sexual conduct was made a condition of a woman's employment, and hostile-environment cases, in which unwelcome sexual conduct interfered with a woman's job performance by creating a hostile or offensive working environment. Here, we go a step further to look at ways these types of sexual harassment can manifest differently in the workplace.

Favoritism or Preferential Treatment

Suppose a supervisor engages in a sexual relationship with a subordinate female worker and favors her by arranging for preferential treatment in the form of salary increases and promotions. May other female subordinates, denied similar raises and promotions, validly claim they have been subjected to acts of sexual harassment in violation of Title VII? The answer is no in some circumstances, yes in others.

A supervisor's isolated acts of preferential treatment in favor of an employee with whom he has a consensual sexual relationship may disadvantage other female workers, but it disadvantages men working under his supervision as well. A female employee denied an employment benefit as a consequence of such favoritism is not treated less favorably because she is a woman. Since women in these circumstances are treated as well or as badly as their male co-workers, the supervisor's conduct, though notably unfair, cannot be said to be discriminatory. Thus, female workers may not validly assert a claim of sexual harassment in this type of setting.

Suppose the relationship is not consensual; rather, the woman has been induced by promises of employment benefits to engage in a sexual relationship with her supervisor. In this setting, the supervisor withholds employment benefits unless the worker submits to his sexual demands. This is a condition of employment that would not be demanded of a male employee, and thus the supervisor's imposition of the condition discriminates and constitutes an act of sexual harassment. Are other women working under his supervision but not directly subjected to the same conditions of employment entitled to relief in a sexual-harassment claim made pursuant to Title VII?

This issue arose for Margaret Toscano, one of a number of applicants for promotion to an administrative position at a Veterans Administration hospital in Delaware. The applicant eventually selected for the promotion was at the time engaged in a sexual affair with the supervisor responsible for the selection. When Toscano sued the supervisor and the Veterans Administration for sexual harassment, she submitted evidence showing that the supervisor demonstrated a total inability to separate his work life from his private life. He described himself as a "lifetime womanizer," and he made little or no attempt to suppress that aspect of his character at the job site. He made telephone calls to proposition female employees at their homes, engaged in suggestive behavior at work, and was wont to telephone female employees working the night shift at the hospital to describe supposed sexual encounters with female workers under his supervision. Although no evidence was offered showing that he explicitly made acquiescence to his sexual advances a condition for promotion, that condition was implicit in his general behavior.

The circumstances confronting Toscano were essentially the same as those confronting any female worker in a sexual-harassment case where sexual favors are demanded as a quid pro quo for job benefits. When her supervisor made sexual favors a condition for promotion, he made it a condition for promotion for all female candidates, and thus he was guilty of sexually harassing each of them. In this type of setting, therefore, favoritism or preferential treatment may constitute a valid basis for a sexual-harassment suit.[1]

If a woman is coerced into submitting to unwelcome sexual advances in return for favored treatment, other women denied employment benefits should easily be able to establish that sex was a condition for receipt of these benefits, that is, a condition of their employment not imposed on men. Therefore, an employer may be held liable to all other female employees who are denied the favored treatment extended to the worker who is directly harassed.

Now suppose a woman works in a place where preferential treatment is extended to a number of female workers, each of whom freely engages in a sexual relationship with her supervisor. Suppose further that neither is this worker the subject of sexual advances nor is her position directly affected by the preferential treatment extended to other women in the office, yet she still finds this type of work environment wholly offensive. Does she have a valid claim for sexual harassment?

This question arose in the case of Catherine Broderick, a staff attorney for the Securities and Exchange Commission's Division of Corporate Finance in Arlington, Virginia. During the entire period of Broderick's employment with the SEC, an atmosphere dominated by sex pervaded her department. Two of the department's supervisors had ongoing sexual relationships with secretaries, and another was engaged in an affair with a staff attorney. All of these women were favored with salary increases, promotions, commendations, and bonus awards. Fully aware that her supervisors bestowed preferential treatment upon those who submitted to their sexual advances, Broderick was grossly offended by the nature of the conditions in which she was required to work, and eventually this environment undermined her motivation and adversely affected her performance. The sexual conduct, pervasive and apparent to all, created a hostile and highly offensive work environment, thus entitling Broderick and other women working in the department to relief under Title VII.[2]

Preferential treatment extended to favored employees in an atmosphere pervaded by sex may form the basis of a sexual-harassment lawsuit, even if the plaintiff, as in the case of Catherine Broderick, is not personally subjected to the harassment. Where sexual harassment is widespread, supervisory and management employees implicitly convey the message that they view women as sexual playthings, thereby creating a working environment that is demeaning to women. Women who find this environment offensive may rely on Title VII for appropriate relief.

In sum, claims of sexual harassment based on preferential treatment are likely to succeed except where the favored employee has entered into a consensual relationship with the provider of the job benefits. Where the relationship is not consensual, but instead a condition for receiving favored treatment, other female workers denied favored treatment may assert a claim for sexual harassment.[3]

Harassment by Nonsupervisory Co-workers

Under certain conditions, employers are liable for the sexually harassing conduct of nonsupervisory employees, just as for that of supervisory employees. An employer will be held responsible for co-worker acts of harassment if it knew, or it should have known, of the conduct.[4] Thus, in most cases involving co-worker sexual harassment, the primary issue under adjudication is the extent of the employer's knowledge of the harassing behavior.

Obviously, if the victim of the harassment reports the offensive conduct to a supervisor or management-level employee, the employer's knowledge will not be an issue in the case. However, as noted earlier, women are not often motivated to disclose immediately acts of sexual harassment committed against them. Except where the harassment is pervasive, the failure to report the harassing conduct of a nonsupervisory co-worker usually proves fatal to the victim's case. Where the harassment is pervasive, however, the court may assume that the employer had to have known of its presence even if it was never reported.

Brenda Lynn Franklin's is a case in point. Franklin, a salesperson for a car dealership, was the only female member of a ten-person sales staff. Franklin alleged that she was continuously harassed by several members of the sales staff. When she sued the dealership for sexual harassment, the defendant-employer asked the court to dismiss her case because she had never reported any of the alleged acts of harassment to her supervisor, and thus management had been unaware of the problem. In effect, her employer contended that it could not be held liable for the objectionable behavior of Franklin's co-workers unless it had direct knowledge of the harassment. The court rejected this argument, observing that the acts of harassment occurred on the showroom floor of the dealership, which, by design, was "a distinctly communal employment forum." If the harassment was as pervasive as Franklin alleged, it must have come to the attention of supervisory or management employees at some point. Accordingly, the court refused to dismiss Franklin's case.[5]

Where workplace harassment is pervasive, the court will charge the employer with "constructive" knowledge of its presence. The court assumes that management must have been aware of the co-worker harassment, whether or not the victim of the harassment reported it.

Harassment by Nonemployees

An employer's duty to provide its employees with a working environment free of sexual harassment may require it to exercise control, not only over its own employees, but over nonemployees as well. Sandra Rodriguez-Hernandez was terminated from her position as office manager of an Occidental International office after she complained she had been subjected to acts of sexual harassment by an executive employee of one of Occidental's most important customers. Occidental sold electric and industrial equipment in Florida and Puerto Rico, and approximately 80 percent of its business in Puerto Rico was with the Puerto Rico Electric Power Authority. Due to the extent of

Occidental's business with the Authority, Omar Chavez, president and sole stockholder of Occidental, undertook special efforts to assure good relations between his company and its major customer.

Chavez primarily employed young, attractive women and instructed them to be especially cordial to Authority employees. Good relations with high-ranking Authority executives, such as Edwin Miranda-Velez, were of first importance to Chavez, and he told Rodriguez that "she should be nice" to Miranda and "keep him satisfied." Rodriguez was also instructed to visit Miranda on each occasion she traveled to the Authority's offices.

Chavez often financed social events for Authority employees, and on one occasion he arranged for a party for them at a local hotel. All female members of Occidental's office in Puerto Rico were directed to attend the event unaccompanied, so that they would be available to dance with Authority executives. Entertainment at the party included a dancing show performed by scantily clad young women.

Not long after, on the occasion of one of Rodriguez's visits to the Authority's offices, Miranda made suggestive comments and unwelcome advances. He invited Rodriguez to dinner and asked her to visit his office after hours and on Friday evenings. On her birthday, he anonymously sent her flowers accompanied by a sexually explicit card, and some time later asked her to go with him to a motel. At that point, Rodriguez complained to Chavez of Miranda's behavior, but Chavez defended Miranda and told Rodriguez that she should respond to Miranda "as a woman." Rodriguez, unwilling to accept this advice, informed Chavez that unless he intervened to force a change in Miranda's behavior, she was prepared to take her complaint to the highest level of Authority executive personnel. Chavez fired her.

Rodriguez's subsequent sexual-harassment claim against Chavez and Occidental culminated in a $200,000 jury award in her favor. When the jury's verdict was later reviewed by an appellate court, it focused on Occidental's liability for Miranda's conduct. The court noted that Chavez conditioned Rodriguez's continued employment on her agreement to accede to Miranda's sexual advances. Because Chavez failed to take any action to curtail Miranda's sexual demands, he in effect made acceptance of those demands a condition of Rodriguez's employment, thus rendering his company liable under Title VII for sexual harassment. In its decision, the court explained: "This is a case in which Rodriguez's employer not only acquiesced in the customer's demands, but explicitly told her to give in to those demands and satisfy the customer. This conduct is clearly an example of quid pro quo sexual harassment, as Rodriguez's employer conditioned her future with the company on her responding to the unwanted sexual demands of a customer."[6]

Acts of sexual harassment committed by an employer's clients and customers often go unreported. Some women decide to ignore the harassment lest they be perceived by their employers as incapable of coping with the conditions of their jobs. Female sales representatives are particularly vulnerable to acts of sexual harassment, as they often must conduct business in hotels and restaurants, and on customers' premises. Since many female workers elect to cope with the harassment of an unruly client or customer rather than seek the intercession of their employer, third-party harassment is far more prevalent than the reported cases indicate.[7]

As in the *Rodriguez* case, even if a woman reports the harassment, her employer may be unwilling to deal with the problem if it believes that doing so will unduly disturb a valued client or customer. This was precisely Chavez's reaction to Rodriguez's disclosure that Miranda was harassing her. But an employer is required to deal with the problem if it knows—or should know—of its existence, and in such circumstances it must protect its employee from further harassment by implementing immediate and appropriate action.[8] What do the courts consider immediate and appropriate action? The unusual case of Kelbi Folkerson supplies the answer.

Folkerson made her living as a mime. She was employed by the Circus Casino in Las Vegas, where she performed as a life-size children's wind-up toy, "Kelbi the Living Doll." Since she was so convincing in her portrayal of a mechanical doll, casino patrons often speculated whether she was human or mechanical, and some tried to touch her to find out. When Folkerson expressed concern to her supervisor that the touching could get out of hand, he directed her to call security whenever she experienced any difficulty of that sort, and as a deterrent to customer touching, the casino provided her with a sign to wear on her back reading, "Stop, Do Not Touch." The casino also furnished Folkerson with a bodyguard of sorts—another performer dressed as a clown—who accompanied her whenever she performed on the floor of the casino. Other employees also were enlisted by Folkerson to call security if they saw that she was in trouble.

Despite these precautions, on one occasion a patron told bystanders, "I will show you how real she really is," and he walked toward her with open arms as though to embrace her. Folkerson floored him with a left to the mouth. The casino then fired Folkerson on the ground that the patron had not sufficiently provoked her to warrant that reaction, but Folkerson alleged that her termination was ordered only because she had opposed and rejected a patron's attempt to sexually harass her. When Folkerson sued the casino alleging sexual harassment, the court agreed that her employer could be held liable for a harassing act committed by one of its patrons, but only if it had acquiesced in the harassment by not taking immediate corrective action when it learned of the existence of objectionable conduct. The facts of the case did not support Folkerson's position. The casino did not acquiesce in touching episodes by its patrons. To the contrary, it undertook reasonable steps to prevent patrons from harassing her. It arranged for its security forces to intervene in the event Folkerson confronted an overly aggressive person, it provided her with a sign designed to deter touching of her body, and it furnished her with bodyguard protection. The court, therefore, dismissed Folkerson's case.[9]

Sexual Harassment and the Sexually Active Plaintiff

Women are often concerned that their sexual history may be opened to examination once they allege workplace harassment. Because the possibility of such disclosure undoubtedly discourages some complainants from prosecuting lawsuits against their harassers, the courts generally look askance at defendant tactics that require inquiry into matters entirely personal to the plaintiff.[10]

The privacy rights of victims of sexual harassment generally have been protected by most courts through the exclusion of any proffered evidence of past sexual conduct with anyone other than the person alleged to have committed acts of sexual harassment against her. The "welcomeness" issue may open the door to inquiries concerning any sort of sexual relationship between the harasser and the victim. However, other inquiries into the past sexual conduct of a plaintiff with persons outside the workplace are barred, even when an employer claims that it relates to her claim of unwelcomeness in the workplace, as Occidental International did in Sandra Rodriguez's case against it and Omar Chavez. Occidental wanted to submit evidence that painted Rodriguez as sexually insatiable, as engaging in multiple affairs with married men, as a lesbian, as suffering from a sexually transmitted disease, as exhibiting flirtatious behavior in Miranda's presence, and as a worker distracted from properly performing her duties by reason of an affair with a married man. The court allowed the submission of evidence allegedly showing that Rodriguez's relationship with a married man had distracted her at work, and it also permitted the introduction of evidence of Rodriguez's alleged flirtatious behavior toward Miranda, but only with respect to whether Miranda's advances were in fact unwelcome to her. It barred defendants' offer of all other evidence relating to Rodriguez's moral character and alleged promiscuity. None of the evidence that the court accepted deterred it from ruling in Rodriguez-Hernandez's favor.[11]

It is not at all unusual for a defendant accused of sexual harassment to endeavor to rake up instances of the plaintiff's past sexual conduct—anything that might possibly prejudice a jury against her. Thus, Congress in 1994 amended the *Federal Rules of Evidence* to prevent misuse of a complainant's sexual history in sexual-harassment and other cases involving sexual misconduct. In a sexual-harassment case, these rules—with some exceptions—bar evidence offered either to prove that a complainant engaged in sexual behavior outside the workplace or to prove her sexual predisposition. The federal rules constitute a major barrier to a defendant bent on introducing a plaintiff's sexual history in the courtroom.[12]

As in the *Rodriguez* case, evidence pertaining to a complainant's behavior regarding the man she claims to be her harasser is relevant to the welcomeness issue. Because defendants very often claim that the alleged harassing conduct was welcomed by the victim, a complainant must be prepared to respond to defendant's inquiries pertaining to her reactions and responses to the harasser's conduct. The defendant may also attempt to show that the complainant spoke, acted, or dressed provocatively, purportedly evidence of her welcomeness to the attentions of the harasser.

Gender Harassment

The courts will consider acts of harassment of a woman as acts of sexual harassment even if they are unrelated to sex, provided they are directed against the woman solely because of her gender. Courts generally refer to this type of harassment as "gender harassment," an issue that arose in the case of Lee Kopp.

Kopp worked for the Samaritan Health System as the lead cardiology technician in the hospital's respiratory-cardiology department. Saadi Albaghdadi, a cardiologist with privileges at Samaritan, had several encounters with Kopp. On two occasions he shouted at her, and on another he threw his stethoscope at her. On still another occasion, after noticing that a medical test report was missing from a patient's chart, Albaghdadi grabbed Kopp by the lapels of her jacket, pulled her close to him, shouted at her through gritted teeth, and shook her violently for approximately thirty seconds before releasing her. Kopp filed a formal complaint against Albaghdadi and later filed suit against him and the hospital. By the time the case reached the court for trial, the litigation record contained testimony from Samaritan employees that recounted numerous instances of Albaghdadi's shouting, swearing, and throwing objects at female employees of the hospital. The record also disclosed that Albaghdadi was prone to shove women around and to use vulgar language when referring to female staff members. Although Albaghdadi also abused male staff members, his abuse of women was far more frequent and serious.

This is a typical gender harassment case. Although Albaghdadi's harassment of Kopp was not of a sexual nature, his abusive mannerisms were as pervasive and as offensive as instances of sexual harassment we have witnessed in the last three chapters. Kopp was singled out for abusive treatment, not because she was a sexual object, but because she was a woman. She was harassed because of her gender.[13]

In another case of gender harassment, Dianne Evans, a life insurance salesperson earning close to six figures as an employee of the Metropolitan Life Insurance Company, was successfully recruited by Durham Life Insurance Company. She achieved even greater success during her first two years at Durham, but when the company was acquired by another insurance company, new management arrived on the scene, and from that point forward, Evans's career proceeded downhill.

When new management assumed control of Durham, Evans was the only full-time female sales agent in an office of thirty agents. Apparently resenting the success she had achieved as a woman, certain male members of the new management set out to undermine her position by depriving her of the staff and other support granted her earlier. Two of them told Evans that she did not fit the company profile for sales agents: Her clothes were too expensive, she dressed too well for the job, and she "made too much money for a goddamn woman." Thereafter, Evans suffered repeated slights from new management. At an awards dinner, the company failed to recognize her sales accomplishments. At a training session, she was publicly mocked on account of her speech and the way she carried herself when she walked. Her supervisors refused to provide her with the legal assistance she had requested, and as a result she lost an important account. They assigned her more than her share of work with lapsed policies—a thankless job, generally distributed proportionately among the sales agents—thus reducing her commission income. Her secretary was fired and not replaced. When management forced her out of her private office, some of her critical files inexplicably disappeared. The result again was a diminution of commission income. She was continually humiliated with sexist remarks and crude sexual and physical touching. After enduring this harassment for several months, Evans concluded that she no longer had a future at Durham, resigned, and sued the company for sexual harassment.

Evans won a favorable trial verdict, and then Durham appealed, arguing that the trial court had erred in aggregating sexual-related and nonsexual-related events in its determination that a hostile environment had existed at the company. The appellate court disagreed: "Some of these events were apparently triggered by sexual desire, some were sexually hostile, some were non-sexual but gender based, and others were facially neutral. . . . Title VII may be applied to all of these types of conduct. . . . Title VII prohibits sex discrimination. Although 'sex' has several common meanings in Title VII it describes a personal characteristic like race or religion. We generally presume that sexual advances of the kind alleged in this case are sex-based, whether the motivation is desire or hatred."[14]

While not always motivated by hatred, gender discrimination is always motivated by a bias against women. In Evans's case, the bias evolved from a perception of women that refused to allow for their success in a business world dominated by men. Evans was harassed because she failed to fit a mold conceived by her male peers. If she had been less successful, she probably would not have been harassed.

In such cases as *Kopp* and *Evans*, the term "sexual harassment" may appear to be a misnomer. But the essence of a sexual-harassment claim is not necessarily constructed upon sexual advances or other incidents having sexual overtones. Intimidation and hostility toward women—merely because they are women—may be as harassing as conduct involving explicit sexual advances. Thus, the courts generally employ the term "gender harassment" to distinguish "nonsexual" harassment from harassment that is sexual or erotic in nature.[15] All such behavior, however, qualifies as sexual harassment.

Fifteen

Employer Liability for Sexual Harassment

Although acts of sexual harassment are committed by individual workers, most courts have ruled that under Title VII individuals are not liable for damages to their victims. Title VII makes it unlawful for an *employer* to discriminate against a woman because of her sex, thus limiting liability to employers.[1] A woman's lawsuit against an employee for sexual harassment will come to naught unless she works in a state where she may rely upon a local anti-discrimination law that provides for recovery against individual defendants.

An employer is liable to a victim of sexual harassment committed by a co-worker or a nonemployee if the employer knew—or the circumstances demonstrate that it should have known—of the harassment. That leaves open a question of significant import for prospective complainants: Under what circumstances will an employer be held liable for the sexually harassing conduct of its supervisors?

Kimberly Ellerth worked in the Chicago office of Burlington Industries, first as a merchandising assistant and later as a sales representative. After about a year on the job, Ellerth claimed that she had been subjected throughout her employment to a series of sexually harassing actions by one of her supervisors. During her pre-employment interview, Theodore Slowik, who held a mid-level management position, asked her sexually suggestive questions and stared at her breasts and legs. After she was hired, Ellerth had intermittent contact with Slowik, and on nearly every occasion he told her offensive, off-color jokes and made other sexually inappropriate comments. While on a business trip, Slowik invited Ellerth to the hotel lounge, an invitation Ellerth felt compelled to accept because Slowik was her boss. During the ensuing conversation, when Ellerth failed to respond to Slowik's remarks about her breasts, he told her to "loosen up" and warned, "I could make your life very hard or very easy at Burlington."

Burlington later considered Ellerth for promotion. During her promotion interview, Slowik expressed reservations concerning her prospects for promotion, commenting that she was not "loose enough," and at that point he reached over and rubbed her knee. When Slowik later phoned her to announce the promotion had been authorized, he said, "You're gonna be out there with men who work in factories, and they certainly like women with pretty butts/legs." During a subsequent telephone call, Slowik said, "I don't have time for you right now, Kim—unless you want to tell me what you're wearing." On another call, he asked if she was "wearing shorter skirts yet" as it "would make your job a whole heck of a lot easier." During her tenure at Burlington, Ellerth did not report any of Slowik's behavior, although she knew that Burlington had a sexual-harassment policy in place. Ultimately, Ellerth resigned in response to criticism leveled against her by another supervisor.

Ellerth sued Burlington Industries for sexual harassment. When her case reached the Supreme Court in 1998, the court had to determine under what circumstances an employer may be held liable for a hostile working environment created by a supervisor. At the outset of its analysis, the court reaffirmed a major distinction between a hostile working environment that culminates in a "tangible employment action" that adversely affects the employment status of the victim, and a hostile working environment that does not.

A "tangible employment action," as defined by the court, constitutes a significant change in the employment status of the victim of the harassment. As a general proposition, only a supervisor, acting with the authority of his employer, possesses the power to effect a tangible employment action. A nonsupervisory employee can cause physical or psychological harm to a co-worker as readily as a supervisor can, but a nonsupervisory employee is not empowered to hire or fire, promote or demote, or increase or reduce another worker's pay. Tangible employment actions fall within the special province of a supervisor who has been empowered by his employer to make employment decisions affecting the status of workers under his control: "Tangible employment actions are the means by which the supervisor brings the official power of the enterprise to bear on subordinates. A tangible employment decision requires an official act of the enterprise, a company act. . . . For these reasons, a tangible employment action taken by the supervisor becomes for Title VII purposes the act of the employer." Thus, the court ruled that when a supervisor harasses a subordinate female employee and thereby creates a hostile working environment that culminates in a tangible employment action adversely affecting the victim's employment status, the employer is liable for the supervisor's conduct.

Ellerth, however, had not suffered the consequences of an adverse tangible employment action. In fact, she had been promoted and had later resigned from the company without ever having complained of Slowik's harassment. Under these circumstances, could Burlington nevertheless be held liable to Ellerth for Slowik's harassing conduct? The Supreme Court answered in the affirmative, but it also provided Burlington with a defense it could elect to assert to insulate itself from liability. To establish this defense, Burlington would be required to prove that (1) Burlington exercised reasonable care to prevent and correct promptly any sexually harassing behavior occurring in its workplace, and (2) Ellerth unreasonably failed to take advantage of preventive or corrective opportunities provided by Burlington to avoid harm from sexual harassment, such as failing to report the harassment in accordance with Burlington's sexual-harassment policy. The court emphasized that this defense is available to employers only where no tangible employment action was taken by the supervisor during the course of the harassment. In all other cases, employers are strictly liable for the harassment of its supervisors.

Because this ruling essentially constituted a new statement of the law, the Court remanded the case for further proceedings, thus providing Ellerth another opportunity to establish Burlington's liability and affording Burlington the opportunity to plead and prove the newly fashioned defense.[2]

The Supreme Court's ruling not only affirmed an old standard of liability for employers but also established a new one. It reaffirmed an employer's liability for a supervisor's acts of sexual harassment that culminate in tangible employment actions adversely affecting the victim of the harassment. It also ruled that an employer may remain liable for a supervisor's conduct even if the harassment does not result in tangible employment actions, but in those circumstances the employer must be given the opportunity to establish a defense that may relieve it of liability for the behavior of its supervisor. The Court, however, placed the burden of proving the essential elements of the new defense squarely upon the employer. Under the law, this type of defense is commonly referred to as an "affirmative defense." Because it allocated to the defendant employer the burden of proving this affirmative defense, the Court afforded the plaintiff employee an enormous advantage in relation to issues involving employer liability for supervisory harassment.

Inasmuch as the question of an employer's liability for supervisory workplace behavior will play a major role in future sexual-harassment litigation, we will examine the Supreme Court's newly fashioned affirmative defense in some detail—after we establish exactly who qualifies as a supervisor.

A supervisor's ability to commit acts of harassment is enhanced by his authority to adversely affect an employee's employment status and her daily work life. A supervisor generally is defined as one who has immediate or successively higher authority over an employee. If an individual is authorized to recommend or order tangible employment actions affecting a worker, such as hiring, firing, promoting, demoting, and reassigning, he qualifies as a supervisor, as does an individual authorized to direct an employee's day-to-day activities.[3]

Again, if the harassing supervisor's actions culminate in a tangible employment action, the new affirmative defense is not available to the employer, who will be held liable for its supervisor's harassment. The Supreme Court defined a "tangible employment action" as a "significant change in employment status, such as hiring, firing, failing to promote, reassignment with significantly different responsibilities, or a decision causing a significant change in benefits."[4] The EEOC's definition, however, is somewhat more expansive, as its definition of a tangible employment action also includes a significant change in a worker's duties, with or without a change in salary or benefits. As an example, a change in duties that blocks an opportunity for promotion would qualify as a tangible employment action under the EEOC definition. But a change in job title probably would not, unless the change signaled a demotion or other downward change in status.[5]

The employment actions taken against Dianne Evans in her sexual-harassment case against Durham Life Insurance Company (chapter 14) included the nonreplacement of her dismissed secretary, the loss of her private office, the unexplained disappearance of files critical to her work, and her assignment of a disproportionate share of work that earned low commission income. None of the four actions falls within any of those specified in the Supreme Court definition, but in combination they resulted in a significant change in Evans's employment status, and thus the court held that the affirmative defense was not available to Durham.[6]

The problems Lisetta Molnar encountered at the East Chicago Community School illustrate the flexibility the courts have employed in determining whether a plaintiff has been the subject of a tangible employment action. Hired as an intern to teach art, Molnar hoped to qualify at the conclusion of her internship for a license as a full-fledged art teacher. Beginning with her first day at the school, her principal, Lloyd Booth, made sexual advances Molnar found offensive. Booth told her he could secure various benefits for her that other interns were not granted, such as a permanent art room and art supplies. Molnar perceived the offer as a sexual advance, which made her very uncomfortable. The unwelcome behavior continued during succeeding weeks, but

Molnar rejected each of Booth's advances. After Molnar had spurned him, Booth ordered the return of all art supplies previously furnished her, and all discussion of a permanent art room ceased. At the end of the school year, Booth gave Molnar a negative performance evaluation, making it less likely she would be granted a teaching license.

When Molnar sued the school for sexual harassment, the court ruled that the affirmative defense was unavailable to the school because Booth had subjected Molnar to tangible employment actions. The clearest tangible employment action, in the court's estimation, was Booth's confiscation of art supplies he had instructed to be furnished to Molnar, supplies she required to perform her functions as an art teacher. The negative performance evaluation also fell into that category of employment action. Even though the school board later reversed Booth's negative evaluation, the temporary derailment of Molnar's career was sufficient to render Booth's original evaluation a tangible employment action. With the affirmative defense unavailable to the school, the jury rendered a verdict in Molnar's favor.[7]

In instances where the victim of harassment did not suffer an adverse employment action, the newly created affirmative defense requires the defendant employer to prove that it exercised reasonable care to prevent acts of sexual harassment in its workplace, and that upon discovering the presence of sexually harassing conduct, it promptly enacted measures to eliminate it. The EEOC suggests that reasonable care generally requires an employer "to establish, disseminate, and enforce an anti-harassment policy and complaint procedure and to take other reasonable steps to prevent and correct harassment."[8] However, even the best-formulated sexual-harassment policy and complaint procedure will not satisfy the employer's burden of proving reasonable care unless the employer effectively implements, maintains, and enforces the policy and the complaint procedure.

Smaller employers may be able to use informal means to fulfill their responsibilities in this regard, while larger employers may need to institute more formal procedures.[9] But regardless of their form, failure to implement, maintain, and enforce an anti-harassment policy and complaint procedure will render it far more difficult for an employer to prove that it exercised reasonable care in preventing and correcting sexual harassment.

Plaintiff employees often charge their employers with ineffective enforcement of their anti-harassment policies. Employers, of course, vigorously defend their enforcement efforts. In one such case, the employer was able to establish that immediately after the plaintiff employee asserted a complaint of harassment, management assured her that sexual harassment would not be tolerated in its workplace and initiated an investigation of the alleged harasser, who was suspended during the investigation and later demoted. The court ruled that the employer had exercised reasonable care in eliminating the harassment and preventing its recurrence.[10]

In another case, a female worker's supervisor periodically subjected her to offensive sexual advances, and on two occasions she filed formal complaints with her manager. The manager verbally warned the supervisor but failed to make a written record either of the complaints or of any efforts to prevent further harassment. To no one's surprise, the harassment continued. The worker then complained to another supervisor, who advised her that nothing further could or would be done to stop the harassment. Although this employer had a sexual-harassment policy in place, it failed to enforce it.[11]

One further issue affects the validity of an employer's reliance upon the affirmative defense. The second prong of the defense requires the employer to show that the plaintiff employee unreasonably failed to take advantage of preventive or corrective opportunities provided by the employer to avoid harm from sexual harassment. Suppose the employer has instituted an antiharassment policy with an adequate complaint procedure, but the plaintiff worker decides not to report her supervisor's harassment. If the worker later sues her employer for sexual harassment, will her case be dismissed because she ignored the complaint procedure?

A case in which this issue arose is that of Kelly Scrivner. Shortly after Scrivner started teaching in the Socorro Independent School District in Texas, her principal began to harass her with lewd and offensive remarks. Some time later, the school district superintendent received an anonymous letter—not written by Scrivner—complaining of the principal's sexual harassment of teachers and his use of vulgar language in the presence of staff and parents. The school district immediately undertook an investigation, interviewing sixty-four teachers and staff members, three of whom stated that the principal had engaged in sexually harassing conduct. However, when Scrivner was interviewed, she denied the principal had sexually harassed her. Based on its investigation, the school district found insufficient evidence of sexual harassment to discipline the principal, but it warned him in a memorandum to refrain from unprofessional jokes and sexual comments.

Six months later, the principal's harassment of Scrivner intensified. At that point, she filed a formal harassment complaint with the school district, and a second investigation was promptly initiated. Eventually, the school district concluded that the principal's conduct could have created the perception of a hostile environment at the school, and it ordered his removal from his position. Scrivner then initiated legal action against the school district.

Scrivner's sexual-harassment claim rose or fell on the validity of the affirmative defense asserted by the school district. Because Scrivner had not suffered a tangible employment action, the school district could escape liability for the principal's acts of sexual harassment if it were able to prove that (1) it had exercised reasonable care in preventing sexual harassment and in acting quickly to eliminate sexual-harassing conduct when it appeared in its workplace, and (2) Scrivner unreasonably failed to take advantage of preventive or corrective opportunities provided by the school district, including its procedures for reporting acts of sexual harassment.

By relying on its two investigations of the principal's conduct, the school district easily established that it had exercised reasonable care in preventing and eliminating sexual harassment from its workplace. The evidence also showed that Scrivner had declined to avail herself of the school district's preventive and corrective policies. She did not complain of the principal's behavior until nearly two years after she first began to experience it. Even when she was presented with an opportunity to disclose the harassment during the first investigation, she chose to lie and report that she had not witnessed any harassing conduct by the principal. By failing to inform the school district of the principal's behavior when given the opportunity, Scrivner acted unreasonably. The court concluded that Scrivner's complaint should be dismissed.[12]

A female worker should not be expected to complain immediately following an initial incident of harassment. Often, she may ignore the first few incidents, provided they are minor, with the hope that such occurrences will cease before she has to file a formal complaint. Then again, she may elect to resolve the issue herself by advising her harasser that his conduct is unwelcome and should cease. If the harassment persists, however, she must report it in accordance with her employer's procedure for reporting sexual-harassment complaints. If she does not, her failure may doom any later sexual-harassment claim.

Even if a defendant employer is held liable to a plaintiff worker for acts of sexual harassment—whether by a supervisor, a co-worker, or a customer or client—under certain circumstances its liability for the worker's damages may be substantially limited, for example, if the employee elects to resign from her employment rather than continue to work in what she considers to be a hostile environment.

If a worker quits and later charges her employer with sexual harassment, her damages may be reduced unless she can demonstrate that she resigned involuntarily, a resignation commonly referred to as a "constructive discharge." Unless a worker's resignation is considered to be a constructive discharge, her back pay and other damages may be limited to those that accrued before she left the company.

A worker's resignation will be considered a constructive discharge if the employer requires the worker to perform her job functions under conditions so difficult that any reasonable person laboring under those conditions would feel compelled to resign. Thus a worker is constructively discharged if she is forced to quit because of intolerable working conditions. What a reasonable person considers to be tolerable or intolerable is an issue often litigated in the courts. If the court determines that a worker resigned under circumstances the court considers less than intolerable, damages that accrue after her resignation may be denied the worker, even if the employer is found guilty of sexual harassment. Conversely, a worker who is constructively discharged may be eligible for the entire panoply of damages and other relief available to any worker unlawfully discharged.

Even if a worker establishes that her working conditions were intolerable, the court will sustain her constructive-discharge claim only if she also proves that the harassment was the primary cause of her resignation. In other words, she must establish a causal link between the harassment and her resignation. Generally, the causal link is established by considering the amount of time that elapses between the harassment and the resignation; the shorter the passage of time, the greater the likelihood the court will determine that the worker resigned because of the harassment and not on account of some other reason.

Michelle McCrackin filed a constructive discharge claim against LabOne, alleging that her supervisor in the company's Message Center Department subjected her to lewd and sexually suggestive leers, unwanted physical touching, and stalking, and that he refused to alter his conduct despite her repeated expressions of discomfort and disapproval. Although management was aware of her supervisor's behavior, it took no action to discipline him or control his behavior. After enduring this treatment for six months, McCrackin complained to two company officials, including the vice president of the Human Resources Department. Other than to suggest that she change the location of her desk to make it easier to avoid her supervisor, no remedial or preventative action was undertaken. Firmly of the belief that the company would not act to alleviate her situation, McCrackin resigned. Her belief was confirmed when she picked up her final paycheck and the human resources vice president commented, "It's not as if you were raped."

McCrackin sued LabOne, alleging that she had been forced to work in an offensive and hostile work environment, ultimately culminating in her constructive discharge. Later in the litigation, LabOne asked the court to dismiss McCrackin's constructive discharge claim, but the court ruled that McCrackin had alleged facts sufficient to show that a reasonable person in her circumstances would have felt compelled to resign. If McCrackin had been subjected to a pattern of leers, touching, and unwelcome advances, as she alleged, then management should have done more than merely suggest ways that McCrackin might mitigate her supervisor's offensive behavior. It should have taken action to eliminate the harassment. Rather than continue to work in such an environment, McCrackin could reasonably and justifiably have felt that she had no alternative but to resign. Her belief that management would do nothing to improve her working conditions was heightened and reinforced by management's indifference to the hostility and offensiveness of her work environment and was buttressed by the human resources vice president's comment concerning rape. The court denied LabOne's motion to dismiss McCrackin's constructive-discharge claim.[13]

If the supervisor's conduct had been the sole element in the case, the court might very well have arrived at a different conclusion. A six-month lapse between the first acts of offensive behavior and McCrackin's resignation suggested that her working conditions might have been less than intolerable. But they became intolerable once she learned that management had no intention of changing them. Immediately after learning that her working conditions would not improve, McCrackin resigned, thus establishing the requisite causal link.

In another case, the court rejected a constructive-discharge claim because the worker's resignation did not occur until six months after the harassment had ended.[14] If a worker intends to assert a constructive-discharge claim, she must act expeditiously, on the one hand, lest an element of uncertainty be introduced about how tolerable or intolerable her working conditions were. Delay may also create doubt about the causal linkage between the harassment and her resignation. But, on the other hand, if she resigns before her employer has had a reasonable opportunity to implement measures to halt the harassment and eliminate a hostile work environment, the court may conclude that the employer, given ample time, would have resolved those problems. In those circumstances, a court would probably rule that the worker had failed to establish that her working conditions were intolerable. Whether to resign and when to resign are decisions requiring the advice of an attorney well versed in this area of the law.

Sixteen
Employer Retaliation against Workers

In enacting Title VII, Congress decreed it unlawful for an employer to retaliate against a worker who either has charged it with a discriminatory policy or practice or has participated in a legal or administrative proceeding relating to one of its employment policies or practices. The law provides workers with protection from acts of employer retaliation committed against them while exercising their rights under Title VII, as well as under the Equal Pay Act. Once a worker has engaged in a protected activity—an action opposing an act of discrimination, such as filing a charge of discrimination, testifying on behalf of a fellow worker who has asserted a claim of discrimination, or participating in an investigation of alleged discriminatory conduct—an employer is barred from retaliating against that worker on account of her participation in that protected activity. Title VII states: "It shall be an unlawful employment practice for an employer to discriminate against any of his employees or applicants for employment . . . because [she] has opposed . . . an unlawful practice . . . or because [she] has made a charge, testified, assisted, or participated in any manner in an investigation, proceeding, or hearing under this subchapter."[1] Employers who retaliate against employees in such circumstances subject themselves to liability for damages suffered by the worker as a consequence of such conduct.

Employer retaliation comes in varied forms, although employers tend to favor discharge over other options, which was the case for Paula Donnellon, who worked for Fruehauf Corporation first as a secretary and later as office manager of its Atlanta office. When a sales representative position opened up in the Atlanta office, Donnellon applied, but Fruehauf selected a male worker with extended sales experience. Donnellon then filed a discrimination charge with the EEOC, alleging that Fruehauf had refused to consider her for the sales position due to her gender. Within a month of her filing, Fruehauf fired Donnellon. This action triggered a second EEOC charge: Donnellon alleged that Fruehauf had discharged her in retaliation for filing the original charge.

Donnellon's discrimination and retaliation charges were eventually tried before a court sitting without a jury. Inasmuch as the worker Fruehauf hired was far more qualified than Donnellon to fill the sales position, the court rejected Donnellon's charge that she had been denied the position because of her sex. The court, however, refused to dismiss her claim that Fruehauf had fired her in retaliation for filing a sex discrimination charge, and it ordered Fruehauf to reinstate Donnellon to her former position with full back pay.[2]

Other forms of retaliation employers use to punish workers for having engaged in protected activities include denials of promotion, demotions, disadvantageous transfers, refusals to grant merited or scheduled pay increases, and unwarranted adverse performance evaluations. Most federal courts have ruled that any materially adverse change in a worker's terms and conditions of employment may provide the basis for a retaliation charge. Even acts that may not adversely affect the worker's economic status, such as an unwarranted reprimand or an act of workplace harassment, may qualify as retaliatory.

Barbara Weeks worked as a tax examiner for Maine's Bureau of Taxation. Two days after bureau officials learned that she had filed a sex discrimination complaint with the Maine Human Rights Commission, they temporarily reassigned her to an entry-level tax examiner position. After Weeks later filed a second sex discrimination complaint, they immediately transferred her to another unit. When Weeks sued for retaliation, the court ruled that the bureau's contention that the reassignment and transfer were merely coincidental to the sex complaint filings "stretches the bounds of credulity." Moreover, Weeks's retaliation claim was buttressed by evidence presented to the court showing that her supervisors had labeled her a "troublemaker" and had warned other workers not to associate with her either inside or outside the office.[3]

Andrea Capaci's employer took another tack. After Capaci filed an EEOC charge of sex discrimination against her employer, her supervisors began to "document all things out of the ordinary or unusual" in her work performance. Although her employer claimed that the supervisors only intended to document anything of importance in Capaci's daily work life that might relate to the EEOC investigation of her charge, the result was a thick file of reports of trivial, petty, and insignificant events that would not have been recorded in the file of any other worker and could serve no purpose other than to harass Capaci. Her employer was held liable for retaliation.[4]

The withdrawal of a favor or privilege extended to a worker by her employer may also constitute an act of retaliation. Fannie Sims filed a sex discrimination claim with the EEOC alleging that her employer paid her less than her male co-workers. Before she filed the claim, Sims had been allowed to report to work late, as she was caring for her invalid mother, but immediately after she filed charges, the company directed her to report to work by "8:00 sharp" or face dismissal. Subsequently, her supervisor monitored her daily arrival times, and three weeks later her employer fired her for repeated lateness.

Sims's employer denied it had discharged her in retaliation for filing the EEOC complaint. Her supervisors argued that they had merely retracted the "friendly courtesies" that they as "friends" had previously extended Sims, allowing her to report to work late because they liked her and knew she was responsible for caring for her mother. But whether they acted as friends or otherwise was of no moment. When Sims's employer altered its previous practice in regard to her work schedule, it adversely affected the terms of her employment, and therefore it was guilty of retaliation.[5]

Title VII retaliation complaints filed annually with the Equal Employment Opportunity Commission nearly doubled between 1992 and 2000, and at that point, almost 25 percent of all Title VII complaints filed with the EEOC charged employers with acts of retaliation.[6] This steep rise reflects an increasing tendency on the part of employers to react negatively and irresponsibly to charges of discriminatory conduct, as well as a willingness on the part of workers to call their employers to task for such retaliation.

A worker need not actually file a formal charge of discrimination to activate the protections against retaliation. A verbal complaint made to a person in the human resources department, or even a threat to file a discrimination claim, may qualify as a protected activity. In one case, a worker sent her supervisor a memorandum accusing him of exhibiting a "sexist mentality" toward her, and advising him that she would not hesitate to seek legal redress if this "sexism" did not cease. The court ruled that although the worker used the terms "sexist" and "sexism" rather than "discrimination," she nevertheless had engaged in a protected activity.[7]

A worker's action undertaken in opposition to an employer's discriminatory conduct is protected so long as the worker acts reasonably and in a good-faith belief that the conduct is discriminatory. When Linda Love, a vice president for advertising employed by Re/Max of America, learned that male employees in positions comparable to hers had been given substantial raises while

she had not, she not only sent a memo to the president of the company requesting a raise but also went one step further. She attached to her memo a
copy of the Equal Pay Act. Two hours later she was fired. A court later ruled
that Love had made a good-faith assertion that the company had violated the
Equal Pay Act, and thus she was entitled to recover damages resulting from
the discharge ordered in retaliation for asserting her EPA rights.[8]

As we have seen in previous chapters, the courts frequently dismiss a
worker's discrimination claim. In these cases, may a worker still proceed with
a retaliation claim? This question arose in the *Donnellon* case against Fruehauf
Corporation, and the decision of the court reflects the position the federal
courts generally have taken with regard to the issue: A charge of retaliation
may be valid even if the employer has not engaged in a discriminatory practice. The worker need only demonstrate that at the time she filed her charge,
she had a good-faith, reasonable belief that the challenged employer practice
violated the law. If an employer then acts adversely to the worker's interest
because she has asserted a discrimination claim, it may be held liable for retaliation, even if the worker's underlying discrimination claim ultimately is determined to have been without merit.

A case in point: After working several years as a loan processor for the Syra-
cuse, New York, office of the Green Tree Credit Corporation, Stephanie Quinn
complained to Green Tree's main office in St. Paul, Minnesota, that two of her
supervisors had sexually harassed her and had forced her to work in a hostile
work environment. Following a subsequent company investigation of the Syra-
cuse office, Green Tree's director of human resources informed Quinn that
no evidence had been uncovered to support her allegations. Quinn responded
by filing a formal charge of sexual harassment with the New York State Division of Human Rights. Ten days later, Green Tree fired Quinn, who then filed
a retaliation charge with the New York State agency. Quinn later filed suit
against Green Tree and her two supervisors, but the court dismissed her sexual-
harassment and hostile-environment claims on the ground that the conduct she
described as sexual harassment was insufficiently serious to support them. But
rather than dismiss Quinn's retaliation charge, the court permitted it to
proceed.

In order for Quinn to establish a claim of retaliation, she had the burden of
proving, as does any other worker who makes such allegations, the three basic elements of a retaliation case: (1) She had participated in a protected activity; (2) she was then subjected to an adverse employment action; and (3) a
causal relation existed between the protected activity and the adverse employment action. Quinn had no difficulty in establishing the second and third elements of proof. Her termination obviously was an adverse employment action,

thus satisfying the second element. The causal connection between the worker's participation in a protected activity and the employer's adverse employment action affecting that worker may in some instances, as in this case, be established through reliance upon the short time lapse between the protected activity and the adverse employment action. An elapse of only ten days between the filing of Quinn's charge with the State Division of Human Rights and the date of her firing satisfied the third element of proof. But it was with the first element of proof that the court had difficulty. When Quinn filed her sexual-harassment claim, did she have a reasonable and good-faith belief that she had been sexually harassed? If she did not, then the filing of her claim was not a protected activity, and her retaliation claim should be dismissed.

The evidence revealed that six months before Quinn had filed her claim, she had consulted with a representative of the State Division of Human Rights concerning the law as it pertained to sexual harassment. It was only after conferring with the state agency that Quinn presented the company with notice that she intended to formally charge it with sexual harassment. Although the acts of sexual harassment alleged in her charge were later held by the court as not severe enough legally to support her charge, they were not totally without substance. The record disclosed that one of her supervisors had told Quinn that she had been voted the "sleekest ass" in the office and that on another occasion he had deliberately touched her breasts with some papers he was holding in his hand. Although this evidence may have been insufficient to legally establish a sexual-harassment claim, the court nevertheless believed that it might have been adequate to persuade Quinn at the time that she had been subjected to acts of sexual harassment:

> To prove that the filing of her particular complaint with the [New York State agency] . . . was a protected activity, Quinn need not establish that she successfully described in that complaint conduct amounting to a violation of Title VII. . . . She need only demonstrate that she had a "good faith, reasonable belief that the underlying challenged actions of the employer violated the law." Thus, it is possible for an employee to reasonably believe that specified conduct amounts to harassment, even when that conduct would not actually qualify as harassment under the law. . . . Though we [hold] that Quinn has failed to adduce facts sufficient to establish Green Tree's liability for sexual harassment, we are satisfied that her complaints of sexual harassment . . . included evidence sufficient to sustain a good faith, reasonable belief that Green Tree stood in violation of the law. [9]

The filing of a discrimination charge with the New York State Division of Human Rights was a protected activity, even though Quinn's sexual-harassment claim ultimately was dismissed. Because her claim was not without substance, and because she had consulted a representative of the state agency charged with administering state laws barring sexual harassment, Quinn could very well have formed a good-faith, reasonable belief that the conduct she experienced amounted to sexual harassment. Although Green Tree was guilty neither of sexual harassment nor of maintaining a hostile work environment, it neverthe-less had to answer for its conduct in discharging Quinn after she engaged in a protected activity.[10]

In my book *Age Discrimination in the American Workplace: Old at a Young Age*, I relate the story of one of my clients who charged her employer with age and sex discrimination, as well as retaliation. Her case aptly illustrates the difficulties employers create for themselves when they unreasonably react to a worker's charge of discriminatory conduct. Since her case eventually was settled pursuant to terms that bar discussion of its details, I use fictitious names in telling her story.

I doubt that I have ever had a more difficult client than Barbara Jones. She was overly critical of everyone and everything, including me and the handling of her case. She was obstinate, intransigent, and uncompromising. Nearly all of our meetings and discussions about her case ended in anger and frustra-tion. On at least four occasions, I pleaded with her to find another lawyer. Al-though she tried, she was unsuccessful in persuading any other lawyer to assume responsibility for her case. She later advised, "You are stuck with me; better make the best of it."

Jones first came to my office convinced she was about to be fired, and not long after, she indeed was terminated. We then filed suit against her former employer alleging age and sex discrimination. During her last few months on the job, Jones felt that both age and sex bias had undermined her employer's decisions affecting her status as an employee. Initially, I evaluated her claims of discrimination as rather weak, but sufficient evidence was on hand to jus-tify proceeding with the case, at least through the initial stages of the litiga-tion. If we were unable to develop more compelling evidence of either age or sex discrimination, we might have to withdraw the case or suffer a court-ordered dismissal. As we proceeded to gather evidence, the likelihood of prov-ing either type of discrimination grew increasingly more problematic. But in addition to age and sex discrimination, we also had charged Jones's employer with retaliation, claiming that her supervisor had deliberately undermined her status with the company after she filed discrimination charges with the EEOC. Evidence supporting the retaliation charge began to mount.

Of course, charging an employer with retaliation is one thing; proving it is another. As we saw in the *Quinn v. Green Tree* case, the complainant is required to prove a causal connection between her participation in a protected activity and the adverse or allegedly retaliatory action affecting her employment. A causal connection may be demonstrated through indirect evidence, such as the close proximity in time between the worker's participation in the protected activity and the employer's adverse employment action, and also through a sudden change in an employer's attitude toward the worker. Similarly, a pattern of employer conduct, such as continuous harassment of the worker, may prove adequate for this purpose.[11]

Jones's employer argued that her termination occurred as a result, not of any discriminatory conduct on its part, but of interpersonal problems Jones had with her co-workers and supervisors. She was described as generally uncooperative, insubordinate, overly opinionated, and argumentative and was portrayed as creating such a disruptive force in the office as to require her termination. My own experience with Jones suggested that this description was not wholly unwarranted, and that many of Jones's problems may have been of her own making. Apparently, a host of Jones's former co-workers was prepared to testify on the employer's behalf and against her at the forthcoming trial. Since Jones's claims of age and sex discrimination were not developing as we had hoped, we decided to shift gears and focus our efforts on proving the retaliation charge.

Unlike most workers subjected to discriminatory conduct, Jones had filed a discrimination charge with the EEOC *before, not after*, her employment was terminated. Many workers delay filing until after they have been fired, but in almost all cases, that is a mistake. Understandably, a worker has no desire to alienate an employer by filing a discrimination charge, as, guilty or not, an employer will almost always react negatively. Thus, the charge itself may precipitate additional discriminatory and adverse actions against the worker. But on occasion, the filing of a charge may generate positive results. In a large company, it may alert upper management to the existence of discriminatory conduct among lower- and middle-management employees that upper management finds reprehensible. Then again, an employer bent on discriminating against a worker may suddenly desist from such conduct upon realizing that continued adverse treatment of the worker may result in an additional charge of retaliation. Although Jones realized none of these benefits, filing a charge prior to her termination had been an astute move, and she was about to reap its benefits.

In accordance with EEOC procedure, a short time after Jones filed her charge, her employer was advised of the details of her discrimination claim. Two weeks later, Jones suffered the first in a series of adverse actions by her employer. The layout of the office in which she and other employees worked consisted of parallel rows of cubicles, each randomly assigned cubicle just large enough for a desk and chair. The cubicle walls were little more than waist high, affording little privacy. Jones's supervisor occupied one of the front cubicles, and Jones sat in one in the rear. Now, the seating arrangement was changed. Her supervisor moved to a rear cubicle, and he assigned Jones to a cubicle immediately in front of his, which allowed him to monitor her daily activities. As the company's most senior worker, Jones was humiliated in the presence of her co-workers when her supervisor daily peered over her shoulder and recorded her every move. It was apparent that after Jones filed the EEOC charge, the decision had been made to fire her, and the change in seating arrangement facilitated the gathering of evidence to support her forthcoming discharge.

After scrutinizing her work for nearly two months, Jones's supervisor issued her a warning notice, citing three incidents of "improper conduct demonstrating a lack of responsibility." All three incidents were based upon false premises, as Jones was able to demonstrate. In fact, while preparing a response to the warning notice, Jones learned that a fellow worker had witnessed one of the cited incidents and had confirmed the falsity of the supervisor's account.

Not long after, Jones received a "marginal" rating on her annual performance evaluation. Her supervisor had manipulated the evaluation to support the allegations asserted in the warning notice and had recognized none of Jones's achievements during the previous year. A few weeks later, as Jones was entering the cubicle area, she accidentally brushed against her supervisor, who was sitting in his cubicle. He accused her of assaulting him. Jones, at least a foot shorter and 150 pounds lighter, was no match for him and, although the accusation obviously was spurious, he fired Jones the following day.

Once these facts were assembled, a clear picture of retaliation emerged. The three basic elements of a retaliation claim were present. After Jones had engaged in a protected activity—the filing of a discrimination charge with the EEOC—her employer had taken adverse employment actions against her. The causal connection was apparent in the close proximity in time between her filing and the first adverse action taken against her. In addition, the sudden change in her employer's attitude toward her—her personality idiosyncrasies, if not applauded, had at least been tolerated—as well as its subsequent pattern of adverse conduct, provided us with proof of a causal connection between the filing of the EEOC charge and the ensuing adverse actions, including her termination.

Ultimately, Jones's case was settled for a figure equal to more than seven years' salary—a sum far in excess of my original evaluation of her case. The strength of the retaliation charge was a significant factor in the employer's decision to settle the case rather than to proceed to trial. If the case had not been settled, we might well have met defeat on the age and sex discrimination charges, but the retaliation charge appeared solid. The employer was unwilling to let a jury decide that issue.

The reaction of many employers to charges of discrimination does not vary much from their responses to charges of fraud, theft, or other criminal activity. Employers are all too prone to strike back at any worker who even utters the word "discrimination." This is particularly true in sexual-harassment cases. Once a supervisor is accused of acts of sexual harassment, he is likely to make life extremely difficult for the victim of his harassment.

In Margaret Toscano's sexual-harassment claim against the Veterans Administration (see chapter 14), Toscano was one of a number of applicants for promotion to an administrative position at a Veterans Administration Hospital, but the applicant eventually selected for the position was having a sexual affair with the supervisor who had been assigned to choose the candidate for promotion. When Toscano complained that the selection had been made on the basis of sexual favors, she was told that no one was interested in her complaint and that she should stop "rocking the boat." The supervisor who had made the promotion decision then started to treat Toscano differently. He halted the daily briefing he had customarily given her and altered her job assignments, thus making it significantly more difficult for her to perform her job functions properly. He also deliberately participated in conduct intended to create the false impression among Toscano's co-workers that she was engaged in an affair with him. The court recognized the supervisor's conduct as retaliatory and ruled accordingly.[12]

In some sexual-harassment cases the retaliatory conduct takes the form of continued and intensifed harassment. Judy Morris, an employee of the Oldham County Road Department in Kentucky, accused her supervisor, Brent Likins, of engaging in sexually harassing conduct. After Morris complained of his conduct, the department transferred Likins and directed him not to communicate with Morris unless a third party was present. Despite this directive, Likins continually telephoned Morris solely, as she alleged, to sexually harass her. Morris also claimed that Likins drove to her work site on several occasions and sat in his car outside her building, staring at Morris's window and making faces at her. On one occasion, he allegedly followed Morris home from work, pulled alongside her mailbox, and "gave her the finger." Morris also claimed that Likins destroyed the television set in her office and on several occasions threw roofing nails on her driveway. The court concluded that Likins's ongoing harassing conduct clearly was retaliatory.[13]

Every action adverse to an employee does not necessarily rise to the level of retaliation. For example, a change in work hours or the assignment of additional or new responsibilities may change working conditions only minimally. Title VII was not designed to address every decision that arguably might have some tangential effect upon the worker's conditions of employment.[14]

Finally, an employer may be held liable for retaliatory acts even after the employment relationship has been terminated.[15] An employer who issues a negative and unwarranted adverse job reference for an ex-worker who had engaged in a protected activity may find itself liable for damages if the negative reference causes the worker to lose a job opportunity.

Seventeen

Proving Sex Discrimination in Court

Proving that an employer *intended* to discriminate against a female worker is critical to establishing liability for sex discrimination (except in disparate impact cases, discussed later in this chapter). The worker's lawyer must produce evidence sufficient to prove that gender was a determining factor in the employer's decision that adversely affected his client—not necessarily the only factor, but a factor that made a difference in the employer's decision.

Proving an employer's discriminatory intent is never easy. Employers have learned to mask acts of employment discrimination with the appearance of business propriety. As the Supreme Court has observed, employers neither admit discriminatory animus nor leave a paper trail disclosing it. Thus, few employment discrimination cases turn on direct or "smoking gun" evidence of sex bias. Employers do not place memoranda in their files that openly admit to an employment decision based on a worker's gender. Even the least sophisticated of employers is careful not to leave a trail of discriminatory conduct, and it would be rare indeed for a corporate executive to take the witness stand and freely affirm he acted adversely to the interests of a female worker solely because of her gender.[1]

Employment discrimination suits involve numerous complex procedures that make establishing a case difficult, since they allow employers to create barriers that block or divert plaintiff workers from achieving their litigation goals. In addition, these procedures do not readily lend themselves to resolving employment discrimination cases. The complexities of corporate decision making often cannot be adequately analyzed in the adversarial framework of the courtroom. But the litigation process nevertheless insists on an either/or explanation—a discriminatory motive either was or was not the basis of a particular employment decision. Moreover, in employment discrimination litigation, "unambiguous villains and victims are increasingly more difficult to identify."[2] How then does a sex discrimination complainant—while avoiding employer-initiated barriers and contending with unwieldy legal procedures— prove that a discriminatory intent, rather than a legitimate business reason, motivated an employment decision that adversely affected her employment status?

Direct Evidence of Discrimination

The legal procedures used in proving sexual-harassment claims often vary from those used in proving other types of sex discrimination cases. The elements of proof required in a sexual-harassment case are more closely allied with those common to other types of litigation, such as those involving tort claims. The claimant in a tort case must prove she suffered an injury or damages directly as the result of the negligent or deliberate act of the defendant, or as a consequence of the defendant's failure to act in circumstances in which the law requires him to act. The claimant in a sexual-harassment case generally establishes her case by proving she suffered an injury or damages directly as the result of a sexual act—unlawful under the precepts of Title VII— committed by the defendant in the workplace. The complainant nearly always relies solely upon direct evidence in proving she was the victim of sexually harassing conduct.

Unlike sexual harassment cases, direct evidence of sex discrimination, more often than not, is unavailable to the plaintiff. Due to current legal and social sanctions, people generally repress demonstrations of overt sexism and bias. Thus, even if an employer is aware of his own gender bias, he is unlikely to express it openly. Even if fellow workers were to observe discriminatory acts committed by their employer, and thus could offer the court direct evidence of those acts, they may be reluctant to come forward to testify on behalf of the complainant for fear of jeopardizing their own careers.[3] As a result, cases that turn on direct evidence of sex discrimination are the exception. Debbie Moore's sex discrimination case against Alabama State University was one of the exceptions.

After Moore had worked in the university's admissions office for eight years, the university promoted her to admissions staff assistant, second in command to the director. Later, when the position of admissions office director became vacant, Roosevelt Steptoe, the university's vice president of academic affairs, asked Moore to assume increased responsibilities, and for a time she shared the duties of the admission office director's position with another employee.

Moore had every expectation that she would be awarded with further promotion, and she eagerly awaited advancement to admissions director. Her application for the director's position, however, was rejected by a committee appointed to screen and interview candidates. Moore alleged that Steptoe's bias against women led him to interfere with the application process, thus undermining her candidacy.

Steptoe played a major role in the university's hiring process; he appointed the committee that screened and interviewed applicants for the director's position, and after receiving the committee's recommendations, he made the final decision. Moore focused on two incidents she claimed epitomized Steptoe's bias against female workers. While walking across campus on one occasion, Moore was confronted by Steptoe who, noticing Moore's pregnant condition, commented, "I was going to put you in charge of that office, but look at you now." Later, Steptoe told Moore he would not consider her for the director's position because she was married with a child, the director's job entailed far too much traveling for a married mother, and, in any event, a woman should stay home with her family.

Moore sued the university for sex discrimination. The primary trial issue focused on Steptoe's comments regarding Moore's pregnancy and her duties as a mother. Did these comments constitute direct evidence of a discriminatory bias against Moore? For statements of this type to be considered direct evidence of discrimination, the law requires that the plaintiff demonstrate that the comments are capable of only one interpretation—that they reflect a discriminatory attitude correlating to the discrimination complained of—and that they were made by a person involved in an employment decision affecting the worker. The court ruled that Steptoe's comments did indeed qualify as direct evidence of discrimination. The comments were made by an official with decision-making authority, neither statement was subject to multiple interpretation, and "neither required any leap of logic or inference" to conclude that an act of discrimination had occurred.[4]

Remarks based on sex stereotypes like those expressed by Steptoe may or may not—depending upon the circumstances—be considered direct evidence of sex discrimination. In one case, a supervisor, in an angry outburst that followed his detection of a deficiency in a woman's job performance, shouted that he did not want any women working in his office. Although inappropriate and illustrative of a negative view of women in general, the remark, in and of itself, was insufficient to be considered direct evidence that established a discriminatory intent regarding that particular worker.[5] In other circumstances, such a remark could very well be perceived as constituting direct evidence of a discriminatory motive.

Indirect Evidence of Discrimination

Since direct evidence of sex discrimination is often not available to assist the worker, the lawyer representing a sex discrimination claimant must search out indirect or circumstantial evidence of sex bias. Soon after enactment of Title VII, the Supreme Court established ground rules for evaluating indirect evidence of discrimination. These rules were based on the Court's observation that an employer invariably responds to a charge of discriminatory behavior with the argument that behind the employment decision that adversely affected the worker lay a legitimate, nondiscriminatory reason. If the worker establishes that the purported nondiscriminatory reason was not the employer's actual reason, or that the employer's reason simply is not credible, the court may assume that the employer proffered such a reason only to cover up an unlawful motive.[6] The Supreme Court explained why it was justified in making such an assumption: "We are willing to presume this largely because we know from our experience that more often than not people do not act in a totally arbitrary manner, without any underlying reasons, especially in a business setting. Thus when all legitimate reasons for an [employer's decision] have been eliminated as possible reasons for [its] actions, it is more likely than not the employer, who we generally assume acts only with *some* reason, based [its] decision on an impermissible consideration such as race [or gender]."[7]

Thus, the task of the worker's attorney is to prove that the employer's stated reasons for its actions were pretexts offered only to cover up discriminatory intent and that the employer has concealed its real reasons. The attorney must prove that the employer's expressed reasons are "pretextual" and were offered by the employer only to cover up its discriminatory intent.

One way to prove intentional discrimination is thus to show that an employer offered a false explanation for its decision that adversely affected the worker. A court or jury may infer from the falsity of the explanation that the employer has dissembled or misrepresented the facts to cover up a discriminatory purpose.

Once the employer's explanation, because of its falsity, is eliminated from consideration, discriminatory conduct may well be the most likely alternative explanation, especially since the employer, who is in the best position to assert the actual reason for its decision, failed to do so. Thus, a court or jury may infer the ultimate fact of discrimination from the falsity of the employer's explanation.[8] A federal appellate court has succinctly explained this rationale: "Resort to a pretextual explanation is like flight from the scene of a crime, evidence indicating consciousness of guilt, which is, of course, evidence of illegal conduct."[9] Thus, in a pretext case, the worker is required to prove that the employer has opted not to express its true reasons for acting as it did. She must prove that the employer's reasons are "pretextual," and these reasons would not have been offered by the employer except to cover up its discriminatory intent.

Many sex discrimination suits involve indirect evidence and focus on the motivation that underlies an employer's decision. Are the reasons advanced by the employer for its employment decision credible? Are they its actual reasons, or was the decision motivated by an impermissible factor, such as the worker's gender? Are the reasons asserted by the employer merely pretexts, proffered by the employer to cover up the true nature of its decision, namely, that it was discriminatory? Even if an employer's reasons did, in fact, serve as one of the bases for its decision, was the employer also motivated to make that decision because of the worker's gender? These are the issues that typically confront juries hearing sex discrimination cases.

In a case that relied upon both direct and indirect evidence, Karen Emmel sued the Coca-Cola Bottling Company of Chicago after it promoted five men to newly created upper-management positions. Because she had not been included among those promoted, Emmel charged the company with violating Title VII. Later, when Coca-Cola again passed over Emmel in a set of similar promotions, she filed a second charge of sex discrimination. The two charges eventually were litigated in a federal court, where a jury found in her favor and awarded her substantial compensatory and punitive damages. Coca-Cola then asked the court to overturn the jury verdict, and when the court refused, Coca-Cola appealed.

Here, in summary, is the evidence the appellate court reviewed. Emmel began her career at Coca-Cola as an account manager, rose to district sales manager, and then was promoted to cold drink specialist, a position that required her to maintain exclusive purchase agreements with existing accounts, develop new business, and increase the services furnished to customers. Subsequently, Coca-Cola created five upper-management positions called area development managers (ADMs). Each of the five employees promoted to ADM positions—all males—had considerably shorter careers with Coca-Cola and much less time in supervisory positions than Emmel. The following year, the company announced the creation of three upper-management "key account executive" positions, and again the three workers promoted to these positions—all males—had shorter careers with Coca-Cola and less supervisory experience than Emmel.

Emmel based her indirect evidence case on her allegations that she was far better qualified than the male workers selected for these positions. One of the men promoted to an ADM position had just over five years' experience with the company, compared to Emmel's twenty years. Another had two and one-half years of supervisory experience; Emmel had eight. In addition to longer service and more supervisory experience, Emmel, unlike some of those promoted, had a positive employment history. While Emmel had won manager-of-the-year awards, one of the promoted male workers received four disciplinary warnings during the four years prior to his promotion. Emmel had a college degree, while some of the promoted employees did not.

In response to Emmel's position, Coca-Cola asserted that it did not base the selection of the workers for promotion on length of service, supervisory experience, or college education, but rather on a selection process designed to determine who was the best person for the job, and in this process it was determined that Emmel was not the best person for any of the eight positions in question. But at the trial, the jurors rejected the company's explanation, finding that the reasons given for the selection of the male employees were not credible and thus were pretexts, either false or not the actual reasons for denying Emmel a promotion.

The appellate court agreed with the jury's finding of pretext and ruled that sufficient evidence had been offered to support it. Included in the evidence were company memoranda pertaining to the promotions that contained statements undercutting testimony given at the trial by company witnesses. The court also was influenced by the fact that the company's explanation presented at the trial for not promoting Emmel differed from the explanation given to Emmel at the time the company rejected her for promotion. The court commented: "If at the time of the adverse employment action the decision maker gave one reason, but at the time of the trial gave another reason which was not supported by documentary evidence, the jury could reasonably conclude that the new reason was a pretextual after-the-fact justification."

As noted, Emmel did not rely solely on indirect evidence. Her case was a mix of both indirect evidence of pretext and direct evidence of sex bias. Direct evidence of sex discrimination surfaced in a remark made by one of the company's vice presidents at the time of Emmel's rejection for promotion to an ADM position. He told Emmel that she had not been awarded the promotion because company officials were averse to the placement of women in upper-management positions. A number of other comments and statements of company executives, each demonstrating a bias against the elevation of women to upper management, also were received in evidence. Based on this evidence, the appellate court ruled that the jury was justified in concluding that a pervasive attitude existed among company executives that women did not belong in the company's upper echelon. Since direct evidence of sex bias as well as indirect evidence of pretext supported an outcome in Emmel's favor, the appellate court declined to overturn the jury's verdict.[10]

Pretext cases that are not buttressed by direct evidence of discrimination are likely to fail unless the evidence of pretext is clear and persuasive. Evidence that an employer treated its workers unfairly or unequally often will turn jurors against an employer, since many, if not most of them, may be reminded of episodes of unfair or unequal treatment suffered during their own work careers. Deborah Kramer produced this kind of evidence in her case against Nebraska's Logan County School District.

Kramer began her teaching career as a substitute teacher in the district and was later certified as a middle school teacher in mathematics, general science, and natural science. Subsequently, the school district assigned her to teach high school science. After she spent two years in that position, the high school principal, Mike Apple, and the school district's superintendent, John Broadbent, recommended to the school board that it not renew Kramer's contract for the following year. The school board then dismissed Kramer on the grounds that she could not get along with school administrators, that her competency was questionable in light of below-average performance evaluations, that she had failed to function as a team player, and that the school district would be better served by employing a more cooperative teacher. Kramer then filed suit against the school district, alleging she had been discriminatorily discharged because of her gender.

At the trial, Kramer offered evidence that Apple had disciplined her more severely than he had disciplined male teachers for similar conduct, and several female teachers testified they also had been treated inappropriately or unfairly because of their gender. Kramer provided the court with copies of written reprimands prepared by Apple that had been placed in her personnel file, but, in direct contravention of school policy, neither had Apple signed them nor had she received copies of them. She also produced evidence that Apple and Broadbent had materially misrepresented the facts when they informed the school board that her performance evaluations were below average, when in fact five out of six of her evaluations were rated average or better. Kramer adduced evidence that fifteen of the seventeen tenured teachers in her school had signed a letter in her support, thus rebutting the "team player" allegation, but Apple and Broadbent failed to present the letter to the school board. Kramer argued that the evidence relating to her competency and to Apple's and Broadbent's unfair treatment of her and other female teachers supported a finding that the reasons given for her dismissal were pretextual, and that Apple and Broadbent, in recommending nonrenewal of her teaching contract, had been motivated by sex bias. The jury agreed and awarded Kramer back pay and compensatory damages.[11]

Another pretext case was that of Pamela Long, an Asian American, holder of a master's degree in accounting and fluent in the Japanese language, who applied to Ringling Brothers–Barnum & Bailey for a controller's position in Japan. Long was willing to relocate to Japan and travel extensively, if necessary, and she possessed sufficient accounting experience and computer capability to perform the functions of the controller's position. Ringling, however, was unwilling to interview her. A recruiting firm later informed Long that Ringling had declined to consider her for the position because she was a woman, that Ringling thought a woman would be ineffective in the controller's position on account of the cultural bias against working women in Japan, and, moreover, that it was concerned about a woman traveling alone in a foreign country. Long filed a legal action against Ringling for sex discrimination.

Ringling hired a man for the position, but at the trial, it denied that it had specifically set out to hire a male. Ringling claimed that Long had not filed her application soon enough to be considered for the position, since insufficient time then remained to train her for the position. But evidence submitted at the trial disclosed that when Ringling received Long's application, the position was still open. In addition, Ringling's witnesses presented conflicting testimony regarding the extent of training required. One testified that a two-month training period was necessary, another that Ringling had no established period of training, and still another that a person with Long's experience would require little training. The court, sitting without a jury, ruled that in view of Long's extensive accounting experience, together with her fluency in the Japanese language, Ringling had more than sufficient time to train her if they were of a mind to. Based on the evidence, the court was persuaded that Ringling's reasons for not interviewing Long were pretextual:

> The Court believes that Ringling has articulated no more than an after-the-fact attempt to legitimize an unlawful discriminatory decision not to interview nor employ Plaintiff. . . . [The evidence] establishes, in the opinion of this Court, that Ringling wanted a male and that Plaintiff was rejected because she was a woman. . . . Having rejected Ringling's proffered reason for not interviewing nor hiring Plaintiff, the Court reaches the ultimate conclusion that Ringling's decisions were motivated by intentional discriminatory considerations, and that Plaintiff did prove by a preponderance of the evidence that Ringling intentionally discriminated against her because of her sex/gender.[12]

In another case, a female worker was allegedly terminated for insubordination and absenteeism, but these were not the reasons given her at the time. In fact, not until an unemployment compensation hearing several months after the worker's discharge did the employer mention the insubordination and absenteeism allegations. When the employer again asserted them at the trial of the worker's sex discrimination case, the court noted that since these were not the reasons provided the worker at the time of her dismissal, they were of doubtful authenticity, and the circumstances suggested that they were fabricated after the fact to justify a decision made on other grounds. Based on these and other facts, the court ruled that the reasons given for the worker's discharge were pretextual, and it awarded judgment in favor of the worker.[13]

A fairly high proportion of pretext cases are dismissed at the summary judgment stage of the litigation or after trial, as was true for Jan Johnson, a resident physician at the Baptist Medical Center in Kansas City, Missouri. Her attending physician, or supervisor, was Lawrence Rues, an associate director of the hospital's family care center. After Johnson had been in the residency program for a year and a half, the hospital informed her that she had failed to meet its minimum standards of acceptable performance, and it presented her with the choice of termination or resignation. Johnson chose to resign, and then sued the hospital for sex discrimination.

Baptist Medical furnished the court with substantial evidence of its displeasure with Johnson's performance. Her evaluation forms for the most part disclosed "needs much improvement" ratings, and recorded faculty comments touched on her weak knowledge base and inability to diagnose and manage patients. Johnson attributed her low marks to Rues and other faculty members she claimed harbored a discriminatory animus toward women. She characterized Rues as "intimidating, abusive, and judgmental" in dealing with her and other female residents, but as "patient and understanding" when dealing with male residents. Johnson also claimed that certain male residents with performance evaluations similar to hers were not asked to leave the program. The evidence revealed, however, that these male residents had fewer unfavorable evaluations than she. Johnson's support for her other allegations was largely hearsay, and she could offer the court little other probative evidence in support of her positions. Johnson thus was unable to establish a case of pretext, and her case was dismissed.[14]

Pretext appears in myriad forms and is often detected only through the vigilance of the affected worker. Because she is better informed than anyone else regarding the particulars of her own job, she generally is in the best position to evaluate the accuracy and truthfulness of the reasons advanced by her employer to justify its adverse employment decision. Her ability to root out the facts underlying the employer's decision often determines whether a pretext case will succeed or fail.

Disparate Impact

Nearly all of the cases reviewed in this book fall into a category of discrimination lawsuits known as "disparate treatment" cases.[15] "Disparate treatment" refers to an employer policy or practice that treats some workers less favorably than others, sometimes because of their gender. A classic example of a disparate treatment case involved the termination of the Nebraska schoolteacher discussed earlier in this chapter. In *Kramer,* the schoolteacher alleged that her principal had disciplined her more severely than male teachers, and other female teachers testified they had been treated inappropriately or unfairly because of their gender. Unequal treatment and disparate treatment are synonymous, and disparate treatment is the most common form of employment discrimination. The disparate treatment of male and female workers underlies a large proportion of sex discrimination cases.

"Disparate impact," as distinguished from "disparate treatment," comes into play in a sex discrimination case when an employment policy or practice that appears on its face to be neutral or nondiscriminatory falls more harshly upon women than upon men. Employment decisions or practices that appear to be fair in form but are discriminatory in practice disparately impact female workers.

Workers who rely on the disparate impact approach to proving discrimination are generally trying to eliminate employment policies or practices that create barriers to job opportunities and advancement or in some other fashion seriously disadvantage women. As an example, an employer, in connection with certain jobs, may establish height and weight requirements that disproportionately disqualify women from consideration and thus disparately impact female applicants for those positions.

In disparate impact cases, an employment policy or practice may have been adopted without a deliberately discriminatory motive, but it may nevertheless constitute the functional equivalent of an act of intentional discrimination. As one court explained it: "In essence, the disparate impact theory is a doctrinal surrogate for eliminating unprovable acts of intentional discrimination hidden innocuously behind facially neutral policies or practices."[16]

Female workers who rely on the disparate impact approach are not required to prove that the employer was motivated by a discriminatory purpose in initiating or implementing the targeted policies or practices. The motivation of the employer is irrelevant to the outcome of this type of case. If the workers can establish that an employment policy disproportionately affects women because of their gender, the employer must show, if it hopes to prevail, that the policy is essential to its business needs. But even if it is essential, the workers may nonetheless carry the day if they can show that the employer has available to it other policies that it could implement, if it wished, that would impact female workers less disadvantageously.

A plaintiff alleging disparate impact in an employer's hiring practices must establish three elements:

1. A significant disparity exists between the proportion of women available for a particular position and the number of women hired for that position.
2. The employer has in place a specific, facially neutral employment practice that affects the rate of hiring women.
3. A causal nexus exists between the employment practice and the disparity.

Once the plaintiff worker has established these three elements, the employer may attempt to justify the challenged practice by showing that it serves a legitimate, nondiscriminatory business objective. But as noted, even if the employer succeeds in establishing such a business need, the worker may still prevail by showing that another employment practice, impacting women less harshly, is available to the employer to satisfy its business objectives.

The disparate impact approach to proving sex discrimination is most often used in broad-based class actions and in connection with EEOC litigation initiated on behalf of a large number of complainants. Nevertheless, an individual worker complainant and her attorney must remain alert to the possibility of taking this approach when circumstances warrant. This is particularly the case when it may not be possible to prove that an employer has intentionally engaged in acts of discrimination.

Employer Defenses

Although a vast number of defenses are available to employers contesting worker claims of sex discrimination, employers assert certain defenses with some regularity, and we will examine two of them, each of questionable validity.

Suppose a female worker is terminated but replaced by another woman. Is she foreclosed from proving that her employer was guilty of sex discrimination by reason of the fact that she was replaced by a woman and not a man? Numerous employers have asserted this defense, usually with little success. Even when a woman is fired and replaced by another woman, she may have been treated differently from her male co-workers. Her employer may have terminated her on account of a single lapse in performance, while it may afford a man working at her side far greater latitude before reaching the stage of dismissal. In these circumstances, who replaces a female worker is largely irrelevant. Thus, even when a female worker cannot claim that her employer replaced her with a man, she may still allege that her employer treated her less favorably because of her gender. That her replacement is a woman demonstrates the employer's willingness to hire women but does not support the employer's claim that the decision to fire the worker was made without discriminatory intent, or that the employer does not discriminate against women in other workplace matters.[17]

Let us take this a step further. An employer discharges a female worker and replaces her with another woman. Moreover, the person who made the decision to fire the worker also is a woman. May the fired women assert a valid Title VII claim? This was the situation Dawn Veatch confronted when she sued her employer, the Northwestern Memorial Hospital in Chicago. Veatch alleged that after sixteen years with the hospital, she was summarily discharged by her supervisor, a woman. The hospital maintained that Veatch should be barred from continuing with her legal action, as she could not assert a valid claim of sex discrimination because a woman made the decision to terminate her and her replacement also was a woman. The court rejected the hospital's position on the ground that the mere fact that one woman fired another does not prove that the decision to fire was free of sex discrimination. The court expanded on that view: "When power and status are distributed unevenly, administrators may sometimes view members of some groups as more easily expendable than others—either because of some misplaced notion of inferiority or because some groups with less power cannot protest adverse treatment as effectively." Thus, a supervisor, man or woman, may discern that a decision that adversely affects a female employee may spawn less opposition and create less friction in the workplace than a decision that adversely affects a male employee. Moreover, a female supervisor working in an institution dominated by males may feel extra pressure not to be soft on female subordinates, and this pressure may motivate her to act less favorably toward female workers. Therefore, the mere fact that Veatch was fired and replaced by a woman did not legally bar her from proceeding with her case.[18]

Another strategy, the "same actor" defense, has recently gained popularity with employers in cases where the same person who hired a female worker later fires her. It is based on the rationale that if the same person both hired and fired a worker, it is unrealistic to assume that discriminatory intent was absent at the time of the decision to hire but present at the time of the decision to fire. As one court observed, from the viewpoint of the employer, "it hardly makes sense to hire workers from a group one dislikes . . . only to fire them once they are on the job." The court then established the following rule: "In cases where the hirer and the firer are the same individual and termination of employment occurs within a relatively short time span following the hiring, a strong inference exists that discrimination was not a determining factor for the adverse action taken by the employer."[19]

A case in point involved Evelyn Sasmor, a senior vice president at Harcourt, Brace & Company, who hired Mary Bradley as an information services manager. Approximately one year later, Sasmor terminated Bradley, allegedly because of performance problems. Bradley later claimed in her sex discrimination case against Harcourt, Brace that Sasmor's real reason for terminating her was that she wanted to give Bradley's position to a man. The court was dubious; if Sasmor had preferred a man in the position, why did she not hire a man in the first instance? Bradley attempted to buttress her case by offering evidence that Sasmor appeared to favor Bradley's subordinate, Tom Jackson, but the court was of the opinion that Sasmor's favoritism of Jackson stemmed from his competence, particularly in light of Sasmor's negative view of Bradley's performance. The court then applied the same-actor defense, holding that where the same actor is responsible for both the hiring and the firing of a discrimination plaintiff, and the actions occur within a short period of time, a strong inference arises that there was no discriminatory motive involved in the decision to fire the plaintiff. The court dismissed Bradley's case.[20]

The same-actor defense has its limitations. In the *Bradley* case, if Sasmor hired Bradley with the intention of firing her as soon as she was able to groom Jackson for the position, application of the same-actor defense would lead to an injustice. If an employer hires a woman in the belief that she will comply with certain sex-based stereotypes relating to a woman's role in the workplace, and later fires her because she declines to comply with those stereotypes, the same-actor defense should not be a factor in the case.

When applying the same-actor defense, the length of time between the hiring and the firing affects the strength of the inference that may be drawn that discrimination was not a factor in the worker's discharge. Over a period of time, an employer may develop an animus or bias that did not exist when its hiring decision was made.[21] On the other hand, an employer who is of a mind to treat male and female workers equally is less likely to change, regardless of the passage of time. Whenever the same-actor defense is asserted, all the underlying facts must be explored before any inferences may properly be drawn.

Eighteen

Compensatory and Punitive Damages

In determining the amount of monetary damages a victim of sex discrimination may recover, the courts apply a fundamental principle common to all employment discrimination cases: The worker who proves she has been discriminated against is entitled to be made "whole." That is, a worker is entitled to be placed in the circumstances she would have been in if her employer had not discriminated against her. Despite the near universal acceptance of the "make whole" standard of relief, the remedies available to female workers for the discriminatory conduct of their employers fall short of that standard in two material respects: A woman may be denied full recovery of the punitive and compensatory damages awarded her by a jury, and, in certain instances, she may even be denied all damages.

Before 1991, Title VII did not specifically authorize the recovery of damages for pain and suffering, commonly referred to as "compensatory damages." The statute also failed to provide for the recovery of punitive damages. Although the remedies provisions of Title VII were broadly stated, almost all federal courts relied on the absence in the statute of any specifically stated provisions for the recovery of either compensatory or punitive damages to deny women recovery of those damages. In sexual-harassment cases, where the primary damages suffered by the victims of the harassment nearly always are of a compensatory and punitive nature, the harassed victims were effectively left without a remedy. Workers who sued their employers for race or national origin discrimination were able to rely on statutes other than Title VII to recover compensatory and punitive damages.[1]

In 1991, Congress admitted its original error and amended Title VII to provide specifically for the recovery of compensatory and punitive damages. Unfortunately, the amendment failed to resolve the issue completely. As a concession to the business community, Congress included in the amendment an adjustable scale of upper limits on the combined amounts of compensatory and punitive damages that are recoverable by a successful litigant. The upper limit, or cap, ranges from $50,000 for small employers with between fifteen and one hundred employees, to $300,000 for employers with more than five hundred employees.[2] Thus, the recovery of compensatory and punitive damages remains limited under Title VII for employment discrimination litigants.

The statutory limitation has proved especially troublesome where a jury finds the conduct of a defendant employer to have been particularly outrageous, as was the case with Connie Reynolds's employer. One of only two female account executives employed by Octel Communications, Reynolds was the only female account executive working in its Dallas office when Octel terminated her after six years of employment. Based on these facts and other evidence that clearly demonstrated a discriminatory bias against women, a jury determined that the company had dismissed Reynolds because of her gender, and it awarded her $150,000 in back-pay damages, $162,000 in front-pay damages, $800,000 in compensatory damages, and $2.5 million in punitive damages. The total award amounted to $3,612,000, but because of the statutory limitation on compensatory and punitive damages, the court was required to reduce the $800,000 compensatory-damages award and the $2.5 million punitive-damages award to a total of $300,000. Thus, instead of the $3,612,000 in damages that the jury determined appropriate, Reynolds ultimately recovered only $612,000. Three million dollars evaporated with the application of the statutory cap.[3]

In another case where the court applied the cap, Mary Ann Luciano sued her employer, the Olsten Corporation, for sex discrimination after three of Olsten's senior vice presidents, adamantly opposed to Luciano's forthcoming promotion to vice president, formulated a new job description for her, incorporating duties in the description upon which she would be evaluated prior to promotion (see chapter 1). They devised a job description designed to ensure an unsatisfactory performance evaluation. Still not satisfied, they later increased Luciano's job responsibilities, while withholding the support staff she required to perform the additional duties.

At the conclusion of the trial of Luciano's sex discrimination case against Olsten, the jury found that the discriminatory conduct engaged in by Olsten officials warranted a substantial award of punitive damages. Allowing for the company's size and wealth, the jury determined that an award of $5,000,002 was adequate to punish Olsten for its conduct and also sufficiently large to deter it from engaging in such conduct in the future. In light of the evidence submitted in support of Luciano's claim that the three senior vice presidents deliberately undermined her position with the company solely to prevent her elevation to vice president, the amount of the punitive-damages award was fully justified. But the court was required by the statutory limitation to reduce the award of more than $5 million to a mere $300,000, a sum hardly sufficient either to punish Olsten for its conduct or to deter its repetition.[4]

The statutory limitation on compensatory- and punitive-damage awards persists as only one of several barriers that successful sex discrimination complainants confront in striving to obtain adequate monetary recoveries. In addition to the statutory obstructions to complete relief, the courts frequently create barriers of their own. Although judges are required to respect juries' damages awards, they are not required to accept them. Judges must ascertain whether the evidence admitted in the case supports the jury's award, and if it does not, they may either reduce the award to that which they consider supportable by the evidence or order a new trial on damages.

The criteria governing a trial judge's evaluation of a jury award have been articulated from a number of perspectives. A jury award should stand without change unless grossly excessive, bearing no rational relationship to the evidence. It should stand unless a miscarriage of justice would result if the court were to fail to intercede. It should stand unless the amount of the award shocks one's conscience and cries out to be overturned. It should stand unless it appears to be so excessive as to suggest that the jury was motivated by passion or prejudice rather than by a reasoned assessment of the evidence presented at the trial.

A judge should refrain from wholly usurping the jury's function in assessing damages and should in all instances uphold a jury's award, provided a reasonable basis exists for the amount awarded. Moreover, a judge may not overturn an award merely because the judge would have granted a lesser amount if the trial had been conducted without a jury. A judge's mere belief or opinion that the jury was unduly generous is insufficient to warrant intercession.

On balance, the application of these standards by the courts has worked in favor of employers and contrary to the interests of worker claimants. Too often, a court's position on damages appears more closely allied with that espoused by the business community. In some instances, judges have appeared unable to relate to common workplace problems, and, court decisions therefore at times appear to be totally divorced from workplace reality. As a result, large jury awards in favor of discrimination claimants are frequently overturned or reduced by the courts. Where a jury decides on a substantial award of compensatory or punitive damages, the claimant should anticipate that the trial and appellate courts will scrutinize it closely.

Although in many instances a court-reduced jury award may not be warranted, on occasion it is clearly justified, as in the case of Tammy Blakey. An airline pilot, Blakey was the first female assigned by Continental Airlines to captain an A300 Airbus aircraft. Later in her employment, Blakey charged Continental with sexual harassment, claiming that pornographic pictures had been placed in the cockpits of its aircraft and that she had been subjected to obscene and harassing comments by fellow workers. The evidence submitted at the trial supported her claim that even though she had informed Continental's managers of these occurrences, company officials had failed to take any measures either to eliminate the pornography or the obscene comments. In addition to awards of back pay and front pay, the jury awarded Blakey $500,000 in compensatory damages for the emotional distress and other pain and suffering she had experienced on the job. Continental claimed that the jury award was excessive and should be overturned.

Blakey testified to her own mental suffering and emotional distress, as did a forensic psychiatrist, testifying as an expert witness, who had reviewed her medical records but had examined her only once. He affirmed Blakey's testimony that she had suffered job-related emotional distress, but he also testified that other events in Blakey's life unrelated to her work—particularly a volatile romantic relationship—contributed to her emotional problems.

Some of Blakey's own testimony also was damaging to her case. For example, she testified she had deferred seeking psychological counseling until three years after the harassing incidents began, and this psychological counseling, when she finally received it, alleviated the symptoms of anxiety and depression she had attributed to the harassing conduct of her co-workers. Although Blakey's treating psychologist also was present in the courtroom during the trial, for some reason not made known to the court, she was not called upon to testify on Blakey's behalf. The trial judge, upon reviewing the evidence in light of the jury's damage award, commented, "This is not the kind of evidence that $500,000 awards are made of."

The evidence tended to show that Blakey's mental suffering and emotional distress were less severe than she claimed, and her mental condition had not occurred entirely as the result of the incidences of sexual harassment. The court concluded that the jury award of $500,000 was grossly excessive and so disproportionate to the emotional distress suffered by Blakey "as to shock the judicial conscience and constitute a manifest injustice." The judge then reduced the compensatory-damages award to $250,000.[5]

The court also intervened when a jury returned a verdict in favor of Shirley

Hughes in her sex discrimination case against the University of Colorado and awarded her compensatory damages. Hughes had worked for the university as director of auxiliary services, but following a budget-reduction process, the university eliminated her position and assigned her to another job, thereby effecting a material reduction in her responsibilities. The evidence submitted at the trial disclosed that the university's actions were discriminatory. The jury subsequently determined that Hughes should be awarded $125,000 to compensate her for the emotional distress and mental anguish she suffered as a consequence of the university's conduct. The university argued that this award was excessive and contrary to reason.

The jury's compensatory-damages award was based solely on Hughes's word, as she did not offer any medical testimony supporting her mental suffering claim. She testified that during the budget-reduction process her supervisor informed her that the university had "no need for her skills," and that as a result she felt devastated and humiliated. She also testified that she believed her supervisor was trying to get rid of her and that her future career plans with the university had been destroyed. She conceded, however, that she had not found it necessary to seek psychological treatment for the emotional problems that ensued. Although the court ruled that the jury had not erred in believing that Hughes had suffered substantial mental distress and anxiety as a consequence of the university's conduct, it decided that the amount of the jury's compensatory-damages award was excessive, and that $50,000 would sufficiently compensate Hughes for her suffering.[6]

Both the *Blakey* and the *Hughes* rulings reflect the concern of federal court judges that employers be afforded adequate protection from overgenerous juries. In both cases, persuasive testimony of serious emotional distress and anxiety was missing from the record. The two decisions reflect judicial skepticism toward emotional distress claims that are unsupported by psychiatric or psychological evaluation and prognosis.

Even with the statutory limitations, a recovery of punitive damages may significantly increase the amount a successful discrimination litigant may reasonably expect to be awarded, particularly in sexual-harassment litigation. The standard to be applied in determining whether punitive damages should be awarded was established by Congress in the 1991 amendment to Title VII. Punitive damages may be awarded to a worker when the defendant employer has acted "with malice or with reckless indifference to the federally protected rights" of its workers.[7] Stated more simply, an employer may be held accountable to its workers for punitive damages if it has acted maliciously or without any concern for the law—that is, for the anti-discrimination protections afforded employees by Title VII. But the Supreme Court later pulled the rug from beneath the 1991 amendment. It limited an employer's liability for punitive damages when it ruled that an employer who has exercised good-faith efforts to comply with the provisions of Title VII may not be held liable for punitive awards assessed in connection with the discriminatory conduct of one of its supervisory employees.[8] Thus, even if a supervisor sexually harasses a young female worker, acting maliciously and without any regard for the law, the worker may be barred from recovering any monetary damages if her employer can prove that it exercised good faith in complying with Title VII. The court's ruling stands the 1991 amendment on its head.

Among cases in which punitive- and compensatory-damage awards have played a major role is one that involved Martin Greenstein, a partner in the Baker & McKenzie law firm, who worked in its Chicago office for many years. In 1987, a secretary in that office complained to the firm's director of administration that Greenstein had sexually harassed her, and she threatened legal action against the firm. After her allegations were reported to the chair of the Chicago office, he prepared a memorandum relating to the secretary's accusations but inexplicably failed to arrange for a copy to be placed in Greenstein's personnel file.

The following year, one of the firm's young female attorneys reported several incidents of sexual harassment by Greenstein. At the time, no investigation was undertaken, but a memorandum outlining the accusations was prepared, and although a copy was placed in the file of the complaining female attorney, again, none was inserted in Greenstein's file.

Later, Greenstein transferred to the firm's office in Palo Alto, California. On five separate occasions during the ensuing three years, female staff members complained of various acts of sexual harassment by Greenstein. Although on each occasion the accusations were reported to Greenstein's superiors, he was not disciplined for any of the charges levied against him.

Rena Weeks began working as Greenstein's secretary in the summer of 1991. Three weeks after being hired, Weeks had lunch with several employees, including Greenstein, at a local restaurant. As they left the restaurant, Greenstein gave Weeks some M&M candies, which she placed in her blouse pocket. As they walked to their car, Greenstein put his arm over Weeks's shoulder, put his hand in her blouse pocket, and dropped more candies in. He then placed his knee in her lower back, pulled her shoulders back, and said, "Let's see which breast is bigger." On another occasion, Weeks unintentionally ran into Greenstein as he was carrying a box through the office. After putting the box down, Greenstein lunged toward Weeks with his hands cupped. When she moved back, crossing her hands over her chest, he asked her if she was afraid that he was about to grab her. On another occasion he did grab her—but this time it was her buttocks, not her breasts. At that point, Weeks reported Greenstein's conduct to the manager of the Palo Alto office. A copy of the office manager's notes of her conversation with Weeks was placed in Weeks's personnel file but not in Greenstein's. The firm then assigned Weeks to work for another attorney, but a few weeks later she resigned from the firm.

When Weeks sued Greenstein and Baker & McKenzie for sexual harassment, the jury had no difficulty in concluding that Greenstein had been guilty of sexually harassing conduct. The jury also ruled that even though Baker & McKenzie had been apprised of Greenstein's conduct on several occasions, it nevertheless continued to employ him, consciously disregarding the continuing threat of sexual abuse of its female employees. The jury awarded Weeks $50,000 in compensatory damages, to be recovered from both Greenstein and Baker & McKenzie, and also granted punitive damage awards of $225,000 against Greenstein and $6.9 million against Baker & McKenzie. The punitive-damage award against the firm was later reduced by the court to $3.5 million, but Weeks was able to recover the entire sum because she and her attorneys had based her lawsuit on violations of California's anti-discrimination law, which, unlike Title VII, does not place a cap on compensatory and punitive damages.[9]

The submission of significant evidence demonstrating that Baker & McKenzie's management knew that Greenstein posed a danger to female employees had undoubtedly persuaded the jury to grant such a huge punitive-damages award against the firm. The firm's failure to take any action to curtail Greenstein's harassing behavior only made this evidence more persuasive. When the firm's managers assigned Weeks to work for Greenstein, they had knowingly placed her in the lion's den.

If the Weeks case had been litigated in federal court under the provisions of Title VII, the jury could very well have found that Baker & McKenzie had acted "with malice or with reckless indifference to the federally protected rights" of its workers. Prior knowledge of a supervisor's predilection for sexually harassing behavior is likely to culminate in a punitive damage award against an employer. Indeed, in another case, a court ruled that an employer's unresponsiveness to complaints that one of its supervisor's conduct was rife with foul language, sexual innuendo, and sexual advances could readily lead to an inference that it had acted recklessly and without regard to the rights of its female workers, thus rendering it liable for punitive damages.[10]

In another example of the awarding of huge punitive damages, nine employees of the Lutherbrook Children's Center School, working in different capacities, complained that they had been subjected to a significant number of incidents of sexual harassment by the school's principal. Following an investigation, school officials suspended the principal for five days without pay, ordered him to submit to a psychological assessment, and placed him on three months' probation. Even after these corrective measures, several instances of inappropriate behavior involving the principal were reported. Regardless, later in the year, the school board gave the principal a satisfactory performance evaluation and an increase in salary.

After the nine workers sued the school for sexual harassment, a jury awarded them punitive damages on the ground that school officials were well aware of the principal's conduct but deferred taking appropriate corrective action. The trial record disclosed that staff members had informed the director of the school on innumerable occasions that the principal had engaged in sexually harassing conduct, but that the director and other school officials had failed to respond in an adequate manner. Furthermore, the principal's satisfactory performance evaluation and increase in compensation demonstrated the school officials' lack of remorse for the harassment and may also have persuaded the principal that he could continue such behavior without fear of meaningful punishment.

On appeal of the jury's findings, the court ruled that the jury was entitled to conclude that the incidents of sexual harassment were the "product of a long-term ostrich-like failure" on the part of the school to deal forthrightly with the principal's treatment of female employees, and that an award of punitive damages in the maximum amount allowed by the statutory cap was appropriate.[11]

In any set of circumstances where an employer's actions or practices are perceived as particularly outrageous, the jury is likely to penalize that employer by granting a worker a huge award of punitive damages. A case in point is Sandra Ortiz-Del Valle, who wanted to be a referee in the National Basketball Association. For many years, the NBA would not even consider hiring a female referee, and when Ortiz-Del Valle filed her application, NBA officials found numerous means to bar her way. They said her experience as a basketball referee was insufficient to qualify her for an NBA position, although they found male applicants with less experience qualified. They said she did not meet the physical-condition qualifications because she was somewhat overweight, although male applicants for referee positions were given an opportunity to lose weight rather than be eliminated from consideration. They said that she lacked experience refereeing National Collegiate Athletic Association men's basketball games, at a time when women were barred from refereeing them.

The jury was not persuaded that the NBA had acted in good faith in rejecting Ortiz-Del Valle's application, and it awarded her $750,000 in emotional distress damages and $7 million in punitive damages. Apparently, the jury was outraged by the evidence of sex discrimination and bias that had been presented to the court. But, as has become common in cases where juries grant large awards, the court, not nearly as outraged, reduced the emotional distress award to $20,000 and the punitive-damages award to $250,000.[12]

The jury at Jane Peckinpaugh's trial also awarded her substantial damages. Peckinpaugh was a news anchor for Channel 3 in Hartford, Connecticut. When the managers of the television station decided not to renew her contract—purportedly because the station needed to drop one of its five anchors, three of whom were female and two male—Peckinpaugh sued for sex discrimination. Evidence introduced at the trial showed that the station managers decided to drop Peckinpaugh after the three female anchors were required to audition for two anchor positions. The two male anchors were not required to participate in the auditions. Obviously, the station managers had decided to drop one of the anchors, and the departing anchor was to be selected from the group of female anchors.

At the trial of her case, Peckinpaugh testified that station executives had refused to consider pairing two women anchors, apparently because they were intent on keeping male-female teams. She also testified that several executives had told her that the station had "too many women." These executives, however, claimed that they had said that the station had "too many anchors." The jury sided with Peckinpaugh, awarding her substantial damages, including $1 million in punitive damages (later reduced to meet the statutory cap).[13]

As we have seen, jury awards of compensatory and punitive damages are often reduced by federal court judges, in some instances in accordance with the limitations established by Congress and in others on the ground that they are so excessive as to suggest that the juries responsible were motivated by passion or prejudice rather than by a reasoned assessment of the trial evidence. Damage awards based on violations of state anti-discrimination laws that contain no provision for the limitation of damages also are ruthlessly slashed by short-sighted judges to a fraction of the amounts determined appropriate by juries.

A *National Law Journal* study revealed that during 1996 and 1997 approximately 80 percent of employment-case jury verdicts of $1 million and more (verdicts that were not subject to statutory caps) were either reduced by the trial court or reversed by an appellate court. The study also found that the greater the award, the more vulnerable it was to reduction by the court. During those two years, juries awarded sixteen verdicts of more than $6 million to plaintiffs who charged discrimination, harassment, wrongful termination, or retaliation. Nine of the sixteen awards were later reduced, two were reversed, and in two cases, a reduction of the jury's award was under consideration. Only three survived the trial court intact, but two of those were on appeal, and the other had been settled.[14]

Why this dismal record? Plaintiff lawyers believe that jurors are more apt than judges to understand and relate to the problems experienced by workers. Jurors themselves may have confronted discrimination in the workplace and are thus sympathetic to the plight of those who suffer the consequences of biased employer practices and conduct. Some judges, on the other hand, appear incapable of relating to worker concerns and seem more disposed to identify with the employer.

The unfavorable attitude of the lower-court judiciary toward jury awards in employment discrimination cases appears to reflect an inclination on the part of the justices of the U.S. Supreme Court to favor the business community. In its 1988–89 term, the Supreme Court decided fourteen employment law cases, and thirteen of those cases were decided in favor of the employer. In all fourteen cases, Justices Rehnquist and Kennedy adopted positions advanced by the employer, and they were joined in thirteen of these cases by Justices White, O'Connor, and Scalia. Justices Brennan and Marshall, on the other hand, most frequently supported the worker's position. As William P. Murphy of the University of North Carolina Law School observed: "It seems obvious that the determinant in employment law cases is something other than dispassionate and objective application of neutral principles. The majority and minority were clearly marching to different drummers."[15]

When it comes to assessing appropriate awards for compensatory and punitive damages, jurors and trial court judges also appear to be marching to different drummers. Workers can only hope that our nation's judges may eventually hear the beat of those other drums.

Nineteen

Back Pay, Front Pay, and Other Remedies

Once a worker proves that her employer has subjected her to discriminatory policies or practices, the court has available to it—in addition to awards of compensatory and punitive damages—an array of remedial provisions to make the worker "whole." Shortly after enactment of Title VII, the Supreme Court established it as a duty of the trial court to apply these remedial provisions to fully effectuate the "make whole" doctrine: "[Title VII] is intended to make the victims of unlawful employment discrimination whole and . . . the attainment of this objective . . . requires that [workers] aggrieved by the consequences and effects of the unlawful practice be, so far as possible, restored to a position where they would have been were it not for the unlawful discrimination."[1]

The most common forms of court-ordered remedial relief include back pay, front pay, reinstatement, injunctive relief, and reimbursement of attorneys' fees.

Back Pay

Back pay is defined as the total loss of compensation suffered by a worker between the date of her subjection to an act of discrimination and the date of the trial of her subsequent sex discrimination suit. In a failure-to-hire claim, back pay is calculated by computing, for that period of time, the difference between what the worker would have earned if she had been hired and what she actually earned in other employment. In a failure-to-promote claim, back pay is the difference between what the worker would have earned in the new position if she had been promoted and the amount she actually earned after having been denied the promotion. In the case of a terminated worker, back pay is the loss of compensation that accrues between the worker's discharge and the trial of her discrimination claim, reduced by the compensation paid her in other employment during the same period. Each calculation entitles the worker to be awarded the amount that will place her in the economic position she would have been in had her employer not committed an act of discrimination.

Back-pay awards encompass not only lost wages, but also other benefits a worker would have received as a normal incident of her employment. As an example, an award of back pay should reflect increases in compensation the worker would have received had she not been discriminated against. In a discharge case, the court may assume that if the employer had not fired the worker, her compensation would have continued to increase at the same rate as in the past. If the worker's employment history discloses annual salary raises averaging 5 percent, that average may be used by the court in calculating the back pay award. The court, however, may elect instead to review the salary history of the worker's replacement and assume that the terminated worker would have received the same salary increases as her replacement.

Courts customarily increase the back-pay award to compensate the worker for reduced pension benefits and increased costs of health and medical benefits and life-insurance premiums. The "make whole" doctrine requires the court to examine all economic circumstances that emerge from an unlawful act of discrimination.

A worker asserting a claim for back pay must exercise reasonably diligent efforts to minimize or mitigate her damages. In the case of a terminated worker, she must try reasonably hard to secure other employment; generally, she must do everything reasonably expected of any unemployed person seeking another position. If a worker obtains a position comparable to that from which she was terminated, back pay will cease to accrue at that point. If she accepts a position that pays less than her pay in her former position, back pay will continue to accrue, but only to the extent that the new rate of compensation is less than that of the old.

An employer may initiate measures to shorten the back-pay period, such as by offering to reinstate the terminated worker. If the worker rejects the offer, the court may deny her recovery of any back pay that accrued after the date of the offer, on the ground that any continued loss of compensation will be the result of the worker's decision not to return to work, not a consequence of her employer's discriminatory conduct. But to avert the continued accrual of back pay effectively, the offer of reinstatement must be made in good faith and without conditions. A requirement that the worker abandon her sex discrimination claim or her claims for lost wages and employment benefits as a condition of the offer will render it invalid.

If at the time of the offer of reinstatement, the claimant has already obtained other employment, she may be reluctant to surrender her current position, especially if she suspects she may be subjected by her former employer to acts of hostility, retaliation, or yet more acts of discrimination. In addition, most terminated workers view offers of reinstatement negatively, as the animosity generated between worker and employer during the course of a discrimination suit often is just too great to permit the employment relationship to be readily reconstituted. Employers are well aware that workers are of this mind, and they often make offers of reinstatement with no expectation that they will be accepted. More often than not, an employer offers reinstatement with the hope that the offer will be rejected, resulting in a limitation in the back-pay damages the worker may then recover. On occasion, however, an employer who sincerely wishes to make amends for past conduct may make a good-faith, unconditional offer of reemployment, and under these circumstances, the worker must weigh the probable reduction in the amount of her back-pay award if she rejects the offer, against the workplace difficulties she may confront if she accepts it.

This dilemma confronted Jacquelyn Morris, who for three years suffered ongoing and pervasive acts of sexual harassment and resigned when her employer, American National Can Corporation, failed to take effective remedial action. After Morris filed a sexual-harassment suit, American National Can offered to reinstate her, assuring her that it would protect her from further harassment. Morris rejected the offer. At the trial of her sexual-harassment suit, Morris asked the court to award her back pay, thus requiring the court to decide whether the back-pay period ended with her rejection of the offer of reinstatement. In light of the egregious conduct to which Morris had been subjected, the court very much sympathized with her desire not to work again for American Can, but the court also was satisfied that the company was sincere in its position that it was prepared to protect Morris from any further harassment. The court ruled, therefore, that back pay did not continue to accrue after Morris rejected the company's offer of reinstatement.[2]

A worker may involuntarily shorten the back-pay period by voluntarily removing herself from the job market. If a terminated worker elects to enroll in college or otherwise further her education or to improve her work skills rather than search for other employment, she may jeopardize her claim for back pay unless she is able to establish to the court's satisfaction that such measures were necessary to enable her to find another job. If, subsequent to her termination, a worker discovers she is unable to work because of illness or disability and thus is incapacitated from earning wages in any position, the back-pay period will be limited solely to that interval of time when she was physically able to work. But suppose the worker's disability is induced by the discriminatory conduct of the employer, as was the case for Weda Annette Ward?

Ward charged her employer with retaliation after she was fired following her complaint that she had been sexually harassed. When the court ruled in Ward's favor on the retaliation charge, the employer contested her claim for back-pay damages, arguing that after she was terminated she suffered a severe, incapacitating depression that made her unemployable. In applying the make-whole doctrine, the court noted that Ward was entitled to be placed in the position she would have been in had no discrimination occurred, and if she had not been subjected to the retaliatory conduct of her employer, she would not have suffered the depression. Because her depression had been caused by her employer's retaliatory treatment, the court refused to limit her recovery of back-pay damages.[3]

Front Pay

In addition to a claim for back pay, a successful sex discrimination claimant may apply to the court for an award of front pay, seeking to recover the loss of salary and benefits she may sustain after the trial of her sex discrimination action ends. While an award of back pay is computed on the basis of what already has occurred, an award of front pay is computed on the basis of what may occur in the future. Thus, an element of uncertainty and speculation is innate to a claim of this nature.

Suppose that a discharged worker files a sex discrimination claim and at the time of the trial, despite her good faith efforts, she has yet to find new employment. In these circumstances, if the worker prevails, she becomes entitled to a front-pay award. In calculating the front-pay award, the court must determine from the evidence at hand the approximate date that it appears likely that the worker will find new employment, as well as the likely rate of her compensation. Based on these determinations, the court will then calculate the award.

Now suppose that this worker has obtained new employment at the time of the trial, but her salary is less than that previously paid by the defendant employer. In these circumstances, the court must determine when it is likely that the worker will again be compensated on a basis equal to that formerly provided by the defendant employer. If that date can be determined with some degree of certainty, the court will then calculate the award.

In either event, the court is dealing with uncertainties, although it is not as if it were asked to look into a crystal ball and predict the future. With evidence of the worker's current circumstances and her realistic prospects for the future, the court should be able to compute a front-pay award. To the extent that a worker is able to furnish the court with facts that reduce the degree of uncertainty and speculation, the more likely she will receive a front-pay recovery.

When Jennifer Passantino was twenty-five years old, she began working for Johnson & Johnson Consumer Products, and over the next eighteen years she rose through the ranks to become one of the company's most successful female sales managers. She was characterized by company executives as a "leader in her field" and was set on a career path leading to an executive position. Despite her success, she was passed over for several promotions. She suspected that the promotion denials may have been attributable to the company's negative attitude toward women in higher positions, and her suspicions were confirmed when her supervisor advised her to consider searching for employment outside the company, as it did not appear that Johnson & Johnson was fully committed to promoting women to executive positions. Passantino then formally complained to management that her advancement had been denied by reason of the company's sex bias.

Ultimately, Passantino sued Johnson & Johnson for sex discrimination, and the jury at her trial returned a huge verdict in her favor, including an award of $2 million in front-pay damages. On its appeal of the jury verdict, Johnson & Johnson argued before the appellate court that the jury's front-pay award was excessive and wholly speculative.

At the time of the trial, Passantino was forty-three years old. Assuming she were to retire at age sixty-five, her expected work life was twenty-two years. Her annual salary was $71,500. Evidence submitted at the trial showed that if Passantino had been allowed to continue on her career path, she would have proceeded to an upper-level management position, where she would have earned $140,000 annually, plus cash and stock bonuses, and stock options worth 200–300 percent of her salary. The court calculated the difference between what Passantino would earn at an annual salary of $71,500 during the twenty-two years of her expected work life and the amount she would have earned over those years if she had been permitted to proceed along her career path. The court's calculation exceeded the $2 million jury award, and thus the appellate court dismissed the company's appeal.[4]

In calculating front-pay damages, Passantino was able to minimize the element of uncertainty, thus rendering it a less significant factor in the court's deliberations. She demonstrated that if she had been allowed to continue along her career path, eventually she would have advanced to an executive-level position, and by submitting evidence of the rate of compensation of workers in such positions, she gave the court the information that enabled it to compute the difference between what she would earn in her current position and what she would earn if promoted to an executive position. By extending the difference in annual compensation over the remaining twenty-two years of her expected work life, Passantino provided the court with the tools it needed to compute a front-pay award. If the element of uncertainty in these calculations had not been reduced, the court might very well have denied any form of front-pay relief.

Reinstatement

The courts have considerable latitude in fashioning appropriate remedies for Title VII violations. Instead of an award of front pay for a terminated worker, the court can order reinstatement of the worker. Reinstatement may be denied, however, where the employer proves that the worker would have lost her position in any event, such as in a downsizing or reorganization. Nor is reinstatement appropriate if the worker's return to the workplace would be disruptive or result in the displacement of an innocent third party. The mere possibility of hostility or resentment on the part of co-workers or management does not preclude reinstatement, but these factors will be included in those a court will consider in determining whether reinstatement is an appropriate remedy.

Although it is sometimes stated that reinstatement is preferred over front pay, courts frequently encounter obstacles that render reinstatement inappropriate. Front pay, if it is susceptible to calculation, is the option more likely to be selected by the court, and this is especially the case where the worker has found another position and has expressed reluctance to return to work for her former employer.

Injunction

Injunctive relief generally is cast as a directive to an employer either to discontinue certain acts or practices, or to perform a specified act. The first usually takes the form of a cease-and-desist order, and the second, an order to compel.

Injunctive relief is less often sought in lawsuits brought by individual complainants than in broad-based class actions and discrimination lawsuits initiated by the EEOC. For example, the EEOC filed a sex discrimination suit against a California hotel, alleging that its general manager and two other of its executive employees sexually harassed female workers, terminated them when they became pregnant, and retaliated against those who complained of these practices. After a trial of these charges, the court concluded that the hotel's female workers had been subjected to severe and pervasive acts of sexual harassment that corrupted the working environment, adversely altering the terms and conditions of their employment.

The EEOC asked the court to order broad-based injunctive relief designed to prevent hotel executives from engaging in similar unlawful conduct in the future. But hotel management challenged the EEOC's claim that an injunction was necessary, arguing that insufficient evidence existed to demonstrate any reasonable likelihood that such conduct would recur. Hotel management also opposed injunctive relief on the ground that it had initiated a training program of its executive employees to deal with discriminatory conduct in the workplace.

The court noted that when an employer takes curative action only after it has been sued, it has failed to provide sufficient assurance that the unlawful conduct will not be repeated. Moreover, the hotel's position ran counter to evidence that disclosed that when the female employees reported occurrences of sexual harassment, hotel executive personnel failed to take prompt remedial action to eliminate or prevent further harassment. In these circumstances, the court concluded that the injunctive relief requested by the EEOC was necessary to protect the hotel's female staff. The court then described the meaningful role that injunctive relief may play in an employment discrimination case: "By seeking injunctive relief, the EEOC not only deters future unlawful discrimination but also seeks to protect aggrieved employees and others similarly situated from the fear of retaliation for filing Title VII charges. By seeking injunctive relief, moreover, the EEOC promotes public policy and seeks to vindicate rights belonging to the United States as a sovereign."[5]

In another case that called for injunctive relief, Sara Sherkow found herself in circumstances where she had no need for a court order enjoining future acts of discrimination, but she desperately needed an injunction to resolve issues that had occurred as a consequence of her employer's past discriminatory conduct. Sherkow, a doctor of philosophy in educational administration, worked for the Wisconsin Department of Public Instruction as a planning analyst. She was heavily involved in the development of a state-funded Special Education Needs Program intended to provide for the educational needs of children who, due to cultural, social, or economic deprivation, were underachievers. Once the program had been developed, the department created the position of education administrator to direct its activities. After that position was filled, the department appointed Sherkow to serve as second in command of the program. Not long after, the newly appointed education administrator resigned to accept another position. Sherkow, along with six other candidates, then applied for the education administrator position. The department interviewed, tested, and rated the seven candidates, ranking Sherkow second. When the first-ranked applicant decided against taking the position, the department passed over Sherkow for the third-ranked candidate, who was a male. He had scored lower than Sherkow on the qualification test, had little experience with special education, while Sherkow's experience in this area was extensive, and had not participated in the development of the Special Education Needs Program in which Sherkow had been very much involved.

Following her rejection for the education administrator position, Sherkow filed a charge of discrimination with the EEOC, contending that the Department of Public Instruction had denied her the education administrator position solely on account of her gender. Then, as it was later described by the court, "an extraordinary thing happened." An evaluation procedure never previously used in the department was established to appraise Sherkow's performance. The department assigned three administrators with little or no knowledge of Sherkow's performance as second in command of the Special Education Needs Program to evaluate her performance in that position. The three administrators proceeded to denigrate all aspects of her performance and severely downgrade her performance rating.

Ultimately, Sherkow's EEOC charges were litigated in court, and at the conclusion of the trial, the court ruled that the department had discriminated against her when it denied her the education administrator position. The court also ruled that after Sherkow lodged a sex discrimination complaint with the EEOC, the department retaliated by creating a bogus performance-evaluation procedure. The court then had to fashion an appropriate form of make-whole relief. First, it directed the department to offer Sherkow the next available position commensurate with her qualifications. Second, it ordered the department to remove from Sherkow's personnel records all evidence of the spurious performance evaluation.[6]

These directives did not succeed in making Sherkow whole. For the court to have made her entirely whole, it would have had to order the department to assign her to the education administrator position, which would have required the department to displace the person then holding that post. Courts, when possible, attempt to minimize that sort of interference with employer internal operations, and the court in this case followed that rule. Thus, the court granted some of the injunctive relief Sherkow required to make her whole, while minimizing disruption to the department's internal operations. It tiptoed around implementation of the make-whole doctrine in order to fashion a remedy less intrusive to the employer.

Another court showed similar reluctance to fully implement the make-whole doctrine in Diane Garza's case against the Brownsville School District in Texas, which refused to hire her as an assistant principal. Although a court later ruled that the school district had engaged in an act of sex discrimination in refusing to hire Garza, it denied Garza's request that the court direct the school district to offer her the next available comparable position. The court reasoned that because Garza had subsequently obtained an assistant-principal position in another school district, she did not need a hiring preference to make her whole. When Garza appealed the court's ruling, the appellate court noted that the assistant-principal position Garza held at the time of the trial paid her less and required more travel time to and from her home than the position she had sought in the Brownsville School District. The appellate court reversed the lower-court ruling and held that Garza should be granted an opportunity to secure an assistant-principal appointment in the Brownsville School District comparable to that denied her.[7]

In a few cases, courts have exhibited less reluctance to interfere with the internal operations of an employer. In one instance, after an employer discriminatorily denied a promotion to a female worker, the court ordered the employer to promote the worker immediately to the position she would have held absent the acts of discrimination, and in the event that such a position was not then available, the court directed the employer to *create* another position for the worker.[8] This form of intercession in the business world in favor of a worker rarely occurs.

Attorneys' Fees

Because many discrimination claims arise out of terminations of employment, and terminated workers generally lack the financial means to support a lawsuit, lawyers must often agree to contingency-fee arrangements with these workers. In this arrangement, the lawyer is paid only if the plaintiff wins, and the fee is set as a percentage of the amount the plaintiff recovers. But a contingency arrangement is not apt to motivate a lawyer to assume responsibility for a case that involves small monetary damages.

In 1967, Congress enacted legislation that authorized a court to award a successful employment discrimination complainant the recovery of her attorney's fees from her employer.[9] Where recovery of a large damage award is improbable, and hence a contingency-fee arrangement is less attractive to an attorney, the statutory-fee award provides the only means for the lawyer to obtain adequate payment for his or her services.

The courts have consistently rejected the notion that an award of attorney's fees must be proportional to the amount of damages the worker recovers.[10] In fact, in some cases, the fee award has far exceeded the monetary damages recovered by the worker. Rather than a windfall for the attorney, such a fee award constitutes a recognition that a worker's right not to be discriminated against commands the protection of the courts regardless of the amount of money involved. In a failure-to-promote case, for example, the worker's losses may be quite small when measured against the cost of suing to protect the worker's rights. Without some means of recovering attorney's fees, failure-to-promote cases would often not be pursued.

The statutory provision for the recovery of attorney's fees by the successful worker complainant has undoubtedly been instrumental in the development of a fairly large cadre of attorneys willing to take on employment discrimination cases. Most of these cases involve complex factual and legal issues and are vigorously defended by employers. While the worker's counsel more often than not is a sole practitioner or a small firm, an employer is more likely to engage one of the large city law firms, with hundreds of lawyers and abundant support staff. In such circumstances, the worker's counsel needs all the assistance he or she can obtain. The fee-award statute is Congress's recognition that the worker and her attorney must be granted financial assistance if the employment discrimination statutes are to be adequately enforced.

Conclusion

As depicted in the cases reviewed in the preceding chapters, the U.S. workplace is not an attractive one for women. But some believe that women could be even worse off. Take, for example, the case involving Tomoko Haneda reported in the *New York Times* in February 2000. Haneda began working for Sharp Electronics in Japan in 1963, hoping to build a career through hard work and continued education. In her spare time, she earned a university degree, but six years passed before Sharp gave her a small promotion. Another twenty-one years then elapsed before she received her next salary increase. After quietly accepting these conditions for years, Haneda sued Sharp in accordance with Japan's anti-discrimination laws and attained a measure of justice when an Osaka court granted her judgment in the sum of $55,000, the largest workplace sex discrimination award in Japanese history. But Haneda was not happy: "This case has made me ill, and I was hospitalized twice. They may have paid me $50,000 in compensation and $5,000 for legal fees, but they didn't pay me what I had asked for, which was the difference between what I've earned all of these years and what I should have earned."[1]

Many Japanese companies maintain separate personnel systems, one for men and another for women. While it is assumed that men will build careers for themselves and advance to higher positions, Japanese working women are typically assigned to low-level clerical, sales, and accounting positions, with little prospect for future advancement. These women are categorized as miscellaneous workers or "office ladies." What is the role of an office lady? "They are expected to be . . . flowers in the workplace, who . . . brighten up the office with their presence, get married sometime during their 20's and leave the workplace to become mothers and homemakers. Those who do stay in a job learn that dressing fetchingly and mastering the art of speaking in an appealing female voice are part of this strategy."[2]

A subsequent *New York Times* article reported that in 2000, approximately 64 percent of Japanese companies failed to hire a single female university graduate for engineering-related positions, and 39 percent failed to hire any female graduates at all.[3]

Compared with Japanese women, U.S. female workers are not doing so badly. After all, women in the United States are not burdened with performing the functions of an "office lady." A "matters could be worse" attitude is popular with some employers and workers, but most U.S. employers and workers firmly believe that any form of workplace discrimination is inappropriate, unlawful, and immoral. Nevertheless, sex discrimination remains prominent in the workplace.

Certain of the reasons for its continued presence are readily identifiable, and others, undoubtedly, are yet undisclosed. An employer's failure to provide adequate oversight and enforcement of its anti-discrimination policies guarantees the continued presence of sex discrimination in its work environment. In companies of this ilk, anti-discrimination policies may be formulated, adopted, and implemented, only to be ignored by mid-level and senior members of management without fear of penalty. That these managers operate by their own rules renders company anti-discrimination policy meaningless and impotent. Women who work in such companies will continue to suffer the consequences of a discriminatory work environment.

Corporate human resources personnel are generally charged with enforcing anti-discrimination policies, but they are frequently denied the power and authority to do so with vigor. Enforcement then becomes an ad hoc application of remedial measures generally insufficient to modify a hostile work environment or prevent future acts of discrimination. The company's anti-discrimination policy is gradually relegated to a matter of low priority, and meaningful enforcement becomes even more problematic.

Sex discrimination also may be sustained, even validated, by factors indigenous to a company's work environment. Working conditions adopted in male-dominated companies often reflect the work and lifestyles of men with limited child-caring and family responsibilities, and jobs structured in this type of work environment often adversely impact female workers. Corporate policies and practices espoused by these companies also contribute to the continuing presence of sex discrimination in the work environment.[4]

The continued presence of sex discrimination in the workplace is also attributable, at least in part, to inadequate administrative procedures devised by Congress for the enforcement of Title VII. When Congress enacted Title VII, it assigned the responsibility for its enforcement to the newly created Equal Employment Opportunity Commission. From the outset, the EEOC has been underfunded, understaffed, and burdened with a workload far greater than it can handle. Because of resulting procedural delays and inadequate investigative processes, workers have generally placed little reliance on the EEOC in obtaining relief from employer discriminatory practices and policies. Many of the legal actions discussed in preceding chapters were initiated and litigated by worker-complainants, acting through their retained attorneys. Although in each of these cases a discrimination charge was filed by the worker with the EEOC as the statute requires, many of these workers litigated their cases with little or no EEOC assistance. Rather, the EEOC's contributions to the eradication of employment discrimination lay in highly effective rule making and in providing guidance for both workers and employers.

Worker-initiated litigation is a cause of far greater concern to employers than is the possibility of EEOC intervention in their policies and practices. Corporate policymakers have little to fear from the EEOC; they are well aware of the agency's ineffectiveness in the area of enforcement. Undoubtedly, the absence of a strong governmental enforcement policy has contributed to the continued presence of sex-discriminatory conduct, policy, and practice in the workplace.

The failure of the EEOC to adequately fill the role first envisioned for it has led to a significant development. As the enforcement of Title VII has shifted from the EEOC to workers and their attorneys, the legal profession has assumed a predominant role in enforcing the statute. In the years to come, the role of the attorney will continue to grow, and as matters now stand, if sex discrimination is ever eradicated from the workplace, it will be the legal profession, acting on behalf of individual worker complainants, that will effect that change.

Vigorous enforcement of Title VII will continue to play a critical part in the preservation and expansion of women's rights in the workplace. As women climb higher in the business world, they stand to lose more in terms of income, prestige, and self-esteem when their employers discriminatorily deny them promotions and block further advancement to executive positions. The higher the level of a woman's achievement, the greater the level of her motivation to contest acts of discrimination, for the incentive to sue grows with the extent of the loss.

However, it may not always be practical or advantageous to sue. Litigation is a time-consuming, emotion-draining, nerve-wracking, and often deeply frustrating process. Before deciding to sue her employer, a woman must carefully consider the stress and pain she and her family will endure during a drawn-out, bitterly contested litigation. But, in addition, she and her attorney must assess the potential for a successful conclusion to the litigation and whether the likely outcome will have warranted the efforts involved in attaining it.

If a woman has been terminated and has been unable to find another comparable position, the decision to proceed with litigation will be easy to arrive at. If a woman is denied a promotion, the decision to proceed is not as clear. If she sues, during the course of the litigation—a process likely to last several years—her employment responsibilities will require her to associate daily with persons she has charged with discriminatory conduct, a difficult situation indeed. And even if she is successful and the litigation culminates in a promotion, through settlement or final judgment, she must still consider whether there exists any likelihood of further advancement. These factors must be measured against those that will follow upon a decision not to sue. If a woman decides not to contest a discriminatory decision adverse to her interests, she may be perceived by her employer as weak or compliant, thus inviting further adverse treatment.

A woman must consider many issues before committing to litigation. Some factors and circumstances personal to the worker will elicit caution and restraint, while others will induce confidence and eagerness to proceed. All must be analyzed, weighed, and balanced one against the other. Whether the decision is to sue or not, a woman's career may be significantly altered.

One additional factor should be considered, a factor that transcends the particular woman called upon to decide. A woman's decision to proceed or not to proceed with litigation will affect, in some way, the workplace status of every other working woman. Ultimately, sex discrimination will be eradicated only if women steadfastly challenge their employers' discriminatory policies, practices, and conduct. As I stated in the introduction, I have written this book to encourage women to commit themselves to accepting that challenge—to contest sex discrimination rather than to acquiesce in it. Thus, in addition to all other factors, she must consider whether she is willing to accept that challenge, not only for herself, but for all working women. If she accepts, all working women will be in her debt.

Notes

Introduction

1. Title VII is codified as 42 U.S.C. Sections 2000e et seq. Discrimination based on age is barred by the Age Discrimination in Employment Act of 1967, 29 U.S.C. Sections 621–634, and discrimination based on disability is barred by the Americans with Disabilities Act of 1990, 42 U.S.C. Sections 12111 et seq.
2. Kathryn Abrams, "Gender Discrimination and the Transformation of Workplace Norms," *Vanderbilt Law Review* 42, 4 (1989): 1183, 1186.
3. U.S. Bureau of the Census, *Statistical Abstract of the United States, 2000* (Washington, D.C.: Bureau of the Census, 2000), table 696, p. 437 (hereafter, *Statistical Abstract 2000*).
4. "2000 Catalyst Census of Women Corporate Officers and Top Earners," *Catalyst Fact Sheet*, available at http://www.catalystwomen.org.

One   Trends in Workplace Discrimination

1. John Markoff, "Hewlett-Packard Picks Rising Star at Lucent as Its Chief Executive," *New York Times,* July 20, 1999. The appointee, Carleton S. Fiorina, was quoted as having said: "I hope that we are at a point that everyone has figured out that there is not a glass ceiling. My gender is interesting but really not the subject of the story here." Fiorina was later reported to have backed off her statement. She said she did not intend her remark to apply throughout corporate America. Reed Abelson, "A Push from the Top Shatters a Glass Ceiling," *New York Times,* August 22, 1999.
2. Steve Lohr, "Setting Her Own Precedents," *New York Times,* July 23, 1999.
3. *New York Times,* November 17, 1999. "It sounds good: the number of women who are chief executives at Fortune 500 companies has doubled the last five months. The trouble is, the number went from two to four, and isn't likely to increase significantly soon." The number increased to five in mid–2001. Claudia H. Deutsch, "Xerox Moves Up an Insider to be Chief," *New York Times,* July 21, 2001.

4. *New York Law Journal,* April 26, 1999.
5. Melody Petersen, "Her Partners Can Call Her Ms. Chairman," *New York Times,* October 9, 1999.
6. *New York Times,* July 21, 1999, referring to a report issued by Catalyst, a nonprofit research organization that focuses on women corporate executives.
7. *Victory v. Hewlett-Packard Co.,* 78 FEP Cases 1718 (E.D.N.Y. 1999).
8. Colorado Women's Bar Association, "Careers and Compensation Study" (N.p.: Colorado Women's Bar Association, 1993); Cathlin Donnell, Nancy Reichman, and Joyce Sterling, "Gender Penalties: The Results of the Careers and Compensation Study," *Colorado Women's Bar Association Executive Summary* (N.p.: Colorado Women's Bar Association, 1998).
9. Leah K. Glasheen and Susan L. Crowley, "More Women in Driver's Seat," *AARP: The Nation,* November 1999.
10. Ibid., referring to U.S. Department of Labor statistics.
11. *Statistical Abstract 2000,* table 696, p. 437.
12. Ibid.
13. Deborah L. Rhode, *Speaking of Sex: The Denial of Gender Inequality* (Cambridge: Harvard University Press, 1997), 9.
14. Richard W. Judy and Carol D'Amico, *Workforce 2020: Work and Workers in the 21st Century* (Indianapolis: Hudson Institute, 1997), 67–68.
15. *Statistical Abstract 2000,* table 700, p. 439.
16. This study was referred to in "The Environmental Scan," in *Good for Business: Making Use of the Nation's Human Capital* (Washington, D.C.: Federal Glass Ceiling Commission, 1995), 13.
17. Natalie Angier, "Pay Gap Remains for Women in Life Sciences," *New York Times,* October 16, 2001.
18. *A Solid Investment: Making Full Use of the Nation's Human Capital* (Washington, D.C.: Federal Glass Ceiling Commission, 1995), 35.
19. Diana Furchtgott-Roth and Christine Stolba, *Women's Figures: An Illustrated Guide to the Economic Progress of Women in America* (Washington, D.C.: AEI Press, 1999), 4–15.
20. Ibid., 18–19.
21. "Environmental Scan," iv, 15–17.
22. *Luciano v. Olsten Corp.,* 912 F. Supp. 663 (E.D.N.Y. 1995), affirmed 110 F.3d 210 (2d Cir. 1997).
23. The term "glass ceiling" appeared in a 1986 *Wall Street Journal* article describing the invisible barriers women confront the closer they approach high corporate executive positions.
24. Glass Ceiling Act of 1991, Title II, Civil Rights Act of 1991.
25. "Environmental Scan," 6.
26. Ibid., 148, 28.
27. Rhode, *Speaking of Sex,* 157. "Most employment discrimination never results in formal complaints. Women often are not sure whether their rights have been violated, whether they can prove a violation, or how to file a complaint. Nor can most women afford the costs of legal action or find lawyers willing to pursue their claims on a contingency fee basis."
28. *Statistical Abstract 2000,* table 645, p. 404.

29. Judy and D'Amico, *Workforce 2020,* 113.

30. Ibid., 52–53.

31. Ibid., 53.

32. *Statistical Abstract,* table 653, p. 409.

Two   Sex Discrimination in Today's Workplace

1. Kate Zernike, "MIT Women Win a Fight against Bias," *Boston Sunday Globe,* March 21, 1999.

2. "A Study on the Status of Women Faculty in Science at MIT," available at http://web.mit.edu.

3. Carey Goldberg, "M.I.T. Acknowledges Bias against Female Professors," *New York Times,* March 23, 1999.

4. Lotte Bailyn's report from the faculty chair, "Momentum of Report Needs to be Extended to Entire Institution," available at http://web.mit.edu.

5. "Study on the Status of Women Faculty," 2.

6. The male culture in the workplace is discussed at some length in Kathryn Abrams, "Gender Discrimination and the Transformation of Workplace Norms," *Vanderbilt Law Review* 42, 4 (1989): 1183.

7. Alfred W. Blumrosen, "The Legacy of Griggs: Social Progress and Subjective Judgments," *Chicago-Kent Law Review* 63 (1987): 1, 17–20.

8. Ibid., 18–19.

9. Deborah J. Vagins, "Occupational Segregation and the Male-Worker-Norm: Challenging Objective Work Requirements under Title VII," *Women's Rights Law Reporter* 18 (1996): 79, 80–85.

10. Nancy McCarthy Snyder, "Career Women in Perspective: The Wichita Sample," in *Women and Careers: Issues and Challenges,* ed. Carol Wolfe Konek and Sally L. Kitch (Thousand Oaks, Calif.: Sage, 1994), 4–5.

11. Vagins, "Occupational Segregation," 81–82.

12. Raymond F. Gregory, *Age Discrimination in the American Workplace: Old at a Young Age* (New Brunswick: Rutgers University Press, 2001).

13. "The Environmental Scan," in *Good for Business: Making Use of the Nation's Human Capital* (Washington, D.C.: Federal Glass Ceiling Commission, 1995), 12.

14. Cynthia Fuchs Epstein, "Glass Ceilings and Open Doors: Women's Advancement in the Legal Profession, a Report to the Committee on Women in the Profession, Association of the Bar of the City of New York," *Fordham Law Review* 64 (1995): 291.

15. Mona Harrington, *Women Lawyers: Rewriting the Rules* (New York: Plume, 1995), 105.

16. MIT has reported some gains for its female staff since the School of Sciences female professors first protested in 1994, but progress appears to have proceeded at less than a snail's pace. Women now make up 18 percent of the faculty, compared with 12 percent in 1994. Women hold only two of MIT's fifty-two institute professorships, its highest faculty honor. Reports issued by faculty-led committees found evidence that women on average still earn less than their male colleagues. Patrick Healy, "MIT Vows to Counter Gender Bias," *Boston Globe,* March 20, 2002.

Three The Federal Anti-Discrimination Laws

1. *Bradwell v. Illinois*, 83 U.S. 130 (1872).
2. *Muller v. Oregon*, 208 U.S. 412 (1908).
3. *Goesaert v. Cleary*, 335 U.S. 464 (1948).
4. Mona Harrington, *Women Lawyers: Rewriting the Rules* (New York: Plume, 1995), 19.
5. Cynthia Fuchs Epstein, *Women in Law* (Urbana: University of Illinois Press, 1993), 84–85.
6. James C. Oldham, "Sex Discrimination and State Protective Laws," *Denver Law Journal* 44 (1967): 344, 350–352. Oldham argued that state protective laws were not preempted by Title VII, a position later rejected by the courts. See chapter 4.
7. Michael I. Sovern, *Legal Restraints on Racial Discrimination in Employment* (New York: Twentieth Century Fund, 1966), 9–15.
8. David L. Rose, "Twenty-five Years Later: Where Do We Stand on Equal Employment Opportunity Law Enforcement," *Vanderbilt Law Review* 42, 4 (1989): 1121, 1127–1128.
9. New York Executive Law, Sections 290 et seq.
10. New Jersey (1945), Massachusetts (1946), Connecticut (1947), Rhode Island (1949), New Mexico (1949), Oregon (1949), Washington (1949), Alaska (1953), Michigan (1955), Minnesota (1955), Pennsylvania (1955), Colorado (1957), Wisconsin (1957), California (1959), Ohio (1959), Delaware (1960), Illinois (1961), Kansas (1961), Missouri (1961), Idaho (1961), Indiana (1963), Hawaii (1963), Iowa (1963), and Vermont (1963). Lex K. Larson, *Employment Discrimination* (New York: Lexis, 2000), 2–29.
11. Alfred W. Blumrosen, *Modern Law: The Law Transmission System and Equal Employment Opportunity* (Madison: University of Wisconsin Press, 1993), 40–41.
12. Rose, "Twenty-five Years Later," 1130.
13. H.R. Report 914, 88th Cong., 1st Sess., 1964.
14. Rose, "Twenty-five Years Later," 1127–1128.
15. Smith's attempt to defeat enactment of Title VII has been widely reported; see Rose, "Twenty-five Years Later," 1131, and Blumrosen, *Modern Law*, 45.
16. Blumrosen, *Modern Law,* 4.

Four After the Enactment of Title VII

1. Title VII, Civil Rights Act of 1964, 42 U.S.C. Section 2000e–2.
2. *Rogers v. EEOC*, 454 F.2d 234, 238 (5th Cir. 1971).
3. Alfred W. Blumrosen, *Modern Law: The Law Transmission System and Equal Employment Opportunity* (Madison: University of Wisconsin Press, 1993), 58.
4. Michael I. Sovern, *Legal Restraints on Racial Discrimination in Employment* (New York: Twentieth Century Fund, 1966), 3.
5. U.S. Bureau of the Census, Department of Commerce, "Current Population Reports," ser. P–50, no. 66 (March 1956), referred to in Jack Greenberg, *Race Relations and American Law* (New York: Columbia University Press, 1959), 154.
6. Deborah L. Rhode, "Perspectives on Professional Women," *Stanford Law Review* 40 (1988): 1163, 1178.

7. David L. Rose, "Twenty-five Years Later: Where Do We Stand on Equal Employment Opportunity Law Enforcement," *Vanderbilt Law Review* 42, 4 (1989): 1136.

8. Harrington, *Women Lawyers*, 107; Blumrosen, *Modern Law*, 184.

9. U.S. EEOC, "Charge Statistics FY 1992 through FY 2000," available at http://www.eeoc.gov/stats/charges.html.

10. *Phillips v. Martin Marietta Corp.*, 400 U.S. 542 (1971).

11. Title VII, 42 U.S.C. Section 2000e–2(e).

12. *Dothard v. Rawlinson*, 433 U.S. 321 (1977).

13. Ibid.

14. However, as recently as February 2000, the New York City Fire Department could count only thirty-six women among its 11,000 members. Kevin Flynn, "Despite Recruiting, Few Women Do Well in Firefighter Tests," *New York Times*, February 3, 2000.

15. *City of Los Angeles Department of Water and Power v. Manhart*, 435 U.S. 702 (1978).

16. *Sprogis v. United Air Lines, Inc.*, 444 F.2d 1194 (7th Cir. 1971).

17. Raymond F. Gregory, *Age Discrimination in the American Workplace: Old at a Young Age* (New Brunswick: Rutgers University Press, 2001).

18. *EEOC v. Sears Roebuck & Co.*, 628 F. Supp. 1264 (N.D. Ill. 1986), affirmed 839 F.2d 302 (7th Cir. 1988).

19. "Introduction to Proposed Guidelines on Employment Discrimination and Reproduction Hazards," 45 Federal Regulations 7,514.

20. *International Union, United Automobile, Aerospace and Agricultural Implement Workers of America v. Johnson Controls, Inc.*, 490 U.S. 187 (1991).

Five Common Forms of Sex Discrimination

1. Alfred W. Blumrosen, "The Legacy of *Griggs*: Social Progress and Subjective Judgments," *Chicago-Kent Law Review* 63 (1987): 1, 17–20.

2. *Sennello v. Reserve Life Insurance Co.*, 667 F. Supp. 1498 (S.D. Fla. 1987), affirmed 872 F.2d 393 (11th Cir. 1989).

3. *Spears v. Board of Education of Pike County*, 843 F.2d 882 (6th Cir. 1988).

4. *Throgmorton v. U.S. Forgecraft Corp.*, 965 F.2d 643 (8th Cir. 1992).

5. *Barbano v. Madison County*, 922 F.2d 139 (2d Cir. 1990).

6. *Luciano v. Olsten Corp.*, 912 F. Supp. 663 (E.D. N.Y. 1995), affirmed 110 F.3d 210 (2d Cir. 1997).

7. *Storey v. City of Sparta Police Department*, 667 F. Supp. 1164 (M.D. Tenn. 1987).

8. See, e.g., *Los Angeles Department of Water and Power v. Manhart*, 435 U.S. 702 (1978).

9. *Price Waterhouse v. Hopkins*, 490 U.S. 228 (1989). In addition to many other law review articles, the case is reviewed in Mary F. Radford, "Sex Stereotyping and the Promotion of Women to Positions of Power," *Hastings Law Journal* 41 (March 1990): 471.

10. *Polacco v. Curators of the University of Missouri*, 37 F.3d 366 (8th Cir. 1994).

11. *Rodhe v. K. O. Steel Castings, Inc.*, 649 F.2d 317 (5th Cir. 1981).

12. *Luciano v. Olsten Corp.*

Six Older Women

1. Age Discrimination in Employment Act, 29 U.S.C. Sections 621–634.
2. Marilyn Webb, "How Old Is Too Old?" *New York Magazine,* March 29, 1993, 66.
3. AARP Women's Initiative, *Employment Discrimination against Midlife and Older Women: An Analysis of Discrimination Charges Filed with the EEOC* (Washington, D.C.: AARP, 1997), 2:13.
4. *Proffitt v. Anacomp, Inc.*, 747 F. Supp. 421 (S.D. Ohio 1990). Once a defendant employer loses a motion to dismiss the worker's claims, the case is frequently settled on terms favorable to the worker. Employers often insist as a condition of the settlement that the terms of the settlement remain confidential. In these circumstances, the final outcome of the case is known only to the parties to the litigation.
5. *Malarky v. Texaco, Inc.*, 559 F. Supp. 117 (S.D. N.Y. 1982), affirmed 704 F.2d 674 (2d Cir. 1983).
6. *Sischo-Nownejad v. Merced Community College District*, 934 F.2d 1104 (9th Cir. 1991).
7. AARP Women's Initiative, *Employment Discrimination against Midlife*, 6.
8. *Palmiero v. Weston Controls*, 809 F Supp. 341 (M.D. Pa. 1992).
9. *EEOC v. Independent Stave Co., Inc.*, 754 F. Supp. 713 (E.D. Mo. 1991).
10. *Arnett v. Aspin*, 846 F. Supp. 1234 (E.D. Pa. 1994).
11. *Good v. U.S. West Communications, Inc.*, 1995 WL 67672 (D.C. Ore. 1995).
12. *Sherman v. American Cyanamid Company*, 996 F. Supp. 719 (N.D. Ohio 1998).
13. *Thompson v. Mississippi State Personnel Board*, 674 F. Supp. 198 (N.D. Miss. 1987).
14. *McFadden-Peel v. Staten Island Cable*, 873 F. Supp. 757 (E.D. N.Y. 1994).
15. *Smith v. Berry Co.*, 165 F.3d 390 (5th Cir. 1999).
16. Ibid. If Smith had prevailed on the sex rather than the age claim, her damages would have been calculated at $174,000.
17. *Blonder v. Evanston Hospital Corp.*, 1992 WL 44404 (N.D. Ill. 1992).
18. *Haskins v. Secretary of Health and Human Services Dep't.*, 35 FEP Cases 256 (W.D. Mo. 1984). The defendant ultimately prevailed, because the plaintiff was unable to prove that she would have been hired even had the hiring policy not been in place.
19. *Statistical Abstract 2000*, table 644, p. 403.

Seven Women of Color

1. Nijole V. Benokraitis and Joe R. Feagin, *Modern Sexism: Blatant, Subtle, and Covert Discrimination,* 2d ed. (Englewood Cliffs, N.J.: Prentice-Hall, 1995), 147.
2. *Statistical Abstract 2000*, table 696, p. 437.
3. "The Environmental Scan," in *Good for Business: Making Use of the Nation's Human Capital* (Washington, D.C.: Federal Glass Ceiling Commission, 1995), 81.
4. *Statistical Abstract 2000*, table 696, p. 437.
5. Benokraitis and Feagin, *Modern Sexism*, 155.
6. "Environmental Scan," 68.
7. Reed Abelson, "Women Minorities Not Getting to the Top," *New York Times,* July 14, 1999.
8. *Jones v. Chicago Research & Trading Group, Ltd.*, 1991 WL 70889 (N.D. Ill. 1991).

9. Kimberle Crenshaw, "Race, Gender, and Sexual Harassment," *Southern California Law Review* 65 (1992): 1467.

10. Peggie R. Smith, "Separate Identities: Black Women, Work, and Title VII," *Harvard Women's Law Journal* 14 (1991): 21, 22–23.

11. Hooks is quoted in ibid., 10.

12. *DeGraffenreid v. General Motors Assembly Division, St. Louis*, 413 F. Supp. 142 (E.D. Mo. 1976).

13. Kimberle Crenshaw, "Demarginalizing the Intersection of Race and Sex: A Black Feminist Critique of Antidiscrimination Doctrine, Feminist Theory, and Antiracist Politics," *University of Chicago Legal Forum* (1989): 139.

14. 42 U.S.C. Section 2000e–2(a).

15. *Jefferies v. Harris County Community Action Association*, 615 F.2d 1025 (5th Cir. 1980).

16. *Graham v. Bendix Corp.*, 585 F. Supp. 1036 (N.D. Ind. 1984).

17. *Lam v. University of Hawaii*, 40 F.3d. 1551 (9th Cir. 1994).

18. *Hicks v. Gates Rubber Co.*, 833 F.2d. 1406 (10th Cir. 1987).

19. Kathryn Abrams, "Title VII and the Complex Female Subject," *Michigan Law Review* 92 (1994): 2479, 2501.

20. *Cruz v. Coach Stores, Inc.*, 202 F.3d. 560 (2d Cir. 2000).

Eight   Women in the Professions

1. Deborah L. Rhode, "Perspectives on Professional Women," *Stanford Law Review* 40 (1988):1163, 1171.

2. Ibid., 1167, quoting *In re Goodell* 39 Wis. 232, 244–245.

3. Ibid., 1174.

4. Wendell Lagrand, "Getting There, Staying There," *American Bar Association Journal*, February 1999, 54.

5. Terry Carter, "Divided Justice," *American Bar Association Journal,* February 1999, 44.

6. Terry Carter, "It's Not Just a 'Guy Thing' Anymore," *American Bar Association Journal,* April 1999, 18.

7. Jonathan D. Glater, "Women Are Close to Being Majority of Law Students," *New York Times,* March 26, 2001.

8. Ritchenya A. Shepherd, "Women: Lonely at Top," *National Law Journal,* July 12, 1999.

9. Deborah L. Rhode, "Equal Rights: Positive Thinking at AALS," *National Law Journal,* November 15, 1999.

10. Linda R. Hirshman, "Battle of the Sexes Rages in Law Schools," *National Law Journal,* August 23, 1999.

11. Ritchenya A. Shepherd, "Business Watch: Top In-House Women Gain Ground," *National Law Journal,* September 6, 1999.

12. Cynthia Fuchs Epstein, *Women in Law,* 2d ed. (Chicago: University of Illinois Press, 1993); Cythia Fuchs Epstein, "Glass Ceilings and Open Doors," *Fordham Law Review* 64 (1995): 291.

13. *Ezold v. Wolf, Block, Schorr and Solis-Cohen*, 983 F.2d 509 (3d Cir. 1993).
14. S. Elizabeth Foster, "The Glass Ceiling in the Legal Profession: Why Do Law Firms Still Have So Few Female Partners?" *UCLA Law Review* 42 (1995): 1631.
15. Ernst Benjamin, *Disparities in the Salaries and Appointments of Academic Women and Men* (Washington, D. C.: American Association of University Professors, 1999).
16. Ibid.
17. Ibid.
18. Edward Wyatt, "Women Gain in the Doctoral Chase," *New York Times,* November 4, 1999.
19. *Sweeney v. Board of Trustees of Keene State College*, 569 F.2d 169 (1st Cir. 1978).
20. *Zahorik v. Cornell University*, 729 F.2d 85 (2d Cir. 1984).
21. *Kunda v. Muhlenberg College*, 621 F.2d 532 (3d Cir. 1980).
22. *Smart v. Columbia Gas System Service Corp.*, 41 FEP Cases 249 (D.C. Del. 1986).
23. "Sexual Inequality Is Found in Medical Faculties," *New York Times,* February 10, 2000.
24. *Jew v. University of Iowa*, 749 F. Supp. 946 (S.D. Iowa 1990).
25. Margaret Burbidge, "Glass Ceilings and Ivory Towers," *American Astronomical Society Status Newsletter,* January 2000; also reported in Natalie Angier, "For Women in Astronomy, a Glass Ceiling in the Sky," *New York Times,* February 15, 2000.

Nine   Pregnant Women

1. Title VII, Civil Rights Act of 1964, 42 U.S.C. Section 2000e–2.
2. For a complainant victory, see, e.g., *Communication Workers v. American Telephone & Telegraph*, 513 F.2d 1024 (2d Cir. 1975).
3. *General Electric Co. v. Gilbert*, 429 U.S. 125 (1976).
4. 42 U.S.C. Section 2000e(k).
5. The statute's provisions are summarized and described in *Maldonado v. U.S. Bank and Manufacturers Bank*, 186 F.3d 759 (7th Cir. 1999).
6. EEOC Title VII Regulations, 29 C.F.R. Section 1604.10; Appendix: Questions on the Pregnancy Discrimination Act.
7. *Urbano v. Continental Airlines, Inc.*, 138 F.3d 204 (5th Cir. 1998).
8. *Geier v. Medtronic, Inc.*, 99 F.3d 238 (7th Cir. 1996).
9. *EEOC v. Hacienda Hotel*, 881 F.2d 1504 (9th Cir. 1989).
10. *EEOC v. Continuity Programs, Inc.*, 841 F. Supp. 218 (E.D. Mich. 1993).
11. *EEOC v. Yenkin-Majestic Paint Corp*, 112 F.3d 831 (6th Cir. 1997).
12. *EEOC v. Red Baron Steak House*, 47 FEP Cases 49 (N.D. Cal. 1988).
13. *Sheehan v. Donlen Corp.*, 173 F.3d 1039 (7th Cir. 1999).
14. Ibid.
15. *Tamimi v. Howard Johnson Co., Inc.*, 807 F.2d 1550 (11th Cir. 1987).
16. *EEOC v. Wal-Mart Stores, Inc.*, 156 F.3d 989 (9th Cir. 1998).
17. *Ahmad v. Loyal American Life Insurance Co.*, 767 F. Supp. 1114 (S.D. Ala. 1991).
18. *Bainlardi v. SBC Warburg, Inc.*, 78 FEP Cases 122 (S.D. N.Y. 1998).
19. *Goss v. Exxon Office Systems Co.*, 33 FEP Cases 21 (E.D. Pa. 1983), affirmed 747 F.2d 885 (3d Cir. 1984).
20. *Kerzer v. Kingly Manufacturing*, 156 F.3d 396 (2d Cir. 1998). When the worker was later discharged while on maternity leave, she sued her employer for pregnancy

discrimination. The employer asked the court to dismiss her case, but the court refused on the ground that the employer's comment raised an inference that the worker was discharged for a discriminatory reason.

21. *Quaratino v. Tiffany & Co.*, 71 F.3d 58 (2d Cir. 1995).
22. *Pacourek v. Inland Steel Co., Inc.*, 858 F. Supp. 1393 (N.D. Ill. 1994).
23. *Fejes v. Gilpin Ventures, Inc.*, 960 F. Supp. 1487 (D. Colo. 1997).
24. *Piantanida v. Wyman Center, Inc.*, 116 F.3d 340 (8th Cir. 1997).
25. *Turic v. Holland Hospitality, Inc.*, 63 FEP Cases 1267 and 64 FEP Cases 786 (W.D. Mich. 1994), affirmed 85 F.3d 1211 (6th Cir. 1996).
26. *Bergstrom-Ek v. Best Oil Co.*, 153 F.3d 851 (8th Cir. 1998).
27. Gloria Allred and Dolores Y. Leal, "Employment: A BFOQ Defense," *National Law Journal*, February 22, 1999, referring to *Tylo v. Spelling*, 55 Cal. App. 4th 1379 (1997).
28. David M. Halbfinger, "Show of Support for Teacher Who Says Pregnancy Blocked Tenure Bid," *New York Times*, April 28, 1999.
29. *New York Times*, May 30, 1999.
30. "EEOC Pregnancy Discrimination Charges—EEOC and FEPAs Combined: FY 1992–FY 2000," available at http://www.eeoc.gov/stats/pregnanc.html.

Ten   Women with Children

1. *Muller v. Oregon*, 208 U.S. 412 (1908).
2. *Jurinko v. Edwin L. Wiegand Co.*, 477 F.2d 1038 (3d Cir. 1973).
3. EEOC Title VII Regulations, 29 C.F.R. Section 1604.4
4. U.S. Bureau of the Census, *Statistical Abstract of the United States, 1998* (Washington, D.C.: Bureau of the Census, 1998), table 654, p. 409.
5. *Coble v. Hot Springs School District No. 6*, 682 F.2d 721 (8th Cir. 1982).
6. *Trezza v. The Hartford*, 78 FEP Cases 1826 (S.D. N.Y. 1998).
7. *Bass v. Chemical Banking Corp.*, 1996 WL 374151 (S.D. N.Y. 1996).
8. *Fuller v. GTE Corp.*, 926 F. Supp. 653 (M.D. Tenn. 1996).
9. *McGrenaghan v. St. Denis School*, 979 F. Supp. 323 (E.D. Pa. 1997).
10. Many legal writers have commented on these circumstances. See, e.g., Kathryn Abrams, "Gender Discrimination and the Transformation of Workplace Norms," *Vanderbilt Law Review* 42, 4 (1989): 1183, 1223; Mary Ann Mason, "Beyond Equal Opportunity: A New Vision for Women Workers," *Notre Dame Journal of Law, Ethics, and Public Policy* 6 (1992): 393.
11. *Coopersmith v. Roudebush*, 517 F.2d 818 (D.C. D.C. 1975).
12. *Fisher v. Vassar College*, 852 F. Supp. 1193 (S.D. N.Y. 1994).
13. Ibid.
14. *Fisher v. Vassar College*, 114 F.3d 1332 (2d Cir. 1997).
15. Ibid., 1383.

Eleven   Sex Discrimination at Stages of Employment

1. EEOC Title VII Regulations, 29 C.F.R. Section 1604.5.
2. *King v. Trans World Airlines*, 738 F.2d 255 (8th Cir. 1984).
3. *Barbano v. Madison County*, 922 F.2d 139 (2d Cir. 1990).

4. *Bruno v. City of Crown Point*, 950 F.2d 355 (7th Cir. 1991).
5. 29 U.S.C. Section 206 (d).
6. *Corning Glass Works v. Brennan*, 417 U.S. 188 (1974), referring to S. Rep. 176, 88th Cong., 1st Sess., 1963.
7. *McMillan v. Massachusetts Society for the Prevention of Cruelty to Animals*, 140 F.3d 288 (1st Cir. 1998).
8. *Houck v. Virginia Polytechnic Institute and State University*, 10 F.3d 204 (4th Cir 1993).
9. *Cherrey v. Thompson Steel Co., Inc.* , 805 F. Supp. 1257 (D.C. Md. 1992).
10. Bureau of the Census, *Statistical Abstract 1998,* table 696, p. 436
11. *Rubin v. Regents of the University of California*, 48 FEP Cases 1130 (N.D. Cal. 1988).
12. *Flucker v. Fox Chapel Area School District*, 461 F. Supp. 1203 (W.D. Pa. 1978).
13. *Bishop v. Wood*, 426 U.S. 341 (1976).
14. *Linville v. State of Hawaii*, 874 F. Supp. 1095 (D.C. Ha. 1994).
15. *Loyd v. Phillips Brothers, Inc.*, 25 F.3d 518 (7th Cir. 1994).
16. *Morley v. New England Telephone Co.*, 47 FEP Cases 917 (D.C. Mass. 1987).
17. *Walsdorf v. Board of Commissioners for the East Jefferson Levee District*, 857 F.2d 1047 (5th Cir. 1988).
18. *Stukey v. United States Air Force*, 809 F. Supp. 536 (S.D. Ohio 1992).
19. *Gobert v. Babbitt*, 83 FEP Cases 1620 (E.D. La. 2000).
20. *Greenbaum v. Svenska Handelsbanken NY*, 67 F. Supp. 2d 228 (S.D.N.Y. 1999).
21. *Sones-Morgan v. The Hertz Corp.*, 542 F. Supp 123 (W.D. Tenn. 1981), affirmed 725 F.2d 1070 (6th Cir. 1984).
22. *Derr v. Gulf Oil Corp.*, 796 F.2d 340 (10th Cir. 1986).
23. *Edwards v. U.S. Postal Service*, 909 F.2d 320 (8th Cir. 1990).
24. *Rodriguez v. Board of Education of Eastchester Union Free School District*, 620 F.2d 362 (2d Cir. 1980).
25. Michael D. Goldhaber, "Women in Skirts, Men in Dockers," *National Law Journal,* June 21, 1999.
26. *EEOC v. Sage Realty Corp.*, 24 FEP Cases 1521 (S.D. N.Y. 1981).
27. *Hearn v. General Electric Co.*, 927 F. Supp. 1486 (M.D. Ala. 1996).
28. *EEOC v. Farmers Brothers Co.*, 31 F.3d 891 (9th Cir. 1994).
29. In one case, however, after a female worker was denied promotion on three occasions, her supervisors refused to talk to her and assigned her excessive work. When she resigned, the court ruled that she had been constructively discharged. *Glass v. Petro-Tex Chemical Corp.*, 757 F.2d 1554 (5th Cir. 1985).
30. *West v. Marion Merrell Dow, Inc.*, 54 F.3d 493 (8th Cir. 1995).
31. *Gartman v. Gencorp., Inc.*, 71 FEP Cases 937 (E.D. Ark. 1996), reversed 120 F.3d 127 (8th Cir. 1997).
32. *Chertkova v. Connecticut General Life Insurance Co.*, 92 F.3d 81 (2d Cir. 1996).
33. *Hurd v. JCB International Credit Card Co., Ltd.*, 923 F. Supp. 492 (S.D. N.Y. 1996).
34. *Tunis v. Corning Glass Works*, 698 F. Supp. 452 (S.D. N.Y. 1988).

Twelve   Increased Sexual Harassment

1. Mona Harrington, *Women Lawyers: Rewriting the Rules* (New York: Plume, 1995), 105.
2. Barbara A. Gutek, *Sex and the Workplace* (San Francisco: Jossey-Bass, 1985), 8–9.

3. Harrington, *Women Lawyers,* 97.

4. Catherine A. MacKinnon, *Sexual Harassment of Working Women* (New Haven: Yale University Press, 1979), 4.

5. *Barnes v. Train,* 13 FEP Cases 123 (D.C. D.C. 1974).

6. *Corne v. Bausch and Lomb, Inc.,* 390 F. Supp. 161 (D.C. Ariz. 1975), reversed on other grounds 562 F.2d 55 (9th Cir. 1977).

7. *Tomkins v. Public Service Electric & Gas Company,* 422 F. Supp. 537 (D.C. N.J. 1976); reversed 568 F.2d 1044 (3rd Cir. 1977).

8. *Barnes v. Costle,* 561 F.2d 983 (D.C. Cir. 1977).

9. *Tomkins v. Public Service Electric & Gas Company.*

10. *Henson v. City of Dundee,* 682 F.2d 897, 902 (11th Cir. 1982).

11. *Meritor Savings Bank v. Vinson,* 477 U.S. 57 (1986).

12. 29 C.F.R. Section 1604.11(a) (1) and (2).

13. "EEOC Policy Guidelines on Current Issues of Sexual Harassment," available at http://www.eeoc.gov/doc. See also *Lancaster v. Sheffler Enterprises,* 19 F. Supp. 2d 1000 (W.D. Mo. 1998).

14. Lex K. Larson, *Employment Discrimination,* 2d ed. (New York: Matthew Bender, 2000), 3:46–6.

15. Stephen Franklin, "More Women Speak Up about Harassment—and Sue," *Chicago Tribune,* January 8, 1999; "Sexual Harassment Charges: EEOC and FEPAs Combined: FY 1992–FY 2001," available at http://www.eeoc.gov/stats/harass.html..

16. Anne C. Levy and Michele A. Paludi, *Workplace Sexual Harassment* (Upper Saddle River, N.J.: Prentice-Hall, 1997), 50.

17. Nijole V. Benokraitis and Joe R. Feagin, *Modern Sexism: Blatant, Subtle, and Convert Discrimination,* 2d ed. (Englewood Cliffs, N.J.: Prentice-Hall, 1995), 31.

18. Marni Halasa, "Officer Wins $2.2 Million in Harassment Suit," *New York Law Journal,* October 2, 2000.

19. *Weeks v. Baker & McKenzie,* 76 FEP Cases 1219 (Cal. Ct. of Appeals, 1998).

20. *New York Times,* July 20, 1999.

21. Monte Williams, "$2.6 Million to End Sex Harassment Suit," *New York Times,* June 4, 1999.

22. EEOC press release, September 7, 1999, available at http://www.eeoc.gov.

23. Reed Abelson, "Can Respect Be Mandated? Maybe Not Here," *New York Times,* September 10, 2000.

24. *Blackmon v. Pinkerton Security & Investigative Services,* 182 F.3d 629 (8th Cir. 1999).

25. *Stoll v. Runyon,* 165 F.3d 123 (9th Cir. 1999).

26. *Jenson v. Eveleth Taconite Co.,* 130 F.3d 1287 (8th Cir. 1997).

27. *Brooks v. City of San Mateo,* 214 F.3d 1082 (9th Cir. 2000).

Thirteen   Hostile-Environment Sexual Harassment

1. "EEOC Guidelines on Current Issues of Sexual Harassment," EEOC Policy Guidance No. 915–050.

2. *Harris v. Forklift Systems, Inc.,* 510 U.S. 17 (1993).

3. *Burns v. McGregor Electronic Industries, Inc.,* 989 F.2d 959 (8th Cir. 1993).

4. *Ellison v. Brady,* 924 F.2d 872 (9th Cir. 1991).

5. Ibid.

6. "EEOC Guidelines on Current Issues of Sexual Harassment," EEOC Policy Guidance No. 915–050.
7. *Meritor Savings Bank v. Vinson*, 477 U.S. 57 (1986).
8. Ibid., 66–67.
9. "EEOC Policy Guidelines on Current Issues of Sexual Harassment."
10. *Bishop v. Interim Industrial Services*, 77 FEP Cases 1598 (N.D. Tex. 1998).
11. *McKenzie v. Illinois Department of Transportation*, 92 F.3d 473 (7th Cir. 1996).
12. *EEOC v. A. Sam & Sons Produce Co., Inc.*, 872 F. Supp. 29 (W.D. N.Y. 1994).
13. *Mallinson-Montague v. Pocrnick*, 224 F.3d 1224 (10th Cir. 2000).
14. *Fall v. Indiana University Board of Trustees*, 12 F. Supp. 2d 870 (N.D. Ind. 1998).
15. "EEOC Guidelines on Current Issues of Sexual Harassment."
16. *Henson v. City of Dundee*, 682 F.2d 897 (11th Cir. 1982).
17. *Kotcher v. Rosa & Sullivan Appliance Center, Inc.*, 957 F.2d 59 (2d Cir. 1992).
18. *Gan v. Kepro Circuit Systems, Inc.*, 28 FEP Cases 639 (E.D. Mo. 1982).
19. *Kahn v. Objective Solutions*, 86 F. Supp. 2d 377 (S.D. N.Y. 2000).
20. *Wolak v. Spucci*, 217 F.3d 157 (2d Cir. 2000).

Fourteen   Other Forms of Sexual Harassment

1. *Toscano v. Nimmo*, 570 F. Supp. 1197 (D.C. Del. 1983).
2. *Broderick v. Ruder*, 685 F. Supp. 1269 (D.C. D.C. 1988).
3. "EEOC Policy Guidelines on Employer Liability under Title VII for Sexual Favoritism"; EEOC Regulations, 29 C.F.R. Section 1604.11(a).
4. EEOC Regulations, 29 C.F.R. Section 1604.11(d).
5. *Franklin v. King Lincoln-Mercury-Suzuki, Inc.*, 51 F. Supp. 2d 661 (D.C. Md. 1999).
6. *Rodriguez-Hernandez v. Miranda-Velez*, 132 F.3d 848 (1st Cir. 1998).
7. Robert J. Aalberts and Lorne H. Seidman, "Sexual Harassment of Employees by Non-Employees: When Does the Employer Become Liable?" *Pepperdine Law Review* 21 (1994): 447.
8. EEOC Regulations, 29 C.F.R. Section 1604.11(e).
9. *Folkerson v. Circus Casino Enterprises, Inc.*, 107 F.3d 754 (9th Cir. 1997).
10. *Priest v. Rotary*, 32 FEP Cases 1064 (N.D. Calif. 1983).
11. *Rodriguez-Hernandez v. Miranda-Velez*.
12. Federal Rules of Evidence 412.
13. *Kopp v. Samaritan Health System, Inc.*, 13 F.3d 264 (8th Cir. 1993).
14. *Durham Life Insurance Co. v. Evans*, 166 F.3d 139 (3d Cir. 1999).
15. *Scannell v. Bel Air Police Dep't.*, 74 FEP Cases 589 (D.C. Md. 1997).

Fifteen   Employer Liability

1. Civil Rights Act of 1964, Title VII, 42 U.S.C. Sections 2000e et seq.
2. *Burlington Industries, Inc. v. Ellerth*, 524 U.S. 743 (1998). See also *Faragher v. City of Boca Raton*, 524 U.S. 775 (1998).
3. "EEOC Enforcement Guidance: Vicarious Employer Liability for Unlawful Harassment," available at http://www.eeoc.gov/docs/harassment. html.
4. *Burlington Industries, Inc. v. Ellerth*.
5. "EEOC Enforcement Guidance."

6. *Durham Life Insurance Co. v. Evans*, 166 F.3d 139 (3d Cir. 1999).
7. *Molnar v. Booth*, 229 F.3d 593 (7th Cir. 2000).
8. "EEOC Enforcement Guidance."
9. Ibid.
10. *Desmarteau v. City of Wichita*, 64 F. Supp. 2d 1067 (D.C. Kan. 1999).
11. *Van Steenburgh v. Rival Co.*, 171 F.3d 1155 (8th Cir. 1999).
12. *Scrivner v. Socorro Independent School District*, 169 F.3d 969 (5th Cir 1999).
13. *McCrackin v. LabOne, Inc.*, 74 FEP Cases 1018 (D.C. Kan. 1995). McCrackin's case was later dismissed on other grounds, 903 F. Supp. 1430.
14. *Smith v. Bath Iron Works Corp.* 943 F.2d 164 (1st Cir. 1991).

Sixteen Employer Retaliation against Workers

1. 42 U.S.C. Section 2000e–3(a). If Title VII were enacted today, Congress would use gender-neutral language.
2. *Donnellon v. Fruehauf Corp.*, 794 F.2d 598 (11th Cir. 1986).
3. *Weeks v. State of Maine*, 866 F. Supp. 601 (D.C. Maine 1994).
4. *Capaci v. Katz & Besthoff, Inc.*, 525 F. Supp 317 (E.D. La. 1981); affirmed in relevant part, 711 F.2d 647 (5th Cir. 1983).
5. *Sims v. Mme. Paulette Dry Cleaners*, 580 F. Supp. 593 (S.D. N.Y. 1984).
6. U.S. EEOC, "Charge Statistics FY 1992 through FY 2000," available at http://www.eeoc.gov/stats/charges.html.
7. *Carter-Obayuwana v. Howard University*, 84 FEP Cases 1365 (D.C. Cir. 2001).
8. *Love v. Re/Max of America, Inc.*, 738 F.2d 383 (10th Cir. 1984).
9. *Quinn v. Green Tree Credit Corp.*, 159 F.3d 759 (2d Cir. 1998).
10. Ibid.
11. *Klimiuk v. ESI Lederle, Inc.*, 84 FEP Cases 971 (E.D. Pa. 2000).
12. *Toscano v. Nimmo*, 570 F. Supp. 1197 (D.C. Del. 1983).
13. *Morris v. Oldham County Fiscal Court*, 201 F.3d 784 (6th Cir. 2000).
14. *Watts v. Kroger Co.*, 170 F.3d 505 (5th Cir. 1999).
15. *Robinson v. Shell Oil Co.*, 519 U.S. 337 (1997).

Seventeen Proving Sex Discrimination in Court

1. See comments made by the Supreme Court in *U.S. Postal Service Board of Governors v. Aikens*, 460 U.S. 711 (1983).
2. Deborah L. Rhode, "Perspectives on Professional Women," *Stanford Law Review* 40 (1988): 1163, 1195.
3. Ibid., 1194.
4. *Moore v. Alabama State University*, 980 F. Supp. 426 (M.D. Ala. 1997).
5. *Heim v. State of Utah*, 8 F.3d 1541 (10th Cir. 1993)
6. *McDonnell Douglas Corp. v. Green*, 411 U.S. 792 (1973).
7. *Furnco Construction Corp. v. Waters*, 438 U.S. 567 (1978).
8. *Reeves v. Sanderson Plumbing Products, Inc.*, 530 U.S. 133 (2000).
9. *Binder v. Long Island Lighting Co.*, 57 F.3d 193 (2d Cir. 1995).
10. *Emmel v. Coca-Cola Bottling Company of Chicago*, 95 F.3d 627 (7th Cir. 1996).
11. *Kramer v. Logan County School District*, 157 F.3d 620 (8th Cir. 1998).

12. *Long v. Ringling Bros.-Barnum & Bailey Combined Shows, Inc.*, 882 F. Supp. 1553 (D.C. Md. 1995).

13. *Gallo v. John Powell Chevrolet, Inc.*, 765 F. Supp. 198 (M.D. Pa. 1991).

14. *Johnson v. Baptist Medical Center*, 97 F.3d 1070 (8th Cir. 1996).

15. The principal issues in Dianne Rawlinson's case in chapter 4 involved the disparate impact of Alabama prison rules upon women. Due to her height and weight, Rawlinson encountered problems when she applied for the position of prison guard.

16. *EEOC v. Joe's Stone Crab, Inc.*, 220 F.3d 1263 (11th Cir. 2000).

17. *Pivirotto v. Innovative Systems, Inc.*, 191 F.3d 344 (3d Cir. 1999).

18. *Veatch v. Northwestern Memorial Hospital*, 730 F. Supp. 809 (N.D. Ill. 1990).

19. *Proud v, Stone*, 945 F.2d 796 (4th Cir. 1991).

20. *Bradley v. Harcourt, Brace & Co.*, 104 F.3d 267 (9th Cir. 1996).

21. *Buhrmaster v. Overnite Transportation Co.*, 61 F.3d 461 (6th Cir. 1995).

Eighteen   Compensatory and Punitive Damages

1. 42 U.S.C. Section 1981.

2. 42 U.S.C. Section 1981a. The complete limitation is as follows: $50,000 for employers with 15 to 100 employees; $100,000 for employers with 101 to 200 employees; $200,000 for employers with 201 to 500 employees; and $300,000 for employers with more than 500 employees.

3. *Reynolds v. Octel Communications Corp.*, 71 FEP Cases 1053 (N.D. Tex. 1995).

4. *Luciano v. Olsten Corp.*, 912 F. Supp. 663 (E.D. N.Y. 1996), affirmed 110 F.3d 210 (2d Cir. 1997). The jury also awarded Luciano $11,400 in compensatory damages for the emotional distress she suffered during her ordeal. If Luciano's attorneys had relied solely on Title VII, this award also would have been subjected to the $300,000 cap. However, they also pleaded violations of the New York State Human Rights Law, and the trial judge allocated the $11,400 award to violations of that statute, thus rescuing it from the $300,000 cap.

5. *Blakey v. Continental Airlines, Inc.*, 992 F. Supp. 731 (D.C. N.J. 1998).

6. *Hughes v. The Regents of the University of Colorado*, 967 F. Supp. 431 (D.C. Colo. 1996).

7. 42 U.S.C. Section 1981a.

8. *Kolstad v. American Dental Association*, 527 U.S. 526 (1999).

9. *Weeks v. Baker & McKenzie*, 76 FEP Cases 1219 (Cal. Ct. of Appeals, 1998).

10. *Knowlton v. Tel-Trust Phones, Inc.*, 189 F.3d 1177 (10th Cir. 1999).

11. *Jonasson v. Lutheran Child and Family Services*, 115 F.3d 436 (7th Cir. 1997).

12. *Ortiz-Del Valle v. National Basketball Association*, 42 F. Supp. 2d 334 (S.D. N.Y. 1996), affirmed 190 F.3d 598 (2d Cir. 1999).

13. *Peckinpaugh v. Post-Newsweek Stations Connecticut, Inc.*, 1999 WL 334838 (D.C. Conn. 1999). See also Mike Allen, "Anchorwoman Wins $8.3 Million over Sex Bias," *New York Times,* January 29, 1999.

14. Margaret Cronin Fisk, "Judges Slash Worker Awards," *National Law Journal*, April 20, 1998.

15. William P. Murphy, "Meandering Musings about Discrimination Law," *Labor Lawyer* 10, 4 (1994): 649.

Nineteen Back Pay, Front Pay, and Other Remedies

1. *Franks v. Bowman Transportation Co.*, 424 U.S. 747 (1976).
2. *Morris v. American National Can Corp.*, 952 F.2d 200 (8th Cir. 1991).
3. *Ward v. Tipton County Sheriff Department*, 937 F. Supp. 791 (S.D. Ind. 1996).
4. *Passantino v. Johnson & Johnson Consumer Products*, 212 F.3d 493 (9th Cir. 2000).
5. *EEOC v. Hacienda Hotel*, 881 F.2d 1504 (9th Cir. 1989).
6. *Sherkow v. State of Wisconsin, Department of Public Instruction*, 630 F.2d 498 (7th Cir. 1980).
7. *Garza v. Brownsville Independent School District*, 700 F.2d 253 (5th Cir. 1983).
8. *Hatcher-Capers v. Haley*, 786 F. Supp. 1054 (D.C. D.C. 1992).
9. 42 U.S.C. Section 2000e–5(k).
10. *City of Riverside v. Rivera*, 477 U.S. 561 (1986).

Conclusion

1. Howard W. French, "Women Win a Battle, but Job Bias Still Rules Japan," *New York Times,* February 26, 2000.
2. Ibid.
3. Howard W. French, "Diploma at Hand, Japanese Women Find Glass Ceiling Reinforced with Iron," *New York Times,* January 1, 2001.
4. Nijole V. Benokraitis and Joe R. Feagin, *Modern Sexism: Blatant, Subtle, and Covert Discrimination,* 2d ed. (Englewood Cliffs, N.J.: Prentice-Hall, 1995), 45.

Index

About the Author

Raymond Gregory, an attorney for more than forty years, has focused his law practice on employment discrimination litigation. He is also the author of *Age Discrimination in the American Workplace: Old at a Young Age* (Rutgers University Press, 2001). He and his wife, Mary, live in Norton, Massachusetts.